To Delroy,
I hope this encourages you to do your own Work.

One Love,

Andy

18th Nov. 2007

Black Theology in Transatlantic Dialogue

Black Religion / Womanist Thought / Social Justice
Series Editors Dwight N. Hopkins and Linda E. Thomas
Published by Palgrave Macmillan

Black Theology in Transatlantic Dialogue

Anthony G. Reddie

First published in 2006 by
PALGRAVE MACMILLAN™
175 Fifth Avenue, New York, N.Y. 10010 and
Houndmills, Basingstoke, Hampshire, England RG21 6XS
Companies and representatives throughout the world.

PALGRAVE MACMILLAN is the global academic imprint of the Palgrave Macmillan division of St. Martin's Press, LLC and of Palgrave Macmillan Ltd. Macmillan® is a registered trademark in the United States, United Kingdom and other countries. Palgrave is a registered trademark in the European Union and other countries.

ISBN-13: 978–1–4039–6863–0
ISBN-10: 1–4039–6863–2

Library of Congress Cataloging-in-Publication Data

Reddie, Anthony G.
    Black theology in transatlantic dialogue / Anthony G. Reddie.
        p.cm.—(Black religion, womanist thought, social justice)
    Includes bibliographical references and index.
    ISBN 1–4039–6863–2
        1. Black theology. 2. Theology—Great Britain. I. Title. II. Series.

BT82.7.R45 2006
230.089′96—dc22   2005056462

A catalogue record for this book is available from the British Library.

Design by Newgen Imaging Systems (P) Ltd., Chennai, India.

First edition: September 2006

10 9 8 7 6 5 4 3 2 1

Printed in the United States of America.

To Sasha
my Niece
You are a wonderful creation of God
who will be a blessing to many
God bless you
your uncle
Anthony

Contents

Series Editors' Preface

With *Black Theology in Transatlantic Dialogue*, black theology is established as an international movement. This book deepens the specific black theology traditions of black South African Allan A. Boesak's *Farewell to Innocence* (1977), *The Gospel Is Not Western: Black Theologies from the Southwest Pacific*, ed. G.W. Trompf (1987), and Dwight N. Hopkins's *Black Theology USA and South Africa* (1989). Anthony G. Reddie gifts us with the first critical comparative analysis between black theology in the United Kingdom of Great Britain (BTUK) and black theology in the United States of America (BTUSA). He adeptly guides the reader through the complex maze of two disciplines (i.e., BTUK and BTUSA). In the book, he charts out their individual and joint maturations: their commonalities and differences in origin, thematic foci, contextual factors, methodological priorities, and doctrinal emphases. Reddie approaches head-on the complicated and sometimes antagonistic relation between black theology and the black church and black (male) theology and womanist theology on both sides of the Atlantic. How do womanists theologians in the United States and in the United Kingdom differ? Likewise, what fusions do we find between the U.K. black theology–black church connection and the U.S. black theology–black church ties? One of the distinct traits of BTUK is its dogged relation with and focus on black churches and poor and working class communities. Unlike BTUSA, which has a tendency to buy into mainstream capitalist notions of scholarship-for-scholarship sake, BTUK always takes seriously the practice of Christian education among ordinary people. Reddie offers an insightful and novel investigation of practical theology. With boldness and astuteness, he warns BTUSA to be mindful of its imperialistic and hegemonic inclination to dominate the myriad and creative manifestations of black theology across the world. BTUSA might be the elder in the global village, but it is not the only sibling. Reddie uses his own life story to signify the lives of other black Caribbean British Christians and, to a certain degree, black Ghanaian British Christians. And, like all good theology (i.e., theology linked to oppressed communities), *Black Theology in Transatlantic Dialogue* provides a positive pathway for this postmodern, fragmented, twenty-first century of ours.

Reddie has constructed a seminal work. One gets a distinct feel that a new voice has emerged, not only in Britain, but internationally. Although black people have been in Britain since Roman times and though African Americans have been in the United States since 1619, this is the first systematic treatment of the development of black theology in Britain and its comparison with BTUSA. Written with the lay reader and nonspecialist in mind, this book speaks to a broad audience—theologians, churches, people who are in search of, comparative analysts, globalization specialists, and anyone excited about listening in on the emergence of a new global discipline.

Because of its interdisciplinary nature and cutting-edge take, Reddie's text embodies the vision of the Black Religion/Womanist Thought/Social Justice series. The series publishes both authored and edited manuscripts that have depth, breadth, and theoretical edge and addresses both academic and nonspecialist audiences. It produces works engaging any dimension of black religion or womanist thought as they pertain to social justice. Womanist thought is a new approach in the study of African American women's perspectives. The series includes a variety of African American religious expressions, that is, traditions such as Protestant and Catholic Christianity, Islam, Judaism, Humanism, African diasporic practices, religion and gender, religion and black gays/lesbians, ecological justice issues, African American religiosity and its relation to African religions, new black religious movements (e.g., Daddy Grace, Father Divine, or the Nation of Islam), religious dimensions in African American "secular" experiences (such as the spiritual aspects of aesthetic efforts like the Harlem Renaissance and literary giants such as James Baldwin, the religious fervor of the black consciousness movement, and the religion of compassion in black women's club movement).

Dwight N. Hopkins, University of Chicago Divinity School
Linda E. Thomas, Lutheran School of Theology at Chicago

Acknowledgments

My initial set of thanks is reserved for three black majority Methodist churches in Birmingham, in the West Midlands area of Britain. First, there is Moseley Road Methodist Church, from where I have learnt what it means to be a black Christian, living and worshipping in Britain. The church has had its high and low points, and at the time of writing, has some very crucial questions to ask of itself regarding the future.

What I have always loved about Moseley Road is the sense of anonymity I have within its holy spaces. My membership of this church predates the scholarly work and subsequent writing for which I am largely known in this country. At Moseley Road, I am simply Anthony, nothing more and nothing less. My so-called accomplishments are recognized and celebrated, but I am not a celebrity; rather, I am simply one of them. Another sojourner trying to make his way through life! Someone attempting to be faithful to God and to those around me!

The other two churches are Lozells Methodist and Villa Road Methodist Churches. It is in these two churches that I began to learn what ministry was all about. It is in these two, seemingly, ordinary urban contexts, that I began to see glimpses of the inherently subversive and prophetic gift, that is, black Christian faith to the ongoing work of God's reign. I know it is invidious to pick out individuals, for all the people in these two churches are special; but I want to highlight Danny Dorsett of Lozells and Syble Morgan of Villa Road. Danny and Syble are very different people, with very different personalities, and yet each in his own way has been an important guide in my ongoing development. Danny has been something of a private confessor, and Syble has been a stern and yet friendly critic of all things "self important" and pompous. To each, and to all the people at all three churches, my heartfelt thanks!

My second set of thanks is extended to the monthly Black Theology in Britain Forum, which meets at the Queen's Foundation for Ecumenical Theological Education, in Edgbaston, Birmingham (United Kingdom) on the last Thursday of every month. This forum has been in existence since the early 1990s and has proved an invaluable space for the nurturing of black theological scholarship and talent. I am grateful to this forum for the confidence it instilled in me when I was doing my doctoral studies in the late 1990s. Also, I should admit that the forum still continues to stimulate my mind and feed my imagination.

In addition to the forum, I would also like to extend particular thanks to Robert Beckford, Inderjit Bhogal, and Emmanuel Lartey. At the outset of my scholarly pilgrimage, each one of these talented and committed individuals challenged me to take up and complete my academic studies. Most importantly, through what they embodied, they demonstrated the need for theology to be engaged, passionate and for it to be done with panache and style. Amongst the holy three, special thanks are reserved for Robert and his particular brand of iconoclastic, no-hold-barred form of truth-telling. The injunction to "write what you like" and to make it "unapologetically black" (my acknowledgment to Steve Biko and Jeremiah Wright for conscripting their terms) that were discerned from my many conversations with Robert have held me in good stead, since we first met in the early 1990s.

It would be remiss of me if I did not acknowledge the continuing support of the Research Centre at the Queen's Foundation in particular and the whole Queen's community in general. I continue to be thankful for the time and space afforded to me by Queen's to reflect and write.

If Queen's are worthy of my thanks, so too is the British Methodist Church. Special thanks are reserved for Formation in Ministry office of the church for providing the infrastructure and moral and financial support that has enabled me to function as a church-sponsored, black theologian. I am the only one who is granted this honor in Britain. Additional thanks are offered to the Pastoral Care and Christian Education and Racial Justice sections of the Connexional Team of the British Methodist Church.

I would like to thank my family, particularly my parents Lucille and Noel Reddie, my siblings Richard, Christopher, and Sandra, my uncle Mervin and auntie Lynette, and their children, Karen, Jason, Andrea, and Lorraine and best of all, my little nephew Noah and niece Sasha, the next generation of my family. They are all special people in my life, and without them I would be a lesser human being.

Finally, of course, there is God, through whom all things are possible; often making a way out of no way. My gratitude to God knows no bounds and cannot be expressed in words.

Thanks to all.

Introduction

All stories start with a beginning. There is an initial moment of departure. A time of encounter when the realization that one is about to embark upon something new and potentially life changing suddenly becomes clear. Such a moment occurred in my life on March 15, 1992. I remember the moment very clearly, as if it happened only yesterday.

I had just begun working as a Youth and Community worker for the Asbury circuit in the Birmingham Methodist district in Britain. The two churches where I was based were black majority Methodist churches— Villa Road and Lozells. Both churches were populated mainly by Caribbean migrants. The membership of one of the churches was mainly Jamaican, the other, predominantly South Caribbean, with St. Kitts, Nevis, and Montserrat featuring heavily in the national identities of the people. I had been employed to work alongside the children and young people associated with the church and in the wider community. Most of the children and young people associated with these churches were black, mainly African Caribbean in terms of their ethnicity.

My previous employment in largely secular Youth and Community work had not equipped me for the realities of working with this client group. In many respects, I could identify with the people linked to the church for I too had African Caribbean roots. My parents had emigrated from Jamaica to Britain in the late 1950s and settled in Bradford, West Yorkshire. I am the eldest child of Noel and Lucille Reddie. Despite my sense of solidarity with the people in the Handsworth and Lozells areas of North Birmingham,[1] neither my academic training in (church) history nor my vocational development as a youth worker had equipped me with the necessary tools to work alongside these often marginalized and dispirited communities.

It was in search of more relevant experience and learning to assist me in the job to which I had been appointed that I went to The Queen's College for Ecumenical Theological Education, in Edgbaston,

Birmingham in 1993. Queen's was (and remains) the only college/ seminary in Britain in which Black Theology is taught as a core component of the curriculum for those training for some form of recognized, authorized ministry. On the staff at Queen's in the early 1990s was Robert Beckford. I shall refrain from saying too much about Robert at this juncture, for I shall speak about his work and legacy at greater length at a later point in the book.

Robert was then the tutor in Black Theology at Queen's. It was to Robert that I went, in the autumn/fall of the following academic year to undertake a preparatory course in black Christian studies. It was there that the journey toward my ongoing work as a black British theologian and religious educator began, leading inexorably to this book.

It was whilst undertaking this one year course that the seeds for my burgeoning interest in black religious studies, specializing in black theological work began. My introduction to the works of James H. Cone, Gayraud S. Wilmore, and J. Deotis Roberts completely reorientated my whole conception of Christianity and what it meant to be a black Christian. I remember opening up my newly purchased copy of *Black Theology: A Documentary History, Vol.1*[2] and being stunned at the range of black scholars on show within this formidably sized text.

In neither of my previous studies had I encountered black scholars. Both History and Youth work had been demonstrably and manifestly white in complexion. Black presence was conspicuous by its complete absence. Undertaking this course whetted my appetite. Further conversations with Robert Beckford gave me the impetus to undertake doctoral work in education and theology at the University of Birmingham.

All Eyes on America

I have shared the "bare bones" of my formative scholarly development in order to explicate the central narrative thread and thematic thrust of this work. As implied by the subtitle of the book, *Black Theology In Transatlantic Dialogue: Inside (Looking) Out*, this work is an attempt to assess the development of black theology within the British context by means of comparison with her older sibling in the United States.

This text seeks to both acknowledge the huge debt black religious scholars from the various alternative locations in which the black experience is housed owe to our African American brothers and sisters, and to critique that ongoing dominance. I have used the term "ongoing dominance" to reflect the cultural, social, and theological influence of African Americans on the development of diasporan African thought.

If one were to identify ten black theologians in the world, approximately seven of them would be African Americans. I am a black British theologian and educator, whose work has been heavily influenced by North American black and womanist theologies. This text seeks to bring these two seminal influences—Britain and the United States—into a dialectical conversation, surrounding the efficacy, influence, and future trajectory of black theology. As the subtitle suggests, I will be writing from within my own context and experience (inside [looking] out), seeking to articulate the development and nature of black theology in Britain, and juxtaposing this with an attempt to assess the impact and effectiveness of black theology in the United States. (outside looking in).

The first four books I read when I began my pilgrimage as a black religious scholar were by African American writers. In addition to *Black Theology: A Documentary History, Vol.1* there was James Cone's ground breaking *Black Theology and Black Power*[3] and *A Black Theology of Liberation*,[4] followed by Gayraud Wilmore's *Black Religion and Black Radicalism*.[5] These books not only gave me an insight into the experience of African Americans within the North American context, but also acted as a mirror through which I could look back at the reflection of my own context.

The development of black theology in Britain has tended to operate (for good or for ill) from within a black Atlantic framework,[6] with North America providing the most durable and resonant of dialogue partners. I have used this ongoing paradigmatic framework as the basis for this book. I want to look at the development of black theology in Britain and the United States by means of a comparative assessment—looking in and looking out. This process is one of comparing and contrasting the ebbs and flows of black theology in two vastly different and yet not dissimilar contexts.

This assessment is a deeply personal one and I take full responsibility for the often tendentious, skewed, partial, and opinionated perspectives that arise from this critical analysis. Like all scholars, I have my own peculiar blind spots and bias. Like all scholars I believe my assessments to be correct, if only to me. But like *all good* scholars, I am forced, in the final analysis to concede that my perspectives are deeply subjective, contingent, and always partial.

The Flow of the Work

Chapter 1: Historical Developments—This chapter seeks to trace the respective developments of black theology in Britain and the

United States. How have they differed? What do these two movements have in common? What can they learn from each other?

Chapter 2: Friend or Foe?: Black Theologians and the Black Church—In both contexts, the black church as the repository for affirming and nurturing the black impulse for freedom has been a key element in the development of black theology. Yet despite its pivotal position within many black communities, the black church has sometimes been as much a hindrance as a strength—a force for conservatism and reactionary thinking rather than a liberative space for antioppressive struggle. So how have black theologians on both sides of the Atlantic engaged with the church? What are the fault lines in the theology and practice of the black church in Britain and the United States?

Chapter 3: Bring on the Sistas—The rise of womanist theology in the 1980s offered a crucial critique and a necessary riposte to the androcentric concerns of black theology. Womanist theology has and remains a challenge not only to "mainline black theology," but also to all black male theologians. How has black theology responded to the challenges and insights provided by womanist theologies? How does womanist theology in Britain and the United States differ?

Chapter 4: Education, Education, Education[7]—Since the late sixties, Christian education, as a branch of practical theology, has attempted to translate the searing insights of Cone, Wilmore, Roberts, Hopkins, Grant, and Williams et al. into workable and sustained models of teaching and learning for black people of African descent. On both sides of the Atlantic, Christian religious educators continue (with varying degrees of success) to bring black theological content into dialogue with pedagogical insights, curriculum issues, and concerns. Has Christian religious education managed to disseminate black theological ideas and themes for the masses?

Chapter 5: Published and Be Damned—Reassessing the Role and Development of the Black Theology Journal—Since its inception in 1998, the journal *Black Theology in Britain: A Journal of Contextual Praxis*, which later became *Black Theology: An International Journal*; has sought to be a conduit between these unequal cousins—Britain and the United States. Whilst the journal was created, initially, to reflect the black British experience, it has always been a home to and indeed has welcomed telling contributions from African American scholars. This chapter will reassesses the role, intent, and effectiveness of the journal in responding to the developments of black theology in Britain and the United States.

Chapter 6: Where We Headed Now?—In this, concluding chapter, I engage in some guess work. What are the new ways in which black theology can be undertaken in the future? How can black theology respond to the challenge of postmodernity and issues of fragmentation as they arise in the twenty-first century?

In undertaking this work, I have taken an unashamedly interdisciplinary approach to the task of detailing a future trajectory for the development of black theology.

What I Bring to the Table!

I am aware that my approach to detailing black theology in Britain is undertaken through two highly influential vistas. In the first instance, I am a black male of African Caribbean descent. My parents are from the Caribbean island of Jamaica. Although I was born in Britain, I have been socialized within and heavily influenced by Caribbean mores and cultural values. I am a black, Caribbean Christian living in Britain. Black theology in Britain, much like the development of black identities, can be viewed as plural, hybrid, and dynamic entities that eschew any simplistic attempt to essentialize or to reify cultures.[8] Black religion and black theology in Britain are very heterogeneous terms that are pregnant with multiple perspectives and possibilities.[9] Indeed, one could quite legitimately theorize in an inordinate fashion and still never exhaust the seemingly endless ways in which one could seek to identify and construct a working paradigm for the nature and intent of black theology in my country. But this work is not simply an attempt to create a comparative framework for the development of black theology in Britain. Rather, in identifying my own formative narrative and ongoing experiences at the forefront of this work, I am, in effect, attempting to tell my own story. The story of being the eldest child of Black migrants in Britain—the story of being a black Caribbean British Christian, in a so-called Christian nation that has not always (some might even say rarely) lived up to such an exalted billing. This is in essence my story told through an expansive lens that seeks to accommodate perspectives from the wider contours of British life and the immensity of experience that is the African American vista residing across the Atlantic.

So, my academic gaze also incorporates a narrative and pastoral dimension. In this work, I am primarily talking about and from black Caribbean and African perspectives. This is not to suggest that other perspectives do not exist or cannot legitimately be called a part of the black theology movement in Britain. But this is my story, and as such, I am writing from within the experience with which I am most familiar.

Second, and perhaps of less import, I am also a British Methodist. In many respects, I am perhaps more Methodist than I care to admit and rather too Methodist than is really good for me. But there you have it. I am a black British Methodist theologian of Caribbean roots. Like my transatlantic colleagues such as Elaine Crawford,[10] I have to attempt to make sense of the dual nomenclatures of being black and Methodist[11] (in terms of the latter, within a White-dominated church).[12]

The flow of this book represents my individual preoccupations and concerns. Doubtless, another scholar would have written this book from an alternative perspective ordering the material differently and no doubt, offering a rather different interpretation of events and the various ongoing developments. I suspect that if I were starting this project all over again, I too might have approached it differently. But for this time and for this place, this is the book I have written, and it represents the best of my efforts at the present moment.

1

Historical Developments

Situating Myself

Like all contextual theologians, it is imperative that I situate myself at the outset of my work. I use the word imperative because my commitment to and utilization of black theology in my scholarly work is not purely an academic affair or some arid intellectual exercise. Having been born into and raised within white majority social and religious settings in the UK, my conception of Christianity until my early twenties was viewed entirely through white European frameworks. The pictures, images, and interpretation of the Christian faith were influenced by Eurocentric sensibilities.

In my early twenties I was on the verge of leaving the Christian church. Neither the liberal racist whiteness of the British Methodist Church nor the conservative blackness of the mainly Pentecostal churches in Britain held much attraction. The former appeared to be enlightened on social issues, but remained steadfastly wedded to white supremacist notions of Eurocentric correctness and superiority,[1] whereas the latter, although more African centered in their modes of operation and cultural expression, was locked into seemingly rigid pseudo nineteenth-century biblical literalism and conservative ecclesiology.

Black theology offered me the rational ground to remain within the Christian church. Having eschewed all opportunities to "candidate" for the ordained ministry within my own church my discovery of black theology and the work of Cone et al. offered me an emotional, spiritual, and intellectual lifeline. In short, black theology gave me a compelling reason to not only remain a Christian, but also undertake black scholarly work in service of the church and the wider world, as an agent of transformative change for the ultimate breaking in of

God's reign. In order to understand the import of that discovery, one should know something of my own formative developments. For, within this sociocultural and political backdrop lie the seeds for the desire to conceive of another way of being a Christian, in a world of rampant white hegemony and neoimperialistic globalization.[2]

My Subjective Agency—Who Am I?

In this section, I want to use my own subjective narrative as a microcosm for the overarching historicocultural and political account of black people in Britain. This narrative interlude is not meant to serve as a definitive rendering of this story, as the experience of black people in Britain is worthy of an entire project in its own right and would be undertaken to better effect by specialized historians, not a theologian. My story is not normative; it is simply my story. Its import, however, lies in the fact that it resonates with the formative experiences of an entire second generation of black people born in Britain of parents who migrated to this country in the mid part of the last century.

I was born in Bradford, West Yorkshire, on October 10, 1964, in the Royal Infirmary. I am the first child of Mr. and Mrs. Noel and Lucille Reddie, who came from Jamaica to Britain separately in 1957 and 1959, respectively. I grew up in a relatively poor area of the city called East Bowling. I was christened in a Methodist church called Prospect Hall. The church was closed in the late 1960s and my family decamped to the central Methodist Mission called Eastbrook Hall.

In some of my previous writings, I have spoken about Eastbrook Hall as a formidable, imposing cradle of Yorkshire Methodism.[3] It was indeed a formidable and imposing place, full of formidable and imposing people—my family was the only black one. The journey from East Bowling, Bradford, to the social space I occupy at the time of writing, that is, the middle class and salubrious area of Moseley, Birmingham, has been an eventful one as is the case with most journeys. You will be pleased to know that I shall spare you the worst excesses of an autobiographical journey down memory lane. I want to reflect for a little while, however, on the means by which this journey has been undertaken. For, as my mother, a redoubtable and determined Jamaican woman of Christian faith is always prone to say, "We haven't gotten where we have by accident."

In order to understand how my journey has been undertaken—the force that has propelled it and the compass that has given it direction—you need to know something of the context in which I was born and was subsequently nurtured. I am instinctively a narrative theologian, and the use of archetypal stories as a means of distilling and capturing truth is one that has always been close to my heart. One of my favorite writers in this regard is Janice Hale. In her book *Unbank the Fire*, Hale describes the journey of her family from rural poverty in the southern states of the United States to professional middle-class respectability, over the course of three generations.[4] The framework of that work has impressed me so much that I have chosen to use it for my initial contextual analysis—the substantive foreground of this chapter.

For my own story, one has to go back to the later period of colonialism in the Caribbean. My parents were born into the endemic poverty of the poor agrarian proletariat of Jamaica. The might of British imperial rule was in the twilight of its political dominance and the visible signs of decline and demise[5] that were to occur two generations on from their birth were already clearly discernible.[6]

My parents were part of an underclass that was poor, deprived, and disparaged.[7] For them, redemption and amelioration from the ills of being black, poor, and uneducated came from the church and the teachings of Christianity.[8] Anne and Anthony Pinn in their book *Black Church History* chart the development of the relationship between black people of the African Diaspora and the Christian faith that was brought from Europe.[9] This chapter, which begins with an outline to the formative background to my own narrative, is predicated on the notion of progressive social, political, and economic improvement through religious teaching and socialization. It can be argued that the most compelling claim for the efficacy of religious teaching and learning for black people of the African Diaspora can be found in the deprived and subjugated bodies of the black slaves whose pitiful existence was affirmed and transformed by the miracle that is faith.[10]

I want to use this metanarrative, that is, black historicity and juxtapose it with my own experiences of growing up in Bradford, West Yorkshire, in Britain. My intention in doing this is to provide a context from which we can depart and make further explorations into the complex meanings and issues that are bound up with the process of highlighting the central import of black theology, to my own development, and also that of all black people in Britain and the United States.

The poverty and frustrations of the Caribbean led my parents, along with hundreds of thousands of their peers, to seek a better life overseas.[11] These people came imbued with values and ideas that were inculcated in the course of their own religious and cultural socialization. The Caribbean in general and Jamaica in particular is a context in which religious matters are discussed and debated with a ferocity and a fervor that make English religious sensibilities look distinctly tame and lacking in conviction.[12] In the worldview of my parents and that of countless black and other poor people, religious knowledge was linked, almost inextricably, with personal growth—a growth that was holistic and all encompassing. The religion into which my parents were socialized was the Christianity of the holiness movement.

My own growth and development can be attributed to the tripartite influences of my parents and Methodism, along with added doses of socialism thrown in for good measure. So the mixture is as follows: take liberal doses of all three, mix in a large tumbler, add a dash of class consciousness, shake and stir, administer on a daily basis for 30 or 50 years and ergo, arises an Anthony Reddie. Of course, it is much more complicated than that; nevertheless, this short-hand description provides the basic ingredients for the sociocultural recipe for my life.

My formative years were spent in a hot-house of religious fervor and social change. In many respects, my story is not unique. Church historians have written extensively about the role of the church in the social and economic improvement of the poor and the underclass.[13] Therefore, I do not intend to delay too long in rehearsing the claims and counterclaims of the church in Britain and her relationship with the deprived and the underclass from the eighteenth century to the present day.

Making certain assumptions about the people who have read my previous work, I know that you will forgive me for being somewhat partisan in my comments. I am a cradle Methodist, but I will do my utmost not to wear it on my sleeve or force you to digest an unpalatable diet of Wesleyan triumphalism. Despite my somewhat trenchant comments directed at the Methodist church in Britain, I need to acknowledge the debt that I owe to my church. From my earliest memories of being marched to church resplendent in my Sunday best, I was conscious of the dour, dutiful, and earnest climate of holiness that permeated the atmosphere of the gathered community of faith that was Eastbrook Hall. Rupert Davies' popular book, which charts the historical developments of Methodism, highlights the potency of Wesley's teaching on holiness and its influence on the religious sensibilities of his initial eighteenth-century followers.[14]

Later generations of Methodists, along with many of her free-church and Nonconformist relatives and their "established" elder sibling were active participants in the development of social and educational programs for the betterment of the poor and deprived. In the area of education,

Cliff's work on the rise and development of the Sunday School Union in Britain charts the important contributions made by Christian faith communities to the creation of educational opportunities for those outside the orbit of seeming privilege, comfort, and affluence.[15]

Education about religion and induction into religion has been identified as being important theological tasks. Writers such as Sedgwick have noted the transformative power and influence of both religious education and "generic" education from within a religious worldview.[16] The work of Douglas Hubery and the former Methodist Division of Education and Youth[17] in the British Methodist church, in recent times has continued to fly the flag for a Christian-inspired view of education, which carries the often benign stamp of Wesleyan holiness.[18]

My education about and induction into the Christian faith was imbued with an aspirant, self-improvement ethic that lies at the forefront of my heightened consciousness. Eastbrook Hall was a highly competitive arena, whose coercive power for social improvement and progress, as a form of pietistic holiness, became all the more pronounced and effective due to the alleged benign nature of its existence. As I have stated on many occasions when giving talks about my past, "growing up in Eastbrook was to live in a world of studious conformity. The rules of belonging were never stated, yet everyone knew what the rules were." I would submit that in this respect, Eastbrook, although undeniably peculiar and idiosyncratic as only Yorkshire folk can be, is a microcosm of British society.

My progress through the church had distinct "knock-on" effects for the other areas of my life. The pressure to conform to the perceived exacting standards of belonging to a respectable and influential city center mission instilled in me a determination to reconcile the disparate worlds of urban poverty on the one hand and religious and social acceptance on the other.[19] This phenomenon is certainly not a new one. The pressure to be "the best I could be," engendered through an environment of self-conscious holiness and added to my parents' determination, saw me through my Ordinary level ("O" levels), and Advanced ("A" levels) examinations and on to university. The necessary skills of applied learning and examination technique were learnt through the rigors of Scripture exams set by the Methodist Youth Department. The good habits of reading and "thinking things through" came principally from my parents and courtesy of a number of willing and patient Sunday schoolteachers. In terms of the latter, I remain deeply indebted to a certain Mr. Salter. I cannot remember much about him, and sadly we lost touch when Eastbrook Hall closed in the mid-1980s. Mr. Salter, if my memory serves right, was a physicist at Sheffield University; he wore his considerable learning not on his sleeve, but buried deep in one of the saggy pockets of a seemingly ill-fitting suit. This white man took a natural interest in my studies and offered weekly encouragement to my parents, insisting that I possessed the necessary skills and ability to go to university. When I left Bradford for the University of Birmingham in the autumn of 1984, I went as a fully paid-up and inducted member of the Methodist church, imbued with and socialized into the whole worldview and the accompanying values of Methodism, which manifested themselves in the studious search for holiness and Christian perfection.

I have now lived in Birmingham longer than I have in Yorkshire, yet the influence of those early years remains. It is indeed true, as the legion of "professional Yorkshire men" in the public eye can testify. You can take the man out of Yorkshire, but you cannot take Yorkshire out of the man. Or in my case, Yorkshire Methodism. The importance of these formative influences has been noted in a previous piece of writing.[20]

The Failed Promises of the White Church

The relative success of my formative years is, in many respects, readily apparent. I would not describe myself as unique in the development and progress I have experienced in the intervening times, from my early years in Bradford, to where I am now. Many others have made that journey.[21] The education and religious nurture I received was more than adequate in many respects, for it allowed me to move beyond the social and cultural limitations that were placed upon me due to circumstances of my birth, such as my ethnicity and social class. But my progress should not disguise the underlying failures and weaknesses of that movement. While it was perfectly adequate in some respects, it was woefully ignorant, naive, and lacking in many others.

My progress was relatively sure footed and I indeed moved into new pastures, far removed from the limitations and frustrations of my origins—areas my parents could hardly conceive. This move gave me enhanced opportunities; however, it did not give me a voice. I had a modicum of success and social improvement, but still no voice. The nature of my belonging—to the much aspired world of the White English middle class, or in the relatively comfortable climate of Methodism, was achieved at the expense of my cultural and ethnic identities.

To belong to British society and that of the church, for a black person, necessitates a denial of one's self. To be black in Britain is to have one's experiences, history, and reality ignored, disparaged, and ridiculed. Being black in Britain is to be rendered an insignificant presence amongst the many who are deemed one's superiors.[22] There is a famous Caribbean aphorism that states, "Who feels it knows it"—to be black in the twenty-first century Britain and the wider world is to find that what I know or have felt is of no consequence to the nation or world as a whole. What I know and have felt is dismissed as untrue and without any social, political, cultural, or theological consequence.

Putting All This into a Wider Context

I have reflected upon my subjective narrative in order to provide a personal microcosm of the larger sociohistorical forces that have shaped and influenced the development of black theology in Britain. This development has been an explicit and implicit response to the ongoing phenomenon of racism within British society in general and in British churches in particular. It can be argued that the formative developments of black theology in Britain have been, for the most part, due to the failed promises of white majority churches in the country. The rhetoric of being "one body in Christ" has often proved more illusionary than actual. I have used aspects of my personal, formative narrative as a form of short-hand for the broader structural issues and questions regarding black negation with regard to white majority ecclesial bodies in Britain.

It is to an assessment of this troubled relationship between black people in Britain and white majority (and white-run) churches that I now turn in order to explicate part of the development of black churches in my country.

Historic Roots

As I have stated previously in this chapter, my parents came to Britain in the mass migratory movement of black people from Africa and the Caribbean in the years following the end of World War II. The 1945 postwar presence of black people in inner cities in Britain and the churches there is a phenomenon that has been described by many sociologists and historians.[23] It is often believed that the existence of black people in Britain can be traced to this period in British history. This influx is perceived as commencing with the arrival of 492 Jamaicans at Tilbury dock on the *Empire Windrush*, on June 22, 1948.

Yet, Ian Duffield, quoting from the *Gentlemen's Magazine of 1764*, describes the large number of black people, estimated at the time, as high as 20,000, living in London at the turn of the eighteenth century.[24]

Peter Fryer describes the sense of alarm within London society in the later Elizabethan age at the apparently large number of black people, which Fryer estimates to be around 10,000 living in the capital at that time.[25] The history of the presence of black people in Britain can be traced to a much earlier period than 1940s onward. This mass migratory movement reached its peak in 1961 when approximately 74,590 blacks entered this country. The year is significant, for in 1962, the Commonwealth Immigrants Act limited greatly black immigration from the Caribbean to Britain.[26]

The experience of poor, marginalized, and oppressed peoples in Christian history and the church has largely been one of struggle, opposition, and invisibility. Black people have often been perceived as problems rather than opportunities. They have been controlled, denigrated, and treated with suspicion. Only in recent history has their presence within white majority churches been celebrated.[27]

In British history, the often submerged presence of black people, such as Mary Prince,[28] Olaudah Equiano,[29] and Ignatius Sancho[30] speaks of an experience that is characterized by an indomitable spirit that yearned for freedom. These pioneering individuals belonged to a community of black slaves who resided, at some point in their lives, in London and were key figures in the Abolition Movement, and yet for the most part they have been written out of British history.[31] More has been written by white abolitionists than the black people who were actually the slaves in question.

In many respects, like that of their U.S. counterparts, the roots of black theology in Britain can be traced to the struggle of black slaves in the seventeenth and eighteenth centuries in their fight for emancipation. The struggles of these black slaves in Britain speak to the corrupt, biased self-serving nature of English Christianity then. The pioneering work of such individuals as Sancho[32] and Prince[33] were valiant attempts to remind the English establishment of the basic tenets of Christianity, which British missionary efforts had exported to their empire throughout this era.

The early struggles of the eighteenth- and nineteenth-century black slaves in Britain have largely been exorcised from the collective memory of this nation. The discontinuity between the era of slavery and the contemporary identity of the nation makes clear the fact that there has been precious little acknowledgment of the role British slavery played in the economic progress of this country making it a global power of wealth and influence.

Sadly, this exorcising of the slave memory within the British experience has led many later generations of black people to believe that their contemporary antiracist struggles form the nascent seeds in the political struggle for liberation rather than an incremental addition to a continuing narrative.[34] The relative lack of data detailing the religious and theological sensibilities of black slaves in eighteenth- and nineteenth-century Britain (in stark contrast to the United States, which is explained later in this chapter) has left a void in the ongoing narrative of the development of black theology in Britain.

It is beyond the scope of this study to mount a detailed examination of the role played by black slaves in the general emancipation movement in Britain, prior to the mid-eighteenth century, or in the development of black theology, in this particular era.[35] It is worth noting, however, that there exists an important story to be told about the development of a prophetic stance on the Christian faith that found expression long before black pastors and scholars began to put pen to paper in a more explicit attempt to create a black theology of liberation for the British context. Just as slave narratives in the United States clearly predate the work of such luminaries as James Cone and J. Deotis Roberts, similarly, prior to the writings of the likes of Paul Grant or Valentina Alexander (more of which is explained later), we had the prophetic steadfastness of such unheralded folk as Olaudah Equiano.

The Self-Conscious Attempt to Create a Liberative Approach to Black Christianity in Britain

The mass influx of black people into Britain between 1948 and 1965 signalled an epoch-making change in the self-understanding of the nation. British churches, in addition to numerous other institutions, were forced to rethink their working models and the assumptions that lay behind such practices. These black people, largely from the many islands of the Caribbean, came to Britain as British passport holders, and were therefore British subjects of her Majesty, the Queen. The churches in particular were faced with having to engage with and accommodate new people, many of whom were communicant members of their denominations and traditions.[36] Many churches rose to the challenge of having to engage with the new dynamic created by this influx of black Christians. Others were less than accommodating.[37]

It is in this ongoing struggle to call white Christianity (often exemplified in the traditional white historic denominations[38]) to account that the more modern roots of black theology in Britain are to be found.

In the first editorial of *Black Theology in Britain*, Emmanuel Lartey, the founding editor offers a wonderful concise resume of the development of black theology in Britain.[39] In it, Lartey differentiates between the developments in black Christian expression as detailed in texts written by the likes of Ira Brooks, Sybil Phoenix, and with the later more expressly theological work by such individuals as Carol Tomlin, and Elaine Foster.[40]

The development of black theology in Britain is evidenced in two parallel tracks or trajectories. On the one hand, one can discern a movement of prophetic, black-consciousness inspired approaches to talking about God in the development of published texts (reports, articles, and books) by black people of faith, dating back to the early 1980s. The second track or trajectory, which will be analyzed extensively in the following chapter, finds expression in the work of black scholars who relate their prophetic scholarly work to the role of black churches[41] and their attempts to articulate a nascent black British theology from within their ongoing practice.

In this chapter, I want to spend a few moments outlining the development of black theology in Britain through early published works and juxtapose these with the development of a self-conscious scholarly approach to black theology, which emerged in the late 1960s in the United States. I want to argue that the development of black theology in Britain as discerned in these published texts from the 1980s and 1990s owes much to the pioneering work of the first generation of scholarly black theologians in the U.S., of whom James H. Cone is the most notable.

Defining One's Terms before We Begin

The essential point of departure between black and white Christianity is our notions of eschatology. *All* black Christians, (irrespective of theological disposition), have a clear sense that the future reign of God will be radically different from the one we presently experience. White male, conservative power, although preeminent in today's world, will not remain so in the new impending future. For many powerful conservative white Christians, the new world to come will be an enhanced version of the current one; with the same people (i.e., people like themselves) calling the shots. Black Christianity is always radical in this regard, whether it is implied and passive or explicit and active.

Before I seek to outline an indicative trajectory for the development of black theology in Britain, it is worth defining a few terms. In the first instance, this text is concerned with the development of black theology, not necessarily black Christian religious experience. One of the difficulties I have often witnessed when talking with white British theologians is their inability to differentiate between the positionality of differing black religious scholars. There is the assumption amongst many white commentators that *all* black Christian religious scholars are black theologians.

When speaking of black theology, I am referring to the specific self-named discipline of reinterpreting Christian traditions and practices in light of liberationist themes and concepts, which arise out of black experiences. This approach is one that makes blackness and black experience the initial point of departure (in partnership with Scripture, not the Bible alone, as sole authority) and uses these sources as the primary hermeneutical lens by which the truth of God's liberating agency is discerned. In effect, blackness becomes the prime interpretative framework for reinterpreting and reimaging God and the Christian faith. Black Christian religious experience refers to the "folk"-orientated approach to Christian traditions that arise out of black experiences, but which do *not necessarily* have a political or explicitly transformative agenda. Neither does this approach necessarily see blackness as a primary hermeneutical lens for reinterpreting the Christian faith, nor is it the case that one necessarily begins with black experience as the normative source for doing theology.

For many, in this camp, salvation has come to mean adherence to the belief in Jesus Christ as Lord and Saviour and is expressed within the context of individual experience and personal salvation. Salvation as understood in terms of liberation, social transformation, and societal reconfiguration is given less emphasis, or in some cases, rejected all together.

I acknowledge that the line of demarcation between these two different perspectives is blurred. There are many commonalities between these two disciplines of black religious scholarship. For example, all black Christian religious experience is implicitly liberationist, even when constrained by conservative doctrines and neoconservative ethics.

One has only to witness the ways in which black Christianity can be theologically conservative and yet be in solidarity with more progressive models of social policy and political engagement. To put it simply, black Christianity, even when conservative (in Britain, often, but not exclusively seen in terms of black Pentecostalism) rarely aligns itself with the dictates of white conservatism, particularly in the areas of social policy and party politics. In the British context most black Christians tend to vote for the "left of center" (British) Labour Party.

Although black Christian religious experience and black theology have a great deal in common, there are, in some cases, significant differences. All black theologians fall within the overall orbit of black Christian religious experience, in so far as black theology thought draws from the common well-spring of black history, culture, ecclesiology, and social and political struggle. Crucially, however, not all that is construed as black Christian religious experience is necessarily black theology.

I am at pains to make this distinction because it has enabled me to be critically selective in my choice of material from which to construct this trajectory. Work by scholars such as Syble Phoenix, Iain MacRoberts, Valentina Alexander, Joel Edwards, Ira Brooks, Carol Tomlin, and others[42] can claim to be important early sources in the development of black theology in Britain. I have decided not to analyze these texts for two reasons. First, some of these authors would not want to be described as being black theologians or have their worked being designated as such. For authors such as Ira Brooks and Joel Edwards, who fall within the black Christian religious experience camp although their work is reflective of African and Caribbean cultures, it does not make blackness and liberation explicit hermeneutical frameworks from which one can reinterpret the Christian faith.

For others, such as Alexander, their work is located within a more explicit liberationist framework, in which blackness is a hermeneutical lens for assessing the truths of the Christian faith; however, it should be noted that her doctoral thesis remains unpublished.

For theological, ideological, and practical reasons, I have sought to confine my assessment to those texts that place issues of black experience and black identity at the foreground of the methodological approach to doing theology and those that are also in the public domain as published documents.

Suffice it to say, of course, that these designations are in no sense absolute and I would not want to give the erroneous impression that the discourse I have just detailed is an uncontested one or even the final word on the matter.

⁻Black Theology in Britain by Way of Published Works

As I have stated previously, it would be incorrect to assert that black theology did not have an existence prior to the published works I am about to describe. For example, in American history, the lives and testimony of black slaves in the United States speak to a form of black theology that existed long before the more self-conscious formal incarnation of the 1960s and 1970s.[43] One of the earliest texts written by a black Christian in Britain that began to articulate a distinct and conscious experience of black religious sensibilities was Gus John's 1976 text *The New Black Presence*.[44] In his British council of churches booklet, John outlines the challenges the nation as a whole and the church in particular encounter as these seek to engage with the growing and settled communities of minority ethnic people living in many of the major conurbations of the country. Gus John can be perceived as a grand patriarch of black theology in Britain.

Many of the challenges articulated by John are taken up with greater alacrity by Robinson Milwood in his 1980 text *Let's Journey Together*.[45] Milwood's text is important, because within it, we begin to see the emergence of many of the themes that will become staple ingredients in the ongoing recipe for an authentic black British theology that is being developed. One of the primary aims of Milwood's text is to challenge white Christians and the governing structures they have created to acknowledge and affirm the presence of black people in society, and predominantly in white ecclesial bodies. Milwood, a black Methodist minister trained in Britain, is certain that the African American model of separate churches on the grounds of race is not the answer for the British context.[46] In one of the early sections Milwood writes,

> Segregation is attractive for sociological and technical reasons . . . Christianity is about reconciliation and liberation. These are not simply themes but actions forming the basis of Christ's teachings, miracles, parables, death and resurrection . . . We know that, as black and white in one church, that this is expected of us. It is not an open option for the Christian to choose: a separatist is *not* a Christian. (Emphasis in the original)[47]

What is instructive about Milwood's text is the sense in which he is still operating within the bounds of what one might term "classical Christianity." There is no reference within the text to the iconic phrase

Black Theology. Nor is there any attempt to offer a radical reappraisal of the central doctrinal formulations of the Christian faith. Rather, his approach is one of reminding, presumably, white Christians, of the need to adhere to the central tenets of Christianity, which speak clearly against any notion of ethnocentric supremacy.

At a later juncture, the author, seeking to expand on his central theme of reconciliation (between God and humankind and between black and white), writes

> The Church must be prepared to engage in a ministry of reconciliation, seeking ways and means of effecting dialogue between rival factions. Reconciliation is a central theme in Christian scripture. In 2 Corinthians 5:18, 19 Paul speaks of "God who through Christ reconciled us to Himself and gave us a ministry of reconciliation; that is, God was in Christ reconciling the world to Himself . . . Christian mission entails working towards a reconciliation amongst estranged elements of humankind.[48]

For Milwood, the Christian faith as classically explicated over the previous 20 centuries contains within it all the essential tools and themes for overcoming the seemingly endemic ills of racism and white supremacy that have led to the breach between black and white in the British context.

Let's Journey Together is notable for the challenging way in which the author asserts the need for black people and their concomitant cultures and identities to be recognized and affirmed within the ongoing life of the church. Forcing black people to adhere to white ethnocentrically constructed norms is not, he argues, a true measure of the acceptance of difference that is the radical intent within the body of Christ.[49]

It is interesting to note that writing in 1998—some 18 years after his pioneering contributions, my work on black theology in Britain, operating from within an educational perspective, asserted not dissimilar notions to Milwood's (unaware of his early work in this respect).[50]

Milwood's text exists as a kind of radical precursor to the explicit forms of Black theological discourse that emerged in the 1990s. In this respect, *Let's Journey Together* is similar in some respects to the important legacy of Howard Thurman and his classic text *Jesus and The Disinherited* in that Milwood's book foreshadows the later emergence of black theology.[51] I think it would be somewhat speculative and,

I dare say, embarrassing for Milwood if I were to compare his own modest text (which runs to some 40 pages) to Thurman's landmark tome. In linking the two, what I hope to elucidate is the dynamic sense of preencounter that exists within each respective text, in terms of their relative positions to the development of black theology in both contexts. Whilst it would be remiss of us to identify Thurman as a black Liberation theologian,[52] there is no doubting the pivotal role he played in providing the canvass on which later theologians could paint their sparkling colors of social and political transformation.

Similarly, within the British context, Milwood can be identified as being a crucial progenitor for the development and articulation of black theology. While neither within this text nor within an important contribution to a later book[53] can Milwood be easily described as a black theologian; there is, however, no doubt as to his importance to the development of black theology in my country. In his conversation with Anita Jackson in *Catching Both Sides of The Wind*, Milwood states,

> I do believe that ultimately mankind should journey together, but in terms of liberation theology, which is biblical, and I think the authentic theology. The God you see in the Old Testament is a God who takes sides. God deliberately segregated his people for the sake of their survival and the survival of the religion.[54]

In the five years between *Let's Journey Together* and his conversation with Jackson, he has begun to articulate the concept of liberation and the biblical injunction for justice as the basic markers for the articulation of a self-conscious model of black theology within Britain. Milwood is now arguing for a "temporary model of separation" in order to ensure the survival of black people in Britain. In his 1994 essay, "Salvation and Liberation," Milwood, using his own praxis as a Methodist minister of two black majority churches in East London as case studies, begins to map out some of the basic building blocks for a nascent black British theology.[55] This work is developed further in a later text in which an increasingly radical theological polemic is beginning to emerge.[56]

In *Liberation and Mission*, Milwood has dispensed completely with the ameliorated and theological moderation of his previous writings. In this text, he takes to task the apparent supine weakness of white English liberal racist attitudes to black people.[57] Milwood remains a key figure in the early development of black theology in Britain.

Remembering the White Folk!

A significant presence in the development of black theology in Britain has been the indefatigable work of committed white scholars. As this text is concerned primarily with the development of black theology in Britain by black people, I want to concentrate my analysis as an insider-looking out, on the voices of black people with whom I share a common experience of marginalization and oppression within the British context. This voice is prioritized, as it has been underrepresented and underreported within the academy. Despite this position, however, it would be remiss of me not to mention the work of particular white people. In this regard, I want to mention briefly three scholars.

First, one has to bear witness to the pioneering work of Roswith Gerloff. Gerloff, a German Lutheran minister, was appointed the first executive director of the Centre for Black And White Christian Partnership. The center was based for many years in Selly Oak area of Birmingham and was an independent Para Church organization with links to the Mission Department of the Selly Oak Colleges and the Theology Department of the University of Birmingham.

Working under the renowned professor of Mission, Walter Hollenweger, Gerloff researched the growing movement of black-led churches in Britain, the majority of which were closely associated with the influx of Caribbean migrants to Britain in the post–World War II period, between 1948 and 1965. Gerloff's pioneering work gave rise to one of the first attempts to identify a black British Theology. Her monumental thesis (in two volumes) became for many years, one of the standard texts detailing the development of black majority church traditions in Britain.[58] The second scholar is the Rev. John L. Wilkinson, presently an Anglican priest at Kings Heath Parish Church, in the Diocese of Birmingham, in the West Midlands area of Britain. Wilkinson is one of the "forgotten heroes" of the developmental process in the emergence of black theology in Britain.

Wilkinson served for many years in black majority Anglican churches in Birmingham. He was instrumental in helping form a black grassroots ecumenical church movement entitled "Claiming The Inheritance."[59] The fruits of his involvement in this multiethnic group of black and white Christians can be seen in a number of ways. First, he initiated the very first black Christian studies course in the British theological education system at the Queen's College back in the early 1990s. This course was a forerunner to the later module in black theology, developed initially by Wilkinson and his later colleague Robert Beckford.[60]

Second, his postgraduate research, which arose from his grassroots engagement with "Claiming The Inheritance," was one of the first such academic pieces of work, seeking to recognize and affirm the black presence in white majority British churches.[61] This thesis was later "converted" into a book.[62]

Third, and finally, I would like to mention briefly Kenneth Leech. Leech is an Anglican priest who has spent most of his working life in inner city contexts in London. In addition to pioneering Christian youth work, involved in a radical ministry amongst those suffering with drug addiction in the 1960s and early 1970s, he has developed an ongoing work as one of the leading urban theologians in Britain.

Prior to his development as an influential scholar, Leech worked as a field officer for the British council of churches. His involvement with urban issues has found expression in his reflections upon the corrosive role of racism in the life experiences of black and white people with reference to the body politic of white majority churches and the British state. Among his most important books are *Struggle in Babylon*[63] and *The Sky is Red.*[64]

Continuing the Story

The development of black theology in Britain through published material, which dates back to the mid-1980s, drew strength and inspiration from the ongoing engagement with African American theologians. In the literature of that time, one begins to see a growing awareness of the importance of black theology and the need for such an enterprise to be developed for and within the British context. The impetus for this growth and development came, chiefly, from African American scholars.

Inheritors Together[65] was a jointly edited pamphlet produced as part of a series entitled "Theology and Racism." This was the second in the series. What is most notable rereading *Inheritors Together* some 20 years after it was published is the fact that it is one of the first texts to link the eradication of the ongoing phenomenon of racism within white majority British churches with the nascent development of black theology in this context. In effect, black theology is now promoted as the most effective antidote and liberative key for unlocking the seemingly perennial stain of racism on the body politic of historic, white majority British churches.[66] The first two sections of the pamphlet are concerned with identifying and illustrating the many ways in which racism has limited and inhibited the presence of black people within (chiefly) the Church of England. The picture they draw is one that echoes many of the themes found in Milwood's discourse. John Wilkinson in his opening essay, "A Study of black Anglicans in Relation to White from Slavery Times to Contemporary Birmingham," states,

> But the heart of Black Christianity lay not with the teaching of the white missionaries but with the form of Christianity which the slaves fashioned for themselves arising out of their *own* experience and needs. (Emphasis added)[67]

Wilkinson's comments penetrate to the very heart of black diasporan Christian experience, a legacy common to both black people in the United States and Britain. Black Christianity is a "steal away"[68] faith that is imbued with subversive countercultural traits that make it somewhat different from White Euro-American religion. John Wilkinson and his wife Renate[69] (who is also ordained) detail the central features of black negation. They outline some positive examples of how white majority British churches might change in order to better accommodate and appreciate the insights and experiences of black Christians.

It is not until the third and final essay in the book that we see the first mention of the term "Black Theology" courtesy of an African American guest writer—James H. Evans, who, at the time of this short text, was the Martin Luther King Jr. Memorial Professor of Theology and Black Church Studies at Colgate Rochester Divinity School, New York. In Britain, Evans is perhaps best known for his African American systematic treatment of black theology entitled *We Have Been Believers.*[70]

In this 1985 pamphlet, it is Evans who offers an outsiders' vista on the development of black religiosity and theology within the British context.[71] Evans's essay is, in many respects, a microcosm of the project with which you are currently engaged, in that he seeks to juxtapose his own (internal) experiences of the United States, alongside an analysis (an outsider's eye) of the British context. Evans highlights most of the salient issues that affect black people in the Church of England (the national established church in England), many of which remain unresolved till now.

In his analysis of the British context, however, Evans goes further than his two white coauthors, for he links the explicit negation of black identity within the white dominated Church of England with a need to develop and articulate a "bottom-up" black theology of liberation for the British context. Evans, in a particularly vibrant section, which reads like the printed text of a rhythmically dynamic sermon, states,

> What is needed is a black theology for Britain. This theology would take account of the particularity of black life in England . . . This theology would be an affirmation of the vitality of the Christian faith seen through black eyes, and perhaps, in the process, call the whole church back to its prophetic mandate.[72]

Evans proceeds to outline some of the central features of this emerging black theology in Britain; he highlights areas of ecumenism, worship and formation, and black hermeneutics and intercultural alliances with white working-class people. Evans's importance to this text lies in the wealth of experience and gravitas he brings to this project. He speaks as an experienced black theological educator and scholar, whose presence inspires a fledgling British community to see beyond the limitations of their immediate context. In many respects, the presence of Evans in this text speaks of a broader engagement between black theologians in the United States and their newer, younger compatriots in Britain, of whom this author is one.

There are many who will argue that one of the weaknesses of black theology in Britain has been its continued reliance upon African American thought in the constructive task of developing resources for one's own context. It is interesting to note that *Inheritors Together* comprises three significant essays, two of which are written by white Anglican authors (the Foreword is by a black Anglican writer), with the third by an African American visitor. Was there no black British voice that could have articulated the insiders' perspective?

Given this context, one might well deduce that the framework of this text simply echoes the ambivalent relationship that continues to exist between white British paternalism and black British invisibility. Recently, black British scholars, such as Robert Beckford, have challenged the British media propensity to engage with and celebrate the contributions of African American scholars, such as Henry Louis Gates and Bonnie Greer (presently residing in Britain) at the expense of home-grown black British talent.[73]

It has often appeared to me that white British paternalism is far happier dealing with African Americans as they represent a kind of "distinguished visitor mentality." This operates at a tacit level where the guest is invited to make a number of pertinent observations safe in the knowledge that they do not belong here, and as such, will offer no ongoing challenge to the structures of white British supremacist thought. The black British presence is, on the other hand, much too close for comfort to be acknowledged and affirmed. The fact is, we belong and exist in this context and many of us have no intention of going anywhere (despite what far-right fascists groups such as the British National Party (BNP) would want to suggest). The relationship between African American black theology and black theology in Britain remains a complex one. Black theology in Britain has rightly looked to her stronger and more established African American cousin for inspiration and guidance, but has this dependence been at the expense of a vitally confident and mature indigenous voice?

Ongoing Developments

Within the literature of the mid-1980s to early 1990s, one can deduce a slowly developing consciousness in terms of a nascent black theology of liberation for the British context. In March 1990, an interdisciplinary and multiagency conference, sponsored by the Community and Race Relations Unit of the British Council of Churches was held, at which major issues pertaining to black people in Britain were discussed.[74] What is interesting to note about *Account of Hope* is the juxtaposing of black British and African American perspectives throughout the two-day conference. In terms of the former, one can cite the work of the Revd. Hewlette (Hewie) Andrew, a black British Methodist minister like Milwood, who in an address to the conference arguing for black self-determination and empowerment, states,

> If it were not for Black churches that are able to hold the people together, to give some sense of value at work, and to make them feel that God is on our side, they (Black people) would all be in mental institutions. And when I myself as a Methodist minister feel very low, and I mean really low, I do not go to a Methodist church to uplift me. I go for spiritual upliftment to what I know I will never get from any white preacher.[75]

What is striking about Andrews's address is that he is clearly articulating an alternative, African-centered expression of Christianity that is wholly at variance with that propagated by white hegemony. Andrews is clear that for black people to achieve their existential liberation within a white dominated and white controlled context, they must begin to create their own ecclesial and educational spaces from which to work out this innate quest for freedom.[76]

Alongside the comments of Andrew are those of another distinguished African American visitor, James Washington of Union Theological Seminary. Washington offers a detailed black Atlantic perspective on the need for collective, self-determined action by black people, drawing upon the work of the black church in the United States.[77] Washington draws upon the multidimensional qualities of black churches in the United States[78] in the areas of education, economic empowerment, civil rights, and of course, spiritual renewal. Washington challenges black people in Britain to gain strength from the multidimensional nature of faith in order to empower and radically transform black communities in this British context. Washington, along with his fellow U.S. compatriots who were guests at the conference, including Dr. Iva Carruthers and the Revd. John Mendez, offer the outsiders' contribution to this British conference, drawing on their own experiences as a means of speaking to this radically different situation.

The development of black theology in the 1990s can be seen in the attempts by particular educators to challenge the status quo in terms of British theological education. In 1992, Raj Patel with Maurice Hobbs and Greg Smith coauthored a report entitled *Equal Partners: Theological Training and Racial Justice*.[79] The report is an empirical analysis of the state of theological education in Britain. In the Foreword, it states,

> Some (seminaries or colleges) have short courses in 'Liberation theology' or 'Black theology'. The great majority, however, it seems from the survey, do not benefit from the kind of teaching about racism which enables them to see it as a profound social, cultural and economic influence in western society which, invading the institutions of the church, is able, only too easily, to render the Gospel of little effect.[80]

Within the report, the most clear clarion call for the development of a black theology of liberation in Britain comes from the Revd. Wesley Daniel, another black Methodist minister in Britain (now living and working within the UMC in New York).[81] Daniel states,

> I want to suggest that a serious look be given to what it means to be minister of and in a multiracial church. The area of preaching the Black tradition is important, pastoral care, music in the Black tradition, the importance of prayers in the Black tradition, Black people's social conditions and the relevance of that in relation to their approach to religion and religious practice.[82]

What is instructive about *Equal Partners* is that it begins to sketch out a role for black theology within British theological education. Whilst it does not offer any formative content for this nascent theological enterprise (indeed, none of the aforementioned texts has done so thus far), it does provide a much needed situational analysis of the white, Eurocentric complexion of the theological education system in Britain.

A Time To Speak and *A Time To Act*—Explicit Black Theology in Britain Comes of Age

As I will indicate, when assessing the development of black theology in the United States from the perspective of an outsider (outside looking in), there are significant Kairos moments, which can be seen to be epoch making events in the emergence of a movement. Clearly, the meeting of negro churchmen in 1966 was one such case in the United States.[83]

In the British context, and of a much more modest vintage (as befits the British character, perhaps) was the emergence of two landmark texts, *A Time To Speak*[84] and its sequel, *A Time To Act*.[85] Along with Robert Beckford's text *Jesus Is Dread* (to which greater reference will be made in the following chapter), these two books remain hugely influential publications in the development of black theology in Britain.

In terms of the central conceit of this text, "inside looking out and outside looking in," these books have been pivotal in shaping my own consciousness, as I sought to make sense of the British context into which I was born. These books predate my entry into the academy and my postgraduate work in education and black theology. These texts served as my early inspiration. They offered the more contextual gaze through which I could interpret the searing insights of my African American heroes James Cone and Gayraud Wilmore.

Both the texts were edited by Raj Patel, a Christian of South Asian descent, and Paul Grant, a black sociologist. Both had connections with a grassroots Christian campaigning group named "Evangelical Christians for Racial Justice," (ECRJ) which was based in Birmingham, in the West Midlands. I have been informed by one of the early participants of ECRJ that the two books that emerged from within its auspices were the product of a number of consultations that were held in and around Birmingham in the late 1980s. The development of black theology in Britain took a more distinctive and formidable turn with the publication of these two books.

What Do I Make of Them Now?

Rereading both texts has brought a number of important issues to light, in terms of my assessment of the development of black theology in Britain. First, it is important to note that despite my self-defined position as a black African Caribbean British subject, black theology in Britain has always occupied a more plural ground than that found in the United States.

In terms of the latter, black theology has become virtually synonymous with the experiences of African American people. A number of scholars have identified the "Black Experience," in which accompanying material productive traits such as black cultures are housed as the repository for the initial point of departure for black theology in North America.[86]

Within a British context, the development of coalition politics[87] and use of a politicized notion of black[88] (i.e., it has become a more plural term denoting an antihegemonic, unified stance amongst all nonwhite people) has enabled differing groups of people to coalesce around this term.

This more pluralistic basis for black theology is reflected in *A Time To Speak* in which South Asian voices are juxtaposed alongside continental African and diasporan African ones. This plural mixing should not be taken as a benign, noncontested space. In one's reading of some of the earlier texts I have cited, it would be fair to report that a number of the writers featured would think of black theology in Britain solely in black African terms. The endemic tensions within the often territorial and tribal nature of minority ethnic communities in the United States fighting for their space and place within the illusory promises of the America dream, offer a radically different context in which the term "black" is used.[89]

In Britain, there remain distinct strains of this tension,[90] but these are less potent (or corrosive) than in the United States, for a whole of host of reasons, one of which, is the fact that race occupies a more concealed and submerged vantage point within the body politic of this nation. In the United States to cite Dubois's[91] now legendary phrase, "the color-line" is the underlying seismic fault that runs through the very thread of the nation.[92]

Alongside the plural identities of the writers is the sense that the editors and authors have "come of age" in their identifying of some of the central features of an authentic black theology in Britain. Also, with the now customary assessment of the U.S. context, written by

Garnet Parris[93] we have essays in womanist theology[94] (the first to my knowledge in a published text (in Britain) and pieces detailing the history of black people in terms of our relationship to Britain.[95]

What is notable about this text, in sharp contrast to those I have identified thus far, is the unapologetic nature of the writing. The ideological intent of this text is demonstrated in the editorial where the joint editors state,

> The contributors to this, the first self-conscious attempt to map out a Black theology in Britain, come from many different backgrounds and speak with different voices and emphases. Even so, we share the commitment to encourage Black Christians to move away from the "thought control" and crumbling fortress of exclusive European theology and political practice. We want the space to express our understanding of God and the love of our people in whatever ways we see fit. This is the first fruit of that concern, but only the first.[96]

Clearly, within an edited text that draws upon a wide range of voices, one would not expect to find a high degree of homogeneity in the writing. What is notable, however, is the degree to which particular writers are grappling with a whole host of societal, political, and economic concerns that should be the rightful purview of black liberation theology. What is lacking, however, is the meaningful critical engagement with central doctrines of the Christian faith. None of the authors attempts to deconstruct or reinterpret any of the basic building blocks of the faith in light of black experience. The emphasis remains on trying to reform historic white Christian practices and the pleading for greater recognition of black people as human beings and fellow members of the body of Christ.

This tendency continues in the sequel to this text, entitled *A Time To Act*. This sequel offers another set of voices in which various aspects of the black theological project are outlined. The authors analyze the mission,[97] of churches,[98] some womanist reflections in the form of a group activity,[99] and some reflections on the unjust nature of immigration control.[100]

My rereading of this text has highlighted two main failings. First, the many contributions, do not explore in any depth the unique contribution of black people to this global phenomenon called Christianity. The various authors, for the most part, have undertaken some fine analytical work, outlining the political and social dimensions of black Christianity in Britain and sought to identify faith as a mobilizing construct in the British context. This approach is highly commendable, given the ways in which, predominantly, black British Pentecostalism has been attacked for its quietist and often passive and conservative spiritualized approach to social and political issues facing black people in Britain.[101]

This text eschews such an approach in favor of a radically political and prophetic outworking of the Christian faith and explores its potential for mobilizing and instituting change, within the British context.

What is lacking in both texts, however, is the significant development of a black hermeneutic. The writers seem to operate from the perspective that there is little that is problematic within the Christian faith. The task, therefore, for black Christians is simply to remind white racists of their myopic perspectives in understanding the central message of Jesus Christ.

This failure, for example, to highlight the need for a black British Christology or to reassess the meaning of salvation, means that these two texts, which are excellent in offering an authentic black British voice, somehow fail to demonstrate how that discourse is nothing more than a colored façade on top of a white supremacist edifice. In a previous piece of work, I have argued against the limited agency of a "colorization" approach, which seeks to offer a reasonable dash of color on top of an unstructured, unchanged white normative template.[102]

One of the central dimensions of black theology is its reimaging of the essentials of God's relationship with human kind in light of existential black experience. Jesus ceases to be an abstract universal symbol, he rather becomes a contextualized and particular agent-provocateur for a form of liberation that is concrete, specific, and historical.[103]

The lack of a black hermeneutic, the exploration of black sources' or norms for undertaking black theology in Britain implies that the effectiveness of these texts in realizing and mobilizing black Christian agency became somewhat blunted.

I wonder whether the sponsorship of these texts offers us a clue as to their limited engagement with the doctrinal heart of normative white Christianity. Both the texts are sponsored in part by Evangelical Christians for Racial Justice. Whilst there is not the space in this text for a detailed discussion on the semantics around such terms as "evangelical," and one has to acknowledge the many ways in which this term can be understood, I have wondered whether the traditional adherence to biblical authority and tradition, which are central convictions of most evangelicals did not hamper the production of these texts at some level.

I dare to suggest this possible fault line, having reflected in one of my previous researches into the ways in which predominantly evangelical theologians and educators have presented the Christian faith in teaching and learning curricula.[104] The need to preserve the purity of the Christian faith may have led to a greater emphasis upon highlighting sociopolitical and economic praxis-orientated forms of analysis as the natural concomitants of vibrant black faith. Yet, as Robert Beckford has shown, often, it is the very adherence to a form of conventional biblical literalism that has stymied the social and political potential of black churches in Britain in the first place![105]

These criticisms, however, should not be taken as a major rebuff for the sterling work undertaken by the two editors and the many contributors to both the volumes. A Time To Speak and A Time To Act remain landmark books in the development of black theology in Britain. My analysis of the development of black theology in my context will continue in the next chapter, when I assess the role of black churches in this ongoing narrative and highlight the seminal role of the most visible black theologian in Britain: Robert Beckford. Now, however, I want to juxtapose this British story alongside my reading of the narrative as it exists within the United States.

Black Theology in the United States—An Outsider looking in

I think it is worth stating, before I begin this assessment, that it is not my intention to either attempt a comprehensive analysis of the development of black theology in the Untied States or to suggest that any such reading by me is a definitive one. In the first instance, Wilmore and Cone's black theology anthologies[106] and a more recent text by Ware[107] lay out the groundwork for this historical and theological work, and these do so more competently than anything I could manage. Second, I am an outsider. This does not mean that I have nothing to say about black theology in the United States, nor does it mean that my comments lack legitimacy or insight. Many scholars have argued that notions of insider and outsider are complex terms that eschew any simplistic discourse around the privileging of knowledge and their resultant claims.[108]

My approach to this black Atlantic task of looking inside out and then outside in is to situate myself as a black British theologian. This is a reflexive form of analysis that says as much about me as it does about the context I attempt to analyze. This form of analysis represents my own intense involvement with black theology in both contexts and is my particular gaze upon both the worlds; as an insider in one and an outsider in the other.

Black Theology in the United States—Distinctive features

It should not need extensive repeating, but by way of a brief summation, it is worth stating that the social, political, and cultural contexts of black people in the United States and in Britain are significantly different. One of these differences is the sheer length of time in which the respective groups of diasporan Africans have lived in their own contexts. Whilst there has been a black presence in Britain since Roman times,[109] the majority of black people in this country, however, trace their close-at-hand engagement to Britain to the mass migratory movements of the last century (1948–1965).[110] Approximately, half a million people made the trip across the Atlantic from the islands of the Caribbean to Britain.[111]

Prior to the passing of the McCarran-Walter Act in the Unite States in 1952, the majority of black people in the Caribbean had emigrated to the States rather than Britain.[112] The majority of these Caribbean migrants came to Britain as British subjects. The countries from which they had traveled were not independent islands, but members of the British Commonwealth, under the direct sovereignty of Her Majesty, Queen Elizabeth the Second of Great Britain. The presence of black people in Britain remains a deeply contentious and politically sensitive issue within the nation. From our earliest times there have been questions about the legitimacy of our presence in the country,[113] which has given rise to white nationalist groups that have regularly called for black and Asian people to be "Repatriated."

Within the U.S. context the black presence dates back to the epoch of slavery. Hence the presence of African Americans in the United States is far longer than the 50 or so years in which the majority of black people have largely been resident within Britain. I have repeated this often-worked discourse because these differing sociohistorical and cultural contexts exert a great deal of influence on the various developments of black theology in each setting.

In my previous analysis on black theology in Britain, I cite Grant and Patel's *A Time To Speak* as the first "explicit" black theological text in this country. I use the term "explicit" intentionally because the text adopts the term *Black Theology* to describe itself. Yet, in the United States, published works by black theologians date back to the 1960s and texts detailing the African American experience go back even further.

The first significant difference between black theology in the United States and in Britain is the fact that it is genuinely theological in the United States. The emergence of black theology in the United States grew out of the social and political upheavals of the 1960s. The oppositional stance of the civil rights and black power movements led to an explicit rejection of white Christianity and the hypocrisy of the latter in terms of its treatment of black people.

The theology that emerged from within the Civil Rights Movement drew on the long legacy of black faith dating back to slavery. Black theology is the summation of 400 years of oppression and alienation of black people in the richest and most powerful country in the world. This theology, to my mind, is captured in part by the words that open Section 2 of the 1966 *Statement by the National Committee of Negro Churchmen* that reads

> It is of critical importance that the leaders of this nation listen to a voice which says that the principal source of the threat to our nation comes neither from the riots erupting in our big cities, nor from the disagreements among the leaders of the civil rights movement, nor even from mere raising for "black power." These events, we believe, are but the expression of the judgement of God upon our nation for its failure to use its abundant resources to serve the real well-being of people, at home and abroad.[114]

The strength of black theology in the United States has been its ability to "name the sin of racism."[115] This struggle has been to challenge the biased self-serving interpretation of the Christian faith that has given voice to and enabled the flourishing of white supremacy. Black people were able to challenge white supremacy through their courageous and unapologetic rereading of the traditional tenets of white Christianity. This latter perspective, by no means popular with all African American Christians, let alone white ones has been for me, the defining quality of black theology in the United States.

This ability to reread and reinterpret can be seen, for example, in the iconoclastic work of James Cone. In a now legendary passage from *A Black Theology of Liberation*, Cone writes,

> In a racist society, God is never color-blind. To say God is color-blind is analogous to saying that God is blind to justice, to right and wrong, to

good and evil. Certainly this is not the picture of God revealed in the Old and New Testaments. Yahweh takes sides.[116]

This early section from Cone's second book reads like an incendiary device within the heart of the body politic of white Christianity. Have not many of us grown up with the notion of God in Christ who can be likened to the genial umpire at a ball game? Jesus is the fair, decent, and "kind sort of chap" who loves everyone and does not take sides. This is the kind of Jesus who will neither get his hands dirty nor involve himself in the nasty, unfortunate, and "can't be helped" forms of racism that have stalked the world and blighted the life experiences of black people for the past half millennium.

In order to affect this form of myopic theological construction, classical white evangelicalism has resorted to a wholesale spiritualization of the central tenets of Christianity. One only has to look at the central heart of the Apostle's and the Nicene Creeds to see the truths of this contention. The creeds tell us everything about what Jesus stands for in terms of his symbolic, universalizing work of atonement, and salvation, but nothing about his liberating praxis as exemplified in his life.[117] In the words of my former academic supervisor, "Jesus' life (and therefore his praxis) disappears in a comma"[118] (that is, "he lived, he died").

Cone seeks to reinterpret the meaning of Jesus' life and ministry in addition to his understanding of salvation. Cone's Christology and Soteriology are shorn of the pious, spiritualized abstractions that have often characterized traditional white dominated understandings of Christianity. This version of faith makes Jesus a supine, pathetic, and nondescript figure who has neither the will nor the desire to effect any semblance of change in the here and now, save for the fact that his death enables people to be "saved"; however, this does not make individuals change their racist practices or views. No wonder black theology did not have any time for this seemingly powerless and pathetic Jesus!

By emphasizing the hyperspiritualized nature of Christ's saving work, white evangelicalism (and by a form of osmosis, black Christianity as well) has been able to replace practice with rhetoric. The doctrinal formulas of Christ's atonement, often mediated via involved and disconnected, premodern cultural concepts, such as "expatiation" and "propitiation,"[119] enables the searing prophetic work of Jesus to be reduced to the point where his followers can assert that they are "naming the name" and are "saved."

In effect, Christian discipleship is reduced to those who are able to say the right words and, make the appropriate cognitive leap of imagination in their identification with Jesus' saving work,[120] but with little inclination to follow his radical, countercultural actions. In short, white evangelicalism has taught us all to "worship Christ" but not to "follow him."

Is it any wonder, then, that confirmed and unapologetic racists could see no contradiction between loving God and hating their neighbor, especially, if that neighbor was black? When the Christian faith is reduced to John Chapter, 14, verse 6, there is little need to follow Jesus' actions, for, according to many, it is not by following Jesus that they can be saved, but by believing in him.

From my first reading of James Cone, back in the early 1990s, I realized that there was a different game in town, one that had new rules and was played in a completely different manner from the old one.

In highlighting Cone at this juncture, it is not my intention to suggest that (1) all of black theology in the United States can be captured in the work of just one man, or (2), that his work is somehow representative of all black Christian expression in the United States. Even within the black theology project, there have been those who have challenged the more polemical nature of some of Cone's pronouncements.[121]

As I reread and reflected on the development of black theology in the United States, I witnessed the extent to which the United States has been engaged in a deeply theological work, often challenging the very basics of traditional received wisdom. In Britain, however, with the notable exception of Robert Beckford's work, most black theologians have been more content to discuss black theology in terms of amendment and adaptation rather than deconstruction and revolution. As I surmised in my rereading of A Time To Speak and A Time To Act and in the work of Milwood and Aldred, one can see a tendency to leave the basic creedal building blocks of Christianity unchanged. Greater emphasis has been exerted on attempting to cajole and amend the practices of white British Christianity rather than denouncing it as being something less than or even antithetical to the Gospel of Christ.

In the work of black religious scholars in Britain, with the exception of Beckford's work,[122] greater emphasis has been given to exploring the social and cultural factors in the development of black religion as opposed to any major discussion on substantive systematic and constructive theological matters. There is relatively little effort to conceive an alternative form of dogmatics for black people, given the historical failings of white Christianity.[123]

I am amazed, for example, at the ways in which black Christians in Britain can display commendable suspicion at the often dissembling and untrustworthy nature of official, hierarchical establishment-bound white Christianity, and yet "swallow whole," the doctrinal assertions of classical Christian faith as developed, expressed, and propagated by the very people they do not trust.

The Christian faith, as we have received it, owes much to a top-down patrician and paternalistic form of imperial control between church and state.[124] Scholars, such as Hood and Byron, have cited this period as one in which many of the demonized notions surrounding blackness first emerged.[125] The introduction to Christianity via the whip and the lash has made diasporan black Christians commendably suspicious of the blandishments of white hegemony. Labels like "evangelical" are white Euro-American terms, not black ones. The tussles against modernity, witnessed in the late eighteenth and nineteenth centuries, stemmed from white *Euro-American problems in terms of epistemology*, and as such, should be left with them. As black people, our genius has been the ability to adhere to Scripture without being tied down by often arcane metaphysics. Black Christianity at its best can overcome the ongoing arguments concerning literalism against symbolic and analogical interpretation.

Somewhere along the line, possibly in the middle part of the last century,[126] many black Christians lost the ability to read Scripture and tradition in a dialectical manner; they could see it only as a single trajectory form of biblicism. I suspect that it is this loss that has led to a greater emphasis upon sociological analysis at the expense of substantive theological articulation. It must be stressed, however, that this emphasis upon sociological analysis as opposed to dogmatic or constructive methodologies is not some without merit or importance. The work of sociologists such as Paul Grant (coeditor of *A Time To Speak* and *A Time To Act*) and the African Caribbean Evangelical Alliance[127] offer a structural and organizational means of analysis in the work and development of black Christianity in Britain in a manner not unlike that provided by the likes of C. Eric Lincoln[128] and Cheryl Townsend Gilkes[129] in the United States.

I have wondered whether this difference is a symptom of the radically alternative contexts in which black theology is practiced in both settings. In the United States, where black people were brought to the shores of the continent in chains and where the legacy of slavery is still represented in the glaring divide between communities and cultures, one witnesses a nation in which race is still the dominant motif in the collective whole.[130] Given the ongoing ravages of racism and white supremacist thought within the United States, one can see the futility of ameliorated and consensus making approaches to black theological thought.[131]

In Britain, where the majority of black people came to the country out of economic necessity, but nevertheless, within the context of one's own agency and volition, we have been seduced by the language of moderation, assimilation, and integration than our African American counterparts. The language of "separate but equal" has never been explicitly sanctioned within the body politic of the nation. As I often tell my white students, there have never been any laws that have told black people where they can or cannot live, work, or study; yet the indices for black unemployment (or underemployment), poor housing, and poor education are virtually the same as those for other nations (chiefly the United States) where such sanctions were in evidence.

To be precise, Britain has hidden her racism under the veneer of apologetic rhetoric and supposed fair play. I have attempted to deal with this carefully concealed and obfuscated dynamic of British racism in some of my previous publications.[132]

I wonder whether the external contexts in which Black theology has been housed within the United States and in Britain has affected the essential character and form of our respective movements.

Black Theology That Arises from African American Experience

One of the first things that strikes the imagination of black theologians living in Britain is the rich historical backdrop on which black theology in the United States is predicated. Black theology, in whatever context it is located, arises out of the rich tapestry of black engagement with the Divine in order to answer the most basic of existential questions,[133] whether within the British context, dating back over a period of approaching 2,000 years[134] or in the United States, in greater mass numbers, in what is approaching an epoch of some 400 years.[135] Black people have sought to use religion as a means of coming to terms with and transforming their world.[136]

What distinguishes these two contexts is the positionality of black peoples' engagement in each context, which, in part, has been influenced by the means by which that activity has come about. In terms of the latter, for example, African Americans came to the United States, a land of economic and religious migrants, by force. In the popularized sloganeering of Malcolm X, "We didn't land on Plymouth Rock, Plymouth Rock landed on us." The migration of the majority of African and Caribbean peoples to Britain, was no less traumatic, but markedly different. It is beyond the scope of this study to detail the psychosocial effects of these differing narratives on the cognitive, affective, and spiritual well-being of black people in each context. I am in no doubt, however, that the various trajectories have exerted some impact on the content and the expression of faith of black people.

In terms of our respective negotiations in the emotional and physical space in which our various spiritualities are housed, whether in Britain or in the United States, it is worth noting that in the latter, one is engaging with a single discontinuity from our ancestral roots. In Britain, for a significant number of black people, their diasporan journeys have taken a 500-year sojourn in the Caribbean.

This period in our histories has led to another complex level of hybridity and syncretistic religiosity on which lies the overlays that is the seemingly homogeneous construction of white British Christianity.[137] This double movement of black people from Africa to the Caribbean and then onto Britain has led to a set of plural identities that have exerted a profound hold on the imagination, religious expression, and sensibilities of black people in Britain. Caribbean and British womanist/feminist[138] scholars such as Marjorie Lewis[139] and Diane Watt[140] have explored the diverse and complex nature of black women's expressions of religiosity and spirituality from a black Atlantic perspective. These expressions of religious identity and spirituality are suffused with African retentive cultures, myriad Caribbean social mores, and British sensibilities within the one complex black female body.[141]

What is interesting to note, looking into the U.S. context from the outside, is the fact that so much of the African American discourse is steadfastly concerned with African Americans. I make this observation, not so much as a criticism, but more of an observation. America is a hugely diverse entity. There has been a long history of black migration to the United States from other contexts in the world. Many of the leading black political leaders, such as Marcus Garvey (who came from Jamaica), for example, were themselves migrants to the United States.

In spite of these plural realities in the United States, it is still common to find black theological texts written with no cognizance of the fact that not all black people or black theologians are African Americans. Ware's recent book on methodologies in black theology is an obvious case in point.[142] The author writes from the assumption that the experiences of black scholars from other contexts (Noel Erskine and Kortright Davis immediately spring to mind) have not made an overly pronounced impact or contribution to black theology in the United States.

Nor is there any sense that African American religious thought has been influenced by and borrowed from the cultural insights and sensibilities of other black peoples. Of course, one can find a number of important examples in which this plurality has been recognized. It would be remiss of me not to mention the work of such scholars as Peter Paris[143] and Anthony Pinn.[144] Pinn is assiduous in highlighting the multiple sources and forms in which African American religiosity is expressed.

In one sense, I can readily appreciate the reasons for this kind of single-trajectory form of discourse. It is clearly the case that slavery and the struggle of African Americans to create something out of nothing has provided the major sociocultural backdrop out of which black theology has emerged and since flourished.

Clearly, it would be an act of the worst kind of churlishness to deny African Americans the right and the necessity to celebrate their story of how they "got over." The contribution of other black peoples to this story is no doubt a relatively small one in comparison to the mighty edifice of the African American experience.

However, the story of black theology in the United States is not solely an African American one. Yes, the dominant voice and expression is indeed African American. But if size and dominance becomes the main, perhaps the only criterion by which contributions are measured, then African American black theology becomes no better than the imperialistic tendencies of corporate America per se, in terms of her relationship to the rest of the world.

If cultural hegemony is wrong, by definition, then it does not suddenly take on a different complexion simply because African Americans are the ones imposing it. One of the critical challenges facing black theology in the United States is to remember that within the dual designation of the term African American is the word "American." By this, I mean, that within the collective and corporate whole that is "project America" lies the potentially prophetic and challenging presence of African Americans who have often called their nation to account and asked it to renounce its aggrandizing tendencies and practices in the world.

This important role, however, should never be assumed or taken for granted. It can become all too easy for African American black theology to become sufficiently immured from internal and external realities that it fails to see the crushing irony, in the casual disregard it holds for other black people, that often becomes a faint echo of the treatment they themselves have received from white Americans.

I have experienced at first hand the sense of becoming invisible and of little worth when in the company of 'some' African Americans at corporate gatherings in the United States. Robert Beckford echoes some of these thoughts when he writes of his experiences as a black British person living in the United States. Remembering some of his formative years in the United States, he writes,

> On most occasions, I was either bullied or patronized by the African-American males with whom I came into contact. In fact the Black males with whom I had an immediate rapport were those, like myself, of Jamaican working-class ancestry (Jamaican-Americans). One thing I learned from that summer was that not all Black young men were the same.[145]

It should not need stating (but I will, in order to ensure that my motives are clearly understood) that my criticisms are not against African Americans per se. I do not want to suggest that African Americans are not hospitable or kind to those among their ranks who do not share their ancestry. I have benefited enormously, both professionally and personally, from the abundant kindness and support of black theologians in the United States. But it is worth reminding my American colleagues (as much to remind myself) that one should always be in the process of constant monitoring and reevaluation of one's assumptions and outlooks.

This is necessary if one is not to fall prey to the subconscious complicit practices and traditions that are something short of the inclusive, liberative spirit that lies at the heart of black theology. In this respect, Cornell West's work on imperialism is of great importance in reminding *all* Americans of the assumptions that arise from the manifest destiny that sits so easily within the body politic of the United States of America.[146]

Specialisation versus Interdisciplinary Practices—A Personal Insight

On my first visit to the American Academy of Religion, I was struck by the number of occasions I met African American religious scholars whose first question upon meeting me was "And what is your discipline?" My usual response was often one of silence followed by a rather stumbling and somewhat incoherent attempt to describe my discipline. The reasons for my difficulty in describing myself were due, in no small measure, to the nature and prevailing culture of the theological academy within Britain.

In my own academic development, I have straddled a number of disciplines. My initial training was in history, specializing in church history. My postgraduate work has been in education and theology. In some respects, I might be described simply as a religious educator; but my scholarly work and training was never solely concerned with the teaching and learning of faith traditions. In many respects, my work involved an intense engagement with constructive and systematic theologians, in addition to biblical specialists. The hermeneutical task of reconfiguring and articulating the Christian faith[147] was undertaken with cognizance of both theological and educational sources.

My twin academic "heroes" on my scholarly pilgrimage have been Grant S. Shockley[148] (an African American religious educator) and James H. Cone (the founding father of Black Liberation theology).

At no point in my development as a scholar have I been overly conscious of being confined to one specific disciplinary box. Whilst education remains a central concern of my research, doctrinal, historical, textual, and pastoral questions have constantly played a part in the construction and development of my academic output.

Within the British context, I think it is fair to say that most black theologians are able to turn their hand to a number of disciplines. This sense of ubiquity is most probably the product of a number of factors.

1. The number of black theologians in Britain is so small that many of us have learnt to add additional strings to our bow in order to augment the particular specialism of our postgraduate work. In the context of my own work, I have taught in the areas of education, practical theology, systematics, missiology, and biblical hermeneutics.
2. As a corollary to the previous point, I have observed the paucity of personnel particularly within British theological education. Many institutions, whether full-time and residential or part-time and non-residential, operate with small faculties. Consequently, it becomes necessary for teaching staff to develop competences in a number of areas, in addition to their particular specialism and training.
3. The often unstructured nature of research programs (doctoral or masters) often enables students to explore seemingly disparate fields of study, with the emphasis upon "pure research" (often little in the

way of structured classroom teaching), which leads to the synthesizing of knowledge from various areas of endeavor.

4. As many black theologians in Britain do not have first degrees in theology, there is a sense that the emergence of their scholarly voice provides an opportunity to develop a greater awareness of foundational issues, in addition to the specialism of the research work.

5. The fact that the theological academy does not seem to "ring-fence" particular disciplines (with the possible exception of biblical studies, about which I discuss a little later) enables many scholars to cross traditional boundaries in the development of their work. The fact that one "can" is usually taken as a "license" to do so.

When I compare this state of affairs with the situation in the United States, the immediate contrast between the two contexts becomes obvious. In the United States, the corporate mass industry, that is, theological education (from M.Div. through to the D.Min., Th.D., and Ph.D.) represents a highly developed pathway in which candidates undertake generic work and then specialize. The creation of scholarly guilds then acts as both a point of focus for the ongoing development of that particular discipline and a form of quality control and perimeter/border within which the nature of the discourse of that discipline is ring-fenced, and subsequently overseen.

It seems to me that crossing academic disciplines in the United States is difficult than it is in Britain. An obvious case in point can be seen with respect to my friend and former colleagues in the black theology in Britain project, Emmanuel Y. Lartey. Lartey (about whom more will be said in the following chapter) is a pastoral theologian by training. His major area of concern is the interpenetration of cultures and identities in the context and discipline of pastoral theology and pastoral care. His seminal text *In Living Colour*[149] has done much to offer a plural, eclectic, and intercultural perspective on the theory and practice of pastoral care in Britain and further afield.

Whilst Lartey has been at the forefront of the development of pastoral theology and care in Britain and on the international stage, his efforts for the development of black theology in Britain have been immense. Lartey is not a specialist systematic or constructive theologian. Yet, his wideranging scholarly interests saw him become the founding father of black theological work in Britain. As we will see in chapter 5, when I assess the development of the black theology journal, the crucial role played by Emmanuel Lartey will become readily apparent.

In the United States, the development of specialist areas of study within the theological academy has been replicated within the particular arena of black theology. It was interesting, for instance, to find a very clear demarcation between those who might describe themselves as theologians (i.e., those who are have specialized in systematics or ethics) and those who do not (namely everyone else).

I have met black religious scholars whose work is at the radical end of the theological spectrum, who, due to the fact that they are not systematic or constructive theologians or ethicists, would not describe themselves as black theologians. Within Britain, where the crossing of academic specialism is more commonplace, the term "Black Theology" has taken on a more generic conception to mean the doing and articulation of theology arising out of the black experience from within a variety of disciplines.

In Britain, for example, there exists within the Midlands[150] a black theology forum (more information of which is given in a later chapter) that meets in the last week of every month. The forum is a dedicated space for black scholars only (but the definition of black is a very plural one as described previously in this chapter). The people attending it (mainly postgraduate students studying at and academics associated with the University of Birmingham) come from a variety of backgrounds. Some are theology students. Others are educationists, psychologists, pastors, and those who defy any form of categorization, but simply want to be part of a radical and creative black space. The meeting is open to all who simply want to relate black religious thinking to life. Black theology is the discipline that unites us. I do not recall one conversation where the legitimacy of any particular discipline has been disputed.

The Benefits of Specialization and the Weaknesses of Generic Approaches

Perhaps the greatest strength of black theology in the United States is the sheer depth in the number of scholars engaged within it auspices. In my previous comments, I have made the claim that, often, it appears that only people within particular disciplines get to identify themselves as black theologians. Quite naturally, I am aware of the obvious dangers of overstating the case based upon the limitations of my own perceptions. I know, for example, of many scholars who are not theologians or ethicists who will identify themselves with the cause and intent of black theology. Biblical scholars such as Cain Hope Felder[151] and Randall Bailey[152] immediately spring to mind. My attendance at the AAR has alerted me to the many scholars who attend the black theology group meetings and whose expertise lie outside the disciplines I have identified thus far. What is instructive about the range of specializations that exists within the United States is the greater number of black theological scholars (whether in systematic or in other areas) than is the case within Britain.

If one takes only those whose areas are systematics or ethics, one can name 20 such individuals. These names range from the elder statesmen (and they most usually are men), such as James Cone,[153] Major Jones,[154] Deotis Roberts,[155] Preston Williams,[156] to the plethora of womanist scholars, such as Karen Baker Fletcher,[157] Kelly Brown Douglas,[158] and Elaine Thomas,[159] who have emerged as theologians in the past 15 years or so.

The benefits of specialization can be seen in the range of methods, approaches, and substantive differences in their respective theologies. Dwight Hopkins has made an important contribution in identifying the plethora of approaches and themes in the work of the so-called second and third generation of Black theologians in the United States.[160]

I have often remarked when giving introductory lectures in black theology to predominantly white students that if I were given a blank piece of paper and 15 minutes, I might possibly be able to name every black theology student and academic in the country, and still have plenty of space left on the page. Black theology in Britain remains at the formative stage. As discussed in my previous historical analysis of select black theology texts in Britain, the first self-conscious pieces of work did not begin to emerge until the early 1990s. Our development is sure footed and is definitely progressing well, but we are beginning from a very recent and small power base.

Perhaps the greatest area where this failure in specialization is best exemplified is in the very technical area of biblical exegesis. There is, to the best of my knowledge, no black biblical specialist within Britain.[161] Many within the black theology in Britain network, such as myself, Michael Jagessar,[162] and Joe Aldred, and others[163] have undertaken biblical hermeneutical work. The depth of African American approaches to biblical studies can be seen in Joseph Brown's *The Blackening of The Bible*[164] in which the author charts the plethora of approaches adopted by African American biblical specialists to interpreting the Bible.

Upon reading this book I was struck at the subtle and carefully nuanced approaches of African Americans in their engagement with biblical texts. The range of various approaches on display reflects the complexity with which black people have engaged with this most sacred of all literature in terms of orientating the entire scope of their cosmos.[165]

Black people in Britain are no less complex in their reading of Holy Scripture. However, the dearth of black scholars who are prepared and able to undertake the necessary years of language training in order to do the detailed exegetical work expected of biblical specialists is the cause of the glaring failure and omission within Black theology in Britain.

It is perhaps worth noting that within the British context, greater emphasis in scholarly work has been given to practical theology than to biblical studies. This disparity may be due to the influence of Lartey as mentioned earlier (whose own specialism was pastoral theology). It may also be a pragmatic choice on the part of some, realizing that it appears somewhat easier to train to be a pastoral theologian than the apparent longer period needed to master biblical languages and learning the art and the science of decoding ancient texts.

Robert Beckford has noted the glaring imbalance in the development of black theology in Britain since the early 1990s.[166] Given the fact that black theology holds the Bible to be one of the basic sources for the undertaking of this discipline,[167] and that Black people are not going to give up on the Bible anytime soon,[168] it is imperative that this ongoing deficiency within the British context is rectified.

In a spirit of mutuality and friendship, it may well be the case that the older sibling, that is, black theology in the United States may offer some pointers and be a symbol for the possibilities that will arise within the British context.

In this chapter I have sought to offer a selective, personal, historical, and contemporary analysis of the respective developments of black theology in Britain and in the United States. In the next chapter I explore the relationship between Black theology and that of the black church in its many guises. This analysis will begin once again within my own context (inside looking out), assessing the work of the black theologians who have emerged from within the black church in Britain, most notably, Robert Beckford. Then I will juxtapose these developments with the situation as I perceive it within the United States (outside looking in). How and to what extent have black theology and the black church made for uneasy bedfellows?

2

Friend or Foe?: Black Theologians and the Black Church

Within the literature of black theology, particular emphasis is placed on the role of the black church as the major (and in some respects, the only) institution that has affirmed and conferred dignity upon the inhibited and assaulted personhood of black people.[1] To put it quite simply, black folk in the African Diaspora might not have survived up to this point had it not been for their God-inspired genius for creating safe ecclesial spaces in which they could seek refuge from the ravages of racism and white supremacy.

In this chapter, I want to take a selective look at the role of black churches work and its importance (or otherwise) with respect to the ongoing development of black theology on both sides of the Atlantic. Once again, this analysis will be a subjective one and will be undertaken partly through the lens of significant black scholars whose work in some ways exemplifies something of the nature and purpose of black churches.

Problematic Nature of Definitions!

Perhaps one of the thorniest problems that we encounter when trying discuss the black church is the question of definition. What do we mean by the term "The black Church"? For reasons that will soon become apparent, this question is somewhat easier to answer within the U.S. context than it is in Britain's. In the United States, the notion of the black church is an ingrained historical, theological, sociological, and experiential reality for many African Americans. The black church has an automatic efficacy that finds expression in myriad forms of discourses and academic courses. The late Grant Shockley, for example, developed a good deal of his scholarly work in Christian education by combining the insights of black theology and educational method-ologies in dialogue with the black church.[2]

In the latter part of the previous chapter, I commented briefly on the importance of the Bible as one of the primary sources and norms for doing black theology. Another important source and norm for undertaking black theology is the black Church.[3] Within the United States, the black church is a normative context out of which black theology (in theory) should arise. Whilst some, particularly those within the pastoral/practical theology domain, have challenged and questioned the relationship between black theology and the black church,[4] there is no doubting that in the United States one is dependent, to some extent, on the other. The term black church when used in the context of the United States is a generic one, seeking to denote and describe particular faith communities in which black leadership, culture, traditions, experience, and spirituality represent the norm, and from which, white, Anglo-Saxon traditions, and expres-sions are largely absent. These churches are termed generic because unlike in Britain, they are not identified to any one denominational or theological slant.

These churches cut across the whole spectrum of church affiliation and the multiplicity of settings in which black life is experienced. The development of the Black church in the United States grew out of the racism of the established churches of white, European origin. The wor-shipping life of these churches displayed discriminatory practices, con-vincing black people to leave in order to form their own faith communities. The denominations most commonly identified with the black Church are *The African Methodist Episcopal Church* (AME), *The African Methodist Episcopal Zion Church* (AMEZ), *The Christian Methodist Church* (CME), *The National Baptist Convention Incorporated*, *The National Baptist Convention of America*, and *The Progressive Baptist Convention and the 'Church of God in Christ'*.[5]

Black Churches in Britain

Black British Pentecostalism

Black churches in Britain in broad terms can be split into three typologies. These are "Classical Pentecostals," "Neo-Pentecostal," and black majority churches, in white historic denominations. The first two typologies are often the most visible (and seen by some as normative), and are those that fall within the Pentecostal camp. In this text, I propose to look at the first and third of the three typologies, namely nationally organized black-led Pentecostal churches and black churches in white historic denominations.

In terms of the former, the largest of these churches are the New Testament Church of God and Church of God of Prophecy. The second of the two typologies are those newer, black-led Pentecostal churches or black majority neo-Pentecostal churches that tend to operate more within a "stand-alone" individualistic context. I have chosen to ignore the second of these first two typologies as these newer black majority neo-Pentecostal churches have not made any discernible contribution to black theology in Britain.

The origins of the first set of churches in this group date back to mass post–World War II migration of predominantly black people from the Caribbean. Whilst some of these people came as communicant members of historic (White) denominations,[6] many, however, arrived as members of established Pentecostal denominations in the Caribbean. A detailed history of this largely untold narrative can be found in the work of black British scholars such as Joe Aldred,[7] Doreen McCalla,[8] and Mark Sturge.[9] These churches have often been perceived as the natural equivalents of the black church tradition in the United States owing to their origin and development, namely, emerging from within a black experience. What complicates this particular perspective, however, is the fact that many of these churches, although emerging from within a black experience, were founded by conservative white Americans in the United States and then established through missionary work in the Caribbean.

Ironically, we now have black majority Pentecostal churches in Britain that are often seen as the natural equivalents of black churches in the United States due to their black majority and their black-run status. Yet the historical developments of these churches are linked to a form of U.S. white ecclesial exclusivism from which black people in the United States had to separate in order to create a version of Christianity that did not oppress them. So ultimately, even Black majority churches in Britain have white roots!

For many years, these churches have been defined using the term "black-led." This term (often used by white commentators, not the adherents themselves) has been a highly contested one. Writers such as Arlington Trotman have challenged the use of such terms to name predominantly black British Pentecostal churches on the grounds that these terms (which define a church on purely ethnic grounds) do not cohere with the self-understanding of the churches and the members themselves.[10] It is interesting to note that the black Church in the United States has never been defined solely on ethnic or racial terms. Rather, they have linked their ancestry and ethnicity alongside their ecclesiological and faith traditions.

One of the defining characteristics of black Pentecostal churches is their style of worship, which draws upon black Diasporan (and Continental) African traditions, some of which are African American in style. The invocation of the spirit within black Pentecostal worship, for example, is fused with an expansive and nontext based liturgy, which has been one of the defining hallmarks of black religiosity. Robert Beckford offers a highly polemical analysis of black British religiosity from a black British Pentecostal perspective on this creative dynamic in which participation and movement is an important means by which the liberative impulse of black life is expressed.[11]

I shall address a number of additional concerns and issues concerning black-led Pentecostal churches by way of an assessment of the work of Robert Beckford, one of the most well known black theologians in Britain. Beckford's formative influences have been within the Pentecostal church in Britain.

White Majority Churches and Black People in Britain

The third broad typology is that of the (white majority) historic churches in Britain. In many respects these churches (often seen in terms of the Anglican or Church of England, Methodist, Baptist, and the United Reformed Church) have natural links with the black churches in the United States, as it was from these ecclesial bodies that the majority of churches in North America (whether black or white) have emerged.

For many years, it has been assumed that black members of these white majority churches were not part of a black church tradition. The black experience was seen to reside within black majority Pentecostalism.[12]

Most of the black members in white majority historic churches in Britain can trace their roots to Africa and the Caribbean. Most of these church adherents attend black majority churches predominantly in inner city urban contexts.[13] These churches operate, in effect, as black enclaves within the overall white majority structure and membership of the ecclesial body as a whole.

The development of black majority churches within these white majority historic bodies has emerged due to demographic changes in inner city areas within the larger cities and towns in Britain, and not through a self-conscious separation along the lines of race, as has been the case in the United States. Research by the Peter Brierley has shown that the majority of black Christians in Britain belong to white majority historic churches (by a factor of almost 2 to 1).[14] These figures are in stark contrast to those in the United States where the majority of black Christians belong to the traditional black church denominations (by a factor of approximately 4 to 1), with a much smaller percentage of believers affiliated to white majority traditions.

Within the literature pertaining to the black church in the United States, the majority of these texts have focused on the formation, history, and praxis of these historic black churches. Less scholarly attention has been directed at those black people who worship within the Presbyterian or the United Methodist Church for example.[15]

The place and role of black people in white majority historic churches remains a deeply contentious issue. David Isiorho, a black Anglican Priest in Britain, has written on the dominant images of "Whiteness" and "Englishness" (the latter often taken as a synonym for the former) in the Church of England, which fail to acknowledge the plural and multiethnic nature of the church.[16] Writing about the seemingly inextricable link between the overarching construct of Englishness and whiteness and that of the Church of England, Isiorho argues that these twin seminal building blocks in the established churches' self-understanding combine in such a way as to exclude black people.[17]

This combination of whiteness being associated with Englishness (and the established ecclesial body being the Church of England) means that it becomes structurally and symbolically difficult for black people to feel a representative part of this white dominated edifice. This exclusionary construct operates in a manner not dissimilar to the still all-too-common conception of Britain as a White country.[18]

In the still powerful imagery of Gilroy's seminal 1992 text *There Ain't no Black in the Union Jack*, Isiorho argues that the conflation of whiteness and Englishness leaves the Church of England as an unreconstructed body of white supremacist assumptions. This point is amplified when he writes,

> For the English, to confront and deal with racism and the racializing process is to erode the national concepts of superiority that centuries of aggressive colonialism have embedded deep within the national psyche. Alongside this is the Church of England as the Church of state and

nation; hence a great deal is at stake when bishops and leaders are challenged about trying to be more accommodating to Black people.[19]

The development of black theology in Britain has become lodged between a number of differing fault lines. On the one hand, black British Pentecostalism, with its black majority space and affirmation of black cultural aesthetics within worship provides a natural repository for the emergence and development of black theology in Britain. But the gains from this tradition are in dialectical tension with a distinct reluctance and inability to adopt the radical, theological, and sociocultural analysis demanded of black liberation theology within their ecclesiological and missiological practices.

In short, black British Pentecostalism often rejects any notion of social and political analysis, in favor of spiritualized and abstracted theology that is content with expressions of personal piety and individual salvation. The reign of God is relegated firmly to heaven and glimpses of it are neither found in nor is there any demand to work for it here on earth.[20]

I am at pains to stress, however, that not all Pentecostal churches fall into this trap. There are some notable exceptions.[21] There are many black Pentecostal churches, however, that do adhere to the theological framework I have just described. Conversely, the work of black and white people within the Church of England has contributed to a fine tradition of fighting for social justice, often utilizing Scripture and adopting a challenging theology to support them in their reforming efforts.[22]

In this regard, the work of Isiorho[23] and Glynn Gordon Carter[24] have made an important contribution to creating a climate in which black theology in Britain can be articulated. What has stunted the development of black theology within the Church of England has been the relationship that exists between a self-consciously radical, bottom-up movement and method for undertaking theological discourse and a top-down hierarchical establishment-bound church that is seen to represent all the worst excesses of the status quo, conformism, and white supremacy.

At a later point in this chapter, I argue that the British Methodism in which black people are located represents the most effective framework for the flourishing of black theology in Britain. Not that this framework is flawless, but the default ecclesiology of British Methodism, allied to this pragmatic approach to mission, has enabled it to construct an explicit radicalism that is manifested in strong programs in racial justice and social and political critique.

Black Theology and the Black Church in Britain

In this section, I want to assess the relationship between black theology and the black church in Britain (drawing from both the first and third typologies) through, first, an analysis of the work of Robert Beckford. Robert Beckford is one of the most important voices in the theological and cultural landscape in Britain. He has written extensively about the muting and denial of the voice attributed to black and minority ethnic people in Britain.[25] I want to talk about his work to decipher the complex relationship between black theology and the black church in Britain.

Beckford's Formative Experiences

I first met Robert not long after he had been appointed tutor in black theology at Queen's College in Birmingham. At the time of his appointment, I was a Youth and Community worker for the Methodist Church in the Asbury circuit in North Birmingham, working with two inner city churches. It was because of Robert's charismatic, persuasive powers that the idea of pursuing postgraduate studies in theologically related work was first implanted in my mind. Prior to that providential meeting, I had intended to change directions and move into social work, as I was coming to the end of my contract with the Methodist Church. It was Robert, in his usual ebullient and inspiring way, who said "Nah man, you don't wanna do that" when I told him of my plans to train to be a social worker. "You should do postgraduate research in theology. The Methodist Church needs some good black theologians. You should do an M.Phil."

Taking Robert's advice to heart, I arranged to visit the University of Birmingham, and the rest, as they say in popular parlance, is history. I share this story because in many respects, it typifies Robert's vivacity and charismatic nature. Being in Robert's presence is never dull or boring. It is this restlessness and sense of perpetual motion that characterizes not only his personality but also his scholarly work. Robert Beckford's scholarly output is very much a reflection of the man himself. His work is vibrant, energetic, very accessible, and hugely entertaining.

My impression of his work, having followed his career since its inception in the early 1990s, is that Robert is not one for long drawn out, densely written theological treatises. The early developments that gave rise to *Jesus is Dread*,[26] for example, seem to mark him out as a black British systematic theologian. I wonder whether the sometimes arcane preoccupations with metaphysical and philosophical minutiae that often characterizes systematic theology soon dissipated this initial enthusiasm.

I believe that Beckford possessed the skills of an excellent systematic or constructive theologian, but I feel that his restlessness and interdisciplinary background (his first degree was in religion and sociology) was always going to take him into more "sexy" academic waters. In many respects, his most complete and coherent work is to be found in his second book (the text that arose from his doctoral thesis) *Dread and Pentecostal*,[27] which incidentally, from my vantage point as one who has taught Beckford to undergraduate students, is his least popular book.

The Contribution of Robert Beckford

Beckford's appointment at The Queen's college meant that he was the first lecturer and tutor appointed to teach black Theology at a theological college/seminary in Britain. Robert taught black theology at Queen's from 1992 to 1998.[28] Beckford's work has been an inspiration to a generation of black theological scholars in the United Kingdom, including me. I would not be doing the work for which I am recognized, were it not for the encouragement and inspiration of Robert Beckford's challenging and committed stance to undertaking theological and cultural thinking in the service of black empowerment.

Robert's Ph.D. thesis (the first of its kind by a black British scholar) was entitled *A Political Theology for the Black Church in Britain*. Robert can be credited with being one of the first black British theological scholars[29] to undertake a systematic analysis of the social and political identity of the black church in Britain, outlining a political black theology of liberation for the British context.

The Public Theologian

Such is Robert's boundless energy and irrepressible spirit that the conventions of doctoral research were never going to be his preferred mode of communication. Whilst he was sufficiently pragmatic to recognize the necessity of completing his Ph.D., Robert wanted to go beyond the strictures of formal academic theology—in many respects, this desire remains one of the ongoing narrative threads, which flows through the heart of his scholarly pilgrimage, and to which, I will return at a later juncture.

It is with much fondness and incredulity that I reflect on the spring of 1998 and public reception afforded to Robert's first book, *Jesus is Dread*.[30] The title alone was a grand political and theological declaration of intent. "Dread," a term that has often been used within generic Caribbean contexts and Rasta sensibilities in particular and taken often to mean either "catastrophe" (in terms of the former) and "powerful and mighty" (in terms of the latter), was juxtaposed with Jesus, the most holy symbol of God's presence in creation! *Jesus is Dread?* I know of many scholars (including me) who would assert that this book[31] is the most innovative and radical contribution to Christology in Britain in the last 30 years.

It is interesting to note that this text emerged prior to Beckford's doctoral thesis. Most budding scholars are content to leave their more incendiary polemics until after they have reached the comparative safety of postdoctoral work, but not Robert. He was firing his theological broadsides before he had received the letter of academic assurance from the faculty board indicating a successfully negotiated Viva Voce.

For many of us, *Jesus is Dread* continues to enthral and delight. It remains a pioneering, iconoclastic piece of work. I sense that Robert remains somewhat sanguine about the relative impact (or lack of it) it has exerted on the black Church in Britain.

With chapters addressing issues of Rastafari, sexuality (including a memorable chapter reflecting on the genitalia of Jesus in an African context), and black popular culture, *Jesus is Dread* remains a difficult text for many conservative Pentecostal churches in Britain.

Robert's later books, *Dread and Pentecostal: A Political Theology for the Black Church in Britain*,[32] *God of the Rahtid: Redeeming Rage*,[33] *God and the Gangs*,[34] and *Jesus out*[35] have a familiar and distinctive seam, namely, linking God-talk with the existential condition of black people in the late twentieth and early twenty-first century. This process of correlating talk about God with the ways in which human identity is constructed and knowledge of self is achieved is undertaken by interrogating popular culture. Beckford is adept at skillfully linking issues related to the varied forms of cultural production alongside the liberative presence of God in the world.

In effect, Beckford asks a series of penetrating questions, first posed by James Cone[36] some 20 years previously, namely, "what does it mean to be a black person in a racist world? Where is God in all this mess and how can our allegiance to God bring about a process of liberation?"

Since nailing his theological colors to the mast with *Jesus is Dread*, Beckford has shown himself to be a fearless disturber of many commonly held (dare one say "lazy") truths. Whether in terms of the spurious superiority of white majority historic Mainline[37] churches,[38] or the innate conservatism and patriarchy of black majority churches in Britain,[39] Beckford has challenged existing or conventional modes of thinking.

A More Detailed Exploration of *Jesus is Dread*

In *Jesus is Dread*,[40] Beckford challenged many of the accepted notions of how and to what purpose human beings have attempted to articulate the relationship between the contingency of humanity and the ultimate reality that is God. Beckford's work in this respect, in seeking to locate the experiences of the flawed, distorted, and humiliated reality of those who are poor, oppressed and without a voice, as the central point in his theological schema, draws upon the insights of such luminaries as James Cone,[41] Gustavo Gutteriez,[42] and Leonardo and Clodovis Boff,[43] and, in some respects, the father of black academic theological work in Britain, Emmanuel Lartey.[44]

It can be argued that *Jesus is Dread* occupies an almost iconic status within the black theological firmament in Britain in a manner not dissimilar to my (outsider's) perceptions on the status granted to James Cone's first book *Black Theology and Black Power*.[45] The importance of Cone's first book, and indeed, the first self-identified text in black theology, is noted in a more recent publication edited by Dwight Hopkins.[46] *Jesus is Dread* is the first fully fledged and articulated black theology text in Britain.

In *Jesus is Dread*, Beckford began the bold experiment of seeking to fuse black approaches to talking about God and God's agency in solidarity with humankind alongside a penetrating analysis of various black cultural forms and aesthetics in Britain. He argues that the muted and submerged voices of the disenfranchised black urban proletariat are the authentic material for an exploration into the sources and locations by which God's liberating presence and actions might be located. This work was an iconoclastic and disturbing text for premillennium Britain. It was a disturber of many commonly held assumptions. Indeed, even his title is a biting critique on the neocolonial, conservative mores of Caribbean societies and the Christians who have been shaped in these sociocultural and political contexts.

Beckford argues that the word "dread" is often taken to mean "an awful calamity" or that which is "terrible and to be avoided,"[47] and often invoked at times of fear and foreboding, was subsequently inverted and given new meaning by the Rastafarian movement that became a potent religious and cultural group in Jamaica.[48]

Time constraints prevent any serious analysis of the Rasta movement in Britain. This religious and cultural movement became one of the most expressive and significant repositories for black self-expression, social, and political dissent.[49]

Jesus is Dread is notable for the creative methodology Beckford employs in his approach to articulating the black experience in Britain through the prism of black religion. Using a variety of sources, such as black expressive cultures and social and literary analysis, he reflects upon the meaning of black Christianity in Britain and across the African Diaspora, identifying the liberational themes and concepts that are inherent within black religiosity.[50] Beckford even suggests that the notable reggae singer and third world icon, the late great Bob Marley, can be understood within the framework of black Diasporan hermeneutics, as a black liberation theologian. Commenting on the inspirational work of Bob Marley, a hero to continuing generations of dispossessed and disenfranchised people, Beckford states,

> Naturally, Marley does not use the traditional theological methods found in your average systematic theological text-book . . . For Marley experience is the basis for exploring the social world. Consequently, he rejects the knowledge-validation processes used in the classroom of traditional education . . . The second aspect of Marley's method is commitment to radical social change. There are two areas of concern in his music: first, the destruction of Babylon, and second, the liberation of the poor.[51]

Beckford's radical identification with Bob Marley, as a liberation theologian, can be interpreted as a commitment to utilizing the seemingly egalitarian resources of popular, expressive cultures, such as music, with a view to enabling black, marginalized, and oppressed people to find a voice for their authentic experiences of struggle.

In his use of multiple and eclectic sources for the articulation of black theology in Britain, Beckford draws upon the similarly creative work of black theologians in the United States who have also mined black religiocultural mores as a means of undertaking liberative black God-talk. So whilst Beckford, in his early work, draws extensively upon the style and the substantive content of Cone's work (Beckford's use of provocative subject headings is a direct case in point, and owes much to the biting polemics of early Cone), he also draws upon insights and methods from scholars such as Gayraud Wilmore,[52] Henry H. Mitchell,[53] and Theophus Smith.[54]

What is interesting to note as a point of comparison with the United States is the highly systematized (and one might argue artificially schematic) methodological framework of Ware's,[55] in which the major black theologians are grouped into one of the three categories. This form of analysis could never be applied to Beckford's work. *Jesus is Dread* incorporates cultural analysis and nonfoundational hermeneutics in the form of Christology, womanist theology, ecclesiology, and elements of church history. Like many of his contemporary black British counterparts, Beckford eschews the seemingly compartmentalization (and fragmentation) of disciplines that seems much more commonplace in the United States, to which reference was made in the previous chapter.

Perhaps the most striking and challenging part of *Jesus is Dread* can be found in an early section of this text, in which the author analyzes the relationship between the major white majority historic mainline churches[56] in Britain and black people of African descent.[57] Beckford asks a number of pertinent and challenging questions about the efficacy of black people seeking to find a voice and a conducive and therapeutic space in which to work out their liberation, from within what have traditionally been seen as oppressive and exclusive bastions of white hegemony.[58]

In this provocative chapter of the book entitled "What Kind of Freed Slaves Worship in the Slave Master's Church? Black Resistance in White Churches in Britain," the author challenges the strategies employed by black people, such as myself, to locate an appropriate space, and as a corollary, to find their authentic voice, from within historically oppressive and discriminatory churches.[59] It seems almost superfluous to remark that Beckford, a black Pentecostal, is not overly taken with the rhetoric, doctrinal assertions, and amended practice of historic mainline churches, in their attempts to engage with issues of racial injustice and social exclusion.

While I have found Beckford's contentions illuminating and helpful, in terms of alerting us to the struggle for an expressive and authentic voice for the poor and the oppressed, his blanket assertions that the slave master's house has not delivered any meaningful or tangible results in this struggle is not particularly accurate.[60]

As I demonstrate shortly, the development of black theology in Britain owes more to black Methodism, within the British Methodist Church, than it does to black British Pentecostalism. For the most part, black British Pentecostalism has studiously avoided any contact with black theology and has certainly not attempted to integrate any of its substantive claims or findings into their ongoing mission or ministry within their ecclesiological framework.

By contrast, my previous research with the "Birmingham Initiative,"[61] and the publication of my first two-volume book *Growing into Hope*[62] were sponsored by the British Methodist Church, along with additional support from the Anglican, Baptist, and the URC traditions. The now widely accepted recognition of the annual Racial Justice Sunday celebration on the second Sunday in September was largely a Methodist-inspired development arising from the landmark report to the British Methodist conference entitled "Faithful and Equal."[63]

One of my previous publications is entitled *Faith, Stories and the Experiences of Black Elders*.[64] In it, I seek to highlight the spirituality and wisdom of the Windrush Generation.[65] This work was sponsored by the Methodist Homes for the Aged—the elder care agency of the British Methodist Church. This book is the first such text that attempts to reflect upon the spirituality and faith of these pioneering black people whose presence underpins the burgeoning strength of black Christian expression in the twenty-first century Britain.[66] The development and support for these groundbreaking initiatives has come from within the auspices of the white majority historic mainline churches in Britain—in effect, from the so-called slave master's house!

In Beckford's third book, *God of the Rahtid*,[67] the author continues with many of the themes evident in his earlier publications. In it, he highlights the means by which black rage destabilizes and deforms the selfhood and humanity of black people in Britain.[68] Beckford advocates a concept he terms "Redemptive Vengeance"[69] as a means of countering the worst excesses of what he describes as "low level rage." The latter is manifested in the seemingly casual incidences of racism that attack the Black psyche and are submerged and internalized within the black self, leading to long-term psychological damage, manifested in such conditions as schizophrenia.[70]

"Redemptive vengeance," according to Beckford, is a process whereby angry and marginalized black people call upon the radical and prophetic resources of a "realized" ideal that is the "Kingdom of God," as depicted in the life and ministry, death and resurrection of

Jesus. Here, Jesus' decisive declaration for and positioning alongside the marginalized and the poor ushers in a new reality, where the destructive forces that distort black humanity, can be challenged and overturned.[71]

Beckford is an outspoken and seemingly fearless champion for the dignity and humanity of black people who, I will submit, represent the voiceless objects in postcolonial Britain. Beckford's work has been instrumental in highlighting the negative effects of racial injustice and institutionalized racism on the black human subject.

Locating Robert Beckford

Beckford's perspective on theology has been informed by his relationship with black British Pentecostalism. His early work, particularly the first two books, owes much to the distinctive emphases of Pentecostalism, echoing many of the relative strengths and weaknesses of that tradition. And yet, I think it is true to say that Beckford has never been limited by either the doctrinal formulations or the cultural traditions of that particular branch of Christianity. His theology has always carried much more of an embodied emphasis than that often found within normative Pentecostalism—hence his focus upon the historical presence of Jesus, which displays an incarnational Christology. I believe that Beckford uses Pentecostalism mainly as a theological framework and shorthand signifier a politicized and sociocultural reading of blackness. In effect, Beckford is not your typical black Pentecostal theologian.

His later works adopted a much more expansive theological and cultural canvass. This is evidenced in later works such as *God of the Rahtid* (my personal favorite—the title would take much too long to explain, suffice to say that it is even *more controversial* than the first book), *God and the Gangs*, and *Jesus Dub* Beckford's persuasive and incisive polemic has enabled many black people to name, the hitherto, often submerged and intuitive sense of anger and frustration, that often defines their existence in this country. Beckford names the one that has often plagued so many of us, and offers theological tools by which such endemic ills can be overcome.

Yet, in the midst of this deserved paean of praise to an iconoclastic scholar, one has to offer a much needed critique of Beckford's canon to date. In the first instance, as a long-time admirer of his work, I have often witnessed at first hand the delicate position Robert holds within the theological academy and the church in Britain. Beckford is an indefatigable opponent of the ethnocentric and patrician arrogance of white, English liberalism, yet if one were to look at the arena in which his work has made the greatest impact, I would suggest it is amongst the very group he so often caricatures and lampoons.

I do not doubt either the sincerity or the necessity of his challenges to the absurdities of white privilege and so-called superiority, but I often feel it would be helpful if he acknowledged his need (as is the case, in reality, for all in scholars) of this constituency.

For all his much vaunted position as a black British Pentecostal theologian, the truth is, Pentecostalism has largely given Robert Beckford and his radical ideas a wide berth. Beckford's theological method, for example, is not consistent with the Pentecostalism he so openly extols. His failure to prioritize the Bible in his theological method puts him at odds with the mainstream of black Pentecostalism in Britain. Ironically, the stridency and polemical nature of many of his arguments have been embraced with more confidence and alacrity by black and white Anglicans, Methodist and United Reformed church members, rather than what might be described as his "home" constituency. Beckford's use of Tillich's notion of corre-lation sits more comfortably within a historic mainline framework and not a Pentecostal one.

Within many black majority churches inside the Pentecostal tradition in Britain, there is a marked reluctance to be explicit about owning their black identity, attributing political and theological significance to the nature of blackness, or even celebrating such, as a major part of their modus operandi. I still carry the bruises from having been heckled and booed at a black majority church conference attended by predomi-nantly black Pentecostal church members. Following my short speech, many in the audience took exception to my assertion that black Christians should identify with their blackness as divinely sanctioned. I was told repeatedly that "God don't see color"—which is strange given that God created this color in the first place! The truth is there are many black British Pentecostal Christians who find Beckford's articu-lation of liberation themes to be either aberrant or simply irrelevant.

I have witnessed Beckford being given a difficult time for his theo-logical emphases, particularly around issues such as social ethics, polit-ical Christology, or inclusive socially orientated missiology—themes that resonate strongly with many aspects of Methodist theology and ecclesiology. I am reminded, at this point, that Beckford was once a member of the Wesleyan Holiness church in his formative years—perhaps he is more of a Methodist than he would care to admit?

Within parts of the Methodist, Anglican, and United Reformed Churches in Britain (amongst black and white), Beckford remains a hero. Within the bulk of black British Pentecostalism, he is persona nongrata. Beckford's work, with its radical intent and creative, interdisciplinary approach (he eschews biblically literalism and fundamentalism and does not use Scripture as a proof text for example) does not sit well with the majority of black British Pentecostal Christians. Within British Methodism and the Church of England, he is the only black theologian, of whom, most of these members have ever heard. I am tempted to ask the difficult question of whether Beckford, for all radical panache, is in effect, a black theologian for white people.

In recent times, Beckford's perspectives have changed. Given his restless energy and boundless intellectual curiosity, it was never going to be the case that traditional academia would be the summit of his ambition. Recently, Robert's primary academic gaze has moved from theology toward the more public arena and glare of cultural studies. In many respects, his primary African American dialogue partner has ceased to be James Cone, and Michael Eric Dyson has replaced him.

As Beckford's interests continue to move into the mainstream media, as a colleague, I am forced to ask two crucial questions regarding his future. First, and by far the most important, relates to the future direction of his work. Since his move from theology to cultural studies, there remains the fear that Beckford's shining talents will be lost to the black theology in Britain project. As the first major black theologian in Britain, Beckford's continued absence is potentially troubling. To understand the import of this point, I simply invite African Americans to imagine what might have been the fate of black theology in the United States had Cone decided to move away from the discipline and head for the bright lights of the media, some time after 1975 and *God of the Oppressed.*

Despite the growing number of able Black religious scholars in Britain, Beckford remains the most visible of our number and is much too good a theologian not to be missed.

Second, to what extent is Beckford now so estranged from mainstream black British Pentecostalism that his work, in terms of an audience, is solely dependent on white liberals and black liberationists, such as myself? Has Beckford lost his "home audience" forever? There are many who will argue that Beckford never carried his core constituency with him in the first place. I think this contention is only partially true, and besides, it fails to take account of the incalculable influence he has exerted on black Christian communities in Britain.

I would imagine that Beckford has inspired more black Christians to look again, in a critical manner, at the Bible, for example, and as a corollary, has challenged many to expect much more from the black church to which they belong and the Christian faith to which they adhere. For this, and for all his many other contributions, Robert Beckford remains the most visible and charismatic black theologian in Britain. In many respects, he remains my primary inspiration within the British context.

The God-Father of Black Theology in Britain—The Legacy of Emmanuel Y. Lartey

Whilst Robert Beckford is the most visible and widely recognized black theologian in Britain, perhaps the most influential in systemic terms has been the Revd. Dr. Emmanuel Lartey. Emmanuel Lartey is a Methodist minister from Ghana, who until his move to the United States was senior lecturer in Pastoral Theology and counselling and director of the Graduate Institute for Religion and Theology at the University of Birmingham. He has been a pioneer in the area of intercultural pastoral care and counselling. His commitment to black theology in Britain has been pivotal in the development of this discipline.

Emmanuel Lartey was my immediate predecessor as editor of the *Black Theology in Britain*[72] journal. Lartey pioneered the first MA course in Black Theology in Britain, within the aforementioned Graduate Institute in Birmingham. His most significant text is *In Living Colour*.[73] In this book, Lartey outlines an approach to pastoral care and counselling that is informed by the cultural contexts in which human existence is located. His method seeks to analyze the overarching situational dilemmas that impinge upon the autonomy of human subjects in their daily struggles to be their true selves.[74]

Lartey's approach to pastoral care and counselling is earthed within his firm commitment to the liberation of poor and oppressed people. This commitment and focus finds its most eloquent expression in a chapter entitled "Liberation as Pastoral Praxis."[75] Lartey, reflecting on this pastoral approach to empowering those who are denied a voice, states,

> The theologian begins from a position of being immersed in the experiences of poverty, marginalisation and oppression. It is from this position that he or she tries to understand and articulate the faith.[76]

Lartey subsequently analyzes the work of such scholars as the Uruguayan Liberation theologians Leonardo and Clodovis Boff,[77] seeking to reflect upon their method for working in solidarity with those who are the "least of these."[78] Reflecting upon the method employed by these authors in their liberation work alongside those who are denied a voice, he writes,

> This basic framework (for their approach) has been extended and adapted by attempts to answer questions like: Who are the poor? Who speaks for the poor? Who has the power and control in the articulation of the experiences of the poor? Who selects what is relevant? Who benefits from the way things are done? Who is excluded? Who is marginalized? . . . At this level it is the poor, the marginalized or the oppressed who speak for themselves, on their own terms and in their chosen manner.[79]

Lartey's commitment to black theology can be seen in three areas. First, as the founding editor of *Black Theology in Britain* (which is analyzed in detail in chapter 5), Lartey helped to create a space in which fledgling black British scholars such as myself could begin to articulate our work. Second, as the first director of the MA course in black theology, Lartey pioneered the development of this discipline as a recognized and accepted part of theological discourse within a university setting. Third, as chair and convener of the monthly black theology in Britain forum (which is now chaired and convened by myself), Lartey assisted in developing a physical and pastoral space in which black religious and theological discourse became normative.

For many of that first generation of black religious scholars, often languishing on white majority postgraduate research programs, finding our work (at best) an object of odd curiosity or (at worst) a matter of ridicule, the black theology forum became a safe space in which one could rehearse the necessary apologetics needed to survive within a theological landscape that is virtually all white. The work of the forum continues, but its initial inception owed much to the organizational, pastoral, and prophetic insights of Lartey.

In keeping with the majority of black theologians in the United States, the thrust of Lartey's work has been within the academy and not in pastoral ministry in the church. Like such luminaries as C. Eric Lincoln, Lartey has had to make the hard decision of prioritizing his work and energies and assessing where he can best serve God and his fellow humans with most distinction.[80] Lartey has not operated within the British Methodist Church at what might be called an explicit or overly visible level. He has not held pastorates. His work has been highly influential within the church, and his engagement with the black Church (both within Methodism and beyond it) has been more pronounced than that of Beckford, in terms of the latter's relationship with Pentecostalism, for example.

What has been notable in Lartey's work, however, has been his commitment (perhaps fuelled by his extensive knowledge of pastoral care) to assist ordinary black people within British Methodism (and beyond) to become conscientized of their innate human subjectivity within a world of white hegemony.

For many years, Lartey was a member of the black support and empowerment caucus within the British Methodist Church, named The Black Methodist Group (BMG), which was later renamed Black Methodists for Liberation and Unity (BMLU). Prior to his departure for the United States in 2002, Lartey was the chair of this group.

Whilst many will argue that Lartey is no more representative of or particularly well known within the various black church movements as are his British or U.S. compatriots, there can be no doubting his desire to attempt to surmount the often huge chasm between academic black theology and the black church.

Bishop Joe Aldred

The third important figure in the black theology in Britain movement is that of Bishop Dr. Joe Aldred. Aldred, like Beckford, operates primarily from within the Pentecostal tradition in Britain. Unlike Beckford, he has been able to construct his contributions to the development of black theology in Britain whilst remaining within the mainstream of black British Pentecostalism. For many years, Aldred was the executive director of the Centre for Black and White Christian Partnership (CBWCP). Centre for Black and White Christian Partnership was a semiautonomous, intercultural organization committed to bringing black and white Christians from varied traditions together in order to bring about improved self-knowledge and reconciliation.

At the time of writing,[81] he was well known as the editor of the "With Power" trilogy.[82] These texts have addressed concerns regarding the destructive power of white hegemonic structures that silence the claims of the poor and the oppressed, particularly if these individuals are black people of African descent. His books have offered principally black men and women an opportunity to express their hopes, fears, and aspirations as people of faith.

Aldred's principal concern has been to open up dialogue between black and white Christians and the various church traditions to which they belong. Aldred's work, which eschews the visceral and polemical panache of that adopted by Beckford, can be likened, in some respects, to the more emollient figure of J. Deotis Roberts in the U.S. context, particularly when compared with James H. Cone. I am aware of the invidious nature of comparisons, so I will not attempt to paint too detailed a portrait of the similarities between the two. But it is interesting to note that whereas Beckford has opted for a more strident and polemical articulation of black theology in Britain, Aldred has opted for dialogue and systemic networking, seeking to change the overall landscape in which theology and ecclesiology is exercised between black and white churches in Britain. Aldred's work is an interesting mix between the studied moderation of Deotis Roberts[83] and the antiessentialist deconstructionism of Victor Anderson.[84]

In terms of the former, Aldred, like Roberts, argues that reconciliation rather than liberation should be the central motif in black theological work. His work is based on a proactive assertion of black people claiming their innate God-given human agency, which provides the main thrust for an authentic Caribbean British theology, as opposed to the more militant and oppositional binary of oppressed-oppressor dialectic often favored by Cone and Beckford.[85] His theology seeks to reject the victim–status paradigm for black people that seem to be a basic norm in black theology.

In terms of the latter, like Victor Anderson, Aldred sees as problematic the concentration within much that is black theology (on both sides of the Atlantic) on racism as the central point of departure. By making racism our main point departure, do we not then construct blackness, first, as purely oppositional (and therefore dependent) upon whiteness? Second, does not this conception of blackness then, as a corollary, become ultimately the handmaiden of the construction of whiteness?[86]

In this regard, Aldred's work differs from that of Lartey and Beckford (and mine), in that the latter are more prepared to deal with the systemic workings of racism and the ways in which structural inequality of British society makes any notion of mutuality and reconciliation, without structural and systematic transformation, something of an illusory promise. In this respect, his work is weakened by the failure to build into his conceptualization for a contextualized Caribbean British black theology any acute sense of constructive social analysis or politicized conscientization. Simply asserting that one is a human being and then claiming equality on that basis, without additional systemic analysis or structural models of conscientization simply leads to debilitating forms of false consciousness and theological escapism. In the famous words of Malcolm X, sitting at a table does not make you a diner if you have no food on your plate! Aldred's notion of respect ultimately fails as it lacks any contextual analysis of the structural imbalances between black people and white hegemony which ultimately makes his conceptualization of "respect" naive.

In the failure to offer a robust broader systemic analysis of white hegemony, Aldred's work does not conform to that of either Roberts or Anderson, both of whom are quite pronounced in their analysis of the structural and systemic ills of corporate America and its effects upon black people and their religious consciousness.

What is interesting is that Aldred's work captures many of the inherent complexities of black British Pentecostalism and the broader area of black Christianity in Britain, which, in some respects, is reflective of the mainstream black Church in the United States. Aldred's indefatigable work for understanding, mutuality, and justice are resonant with concepts and themes that are commonplace within black consciousness and black self-determination modes of thinking and being. Consequently, Aldred is not unlike all black theologians in Britain or the United States, in that he is highly conscious of his blackness and the realities of such dimensions in his ongoing engagement with white people and white church structures. Aldred is the most "institutional" of the black religious scholars in Britain. His work has offered a moderate, professional, and respectable vista for black Christianity in Britain and has been able to operate within the heartland of black Church life in a manner that has eluded both Beckford and Lartey.

Fault lines in the theology of the Black Church

Having analyzed the work of three of the most well-known black theologians in Britain and their relationship with the black church, I now want to turn my attention to the black church itself. Why has there been something of a breach between black theologians and the black church on both sides of the Atlantic? In the first instance, I feel that the default theology of many black churches has made life difficult for a number of black theologians.

I remain intrigued at the extent to which black Christians, in black majority churches in both contexts, have remained wedded to a form of nineteenth-century white evangelicalism. A number of black scholars have demonstrated the extent to which Christianity as a global phenomenon has drunk deeply from the well of Eurocentric philosophical thought at the expense of African or other overarching forms of epistemology.[87] For the most part, the development of Christian doctrine tells us more about the attempts of state imperial power to construct notions of God to fit their already highly developed worldviews than it does about God's own self.

This conflation of human interests with those of God was a significant hermeneutical key for enabling white power to construe a version of the Christian faith as consonant with their own subjective values at the expense of the African self.[88] Clarence Hardy, in his analysis of James Baldwin's theology and theodicy, seeks to highlight (via Baldwin's own fiction and nonfiction) the fault lines inherent within black evangelical Christianity in the United States.[89] Commenting on the pernicious nature of the bloodthirsty atonement theories, which negate the legitimacy of the "preconverted self" Hardy writes,

> In his first novel (*Go Tell it on the mountain*) the possible connections of self-loathing and conversion are suggested, but here, before his novel is even published, Baldwin demonstrates just how closely aligned he believed the psychology of black self-hatred to be with the very act Christian conversion itself.[90]

The supreme irony at the heart of black Christianity worldwide is its continuing adherence to a form of premodern white European Evangelicalism that is a product of a post-Reformation biblicism. This framework is one that speaks more of Eurocentric notions of top–down patrician control than of the very life-giving qualities of the Gospel in and of itself, shorn of its cultural appropriations. As Cone reminds us, Luther, for all his reforming zeal, did not side with the peasants in their revolts against tyrannical rule![91] Black people have held onto something that came from a source, which we have come to see as one not to be trusted in any circumstances.

So in effect, black people on both sides of the Atlantic have learnt how to utilize a hermeneutic of suspicion in terms of white supremacist overlays on the Gospel, but have been most reluctant to critique the very substance of the Gospel, as we have received it: admittedly, from a most tainted of sources, particularly when it speaks against our innate selfhood and wider contextual experiences.

Two brief examples, I believe, will highlight this point. One concerns the practice of biblical literalist readings of Scripture, and the second is concerned with issues of Jesus as being the only means of salvation.

In terms of the first example, it is interesting to note the wholesale inconsistency with which *all* people read the Bible, particularly those who claim to read it literally, as if it were the *actual words* of God. As Miguel De La Torre reminds us, if the Bible were the literal word of God, then God would be guilty of genocide, patricide, regicide, and a host of other "cides" one could care to mention.[92]

Torre begins his argument for a critical, liberationist-marginal reading of scripture by pointing to the fact that the Bible calls for disobedient children to be executed (Leviticus 20:9).[93] I have yet to meet any black Christian who reads this text literally! He continues by reminding us that the Bible is not the fullest revelation of God as that honor falls upon Jesus. Jesus is the norm by which all the other elements of the Bible are to be interpreted.[94] Black Christian faith needs to rediscover the practice of radical readings against the text where Jesus, "who is one of us," becomes our key hermeneutical device for unlocking the apparent fixity of the "Word." At this point, I am reminded of the salient words of my friend and colleague Inderjit Bhogal who has been known to remark, "[the] word became flesh and we have turned it back into (fixed) words again."

Having mentioned the importance of Jesus, it is fascinating to see the ways in which black churches on both sides of the Atlantic have adhered to a Christian supremacist view of the world by means of an often exclusive Johannine Christology. Through ahistorical and decontextualized readings of John 14:6, Jesus becomes the only means by which people might be saved. This particular reading of Jesus stands at a variance with the many examples, such as the "Good Samaritan" (Luke 10:25–37), where the praxis of the "Jesus Way" seem to reside within someone who does not renounce his existing belief structures or claim "Jesus as Lord." Rather, it is found in some one who acts in solidarity with those in need.[95]

The extent to which the black church has traditionally been loathe to engage in interfaith dialogue has been, to a great extent, influenced by the strictures of normative, classical Christianity, in which the benefits of salvation are confined to those who acknowledge Christ's atonement on the cross. This particular fault line, in black churches in Britain and in the United States, has led to a form of disengagement with those religious communities (Islamic groups, for example) with whom one appears to have more in common (particularly within White dominated societies) than is the case with other, often powerful conservative white Christians.

The emphasis on doctrinal purity or orthodoxy within many black churches in Britain and the United States runs counter to our own histories. The black church did not come into existence (in the United States and the Caribbean) in order to replicate the arcane sterility and antimodernist resistance of many forms of white evangelicalism.[96] The roots of the black church lie in a radical appropriation of the Gospel in order that those who are the "least of these" (Matthew 25:31–46) might live, and have that life in all its fullness (John 10:10). That work was a praxis-orientated one and was not mindful of either doctrinal purity or biblical literalism.[97]

What is instructive about the continued rise of black neo-Pentecostalism in black churches on both sides of the Atlantic is the fact that it is not culturally or ethnically specific. Writing with reference to fundamentalist approaches to reading the Bible, Wimbush writes,

> The intentional attempt to embrace Christian traditions, specifically the attempt to interpret the Bible, without respect for the historical experiences of persons of African descent, radically demarcates this reading and this from all others.[98] (That have preceded it—my addition.)

The black church, in terms of strict adherence to classical Christian doctrines, aided and abetted by a literalist reading of the Bible has become (at worst) a thinly colored coating of the white Christianity to which it was once in opposition. The rise of mega ministries such as Creflo Dollar in the United States and Kingsway International Christian Centre in Britain are now offering an attractive prosperity-led, noncontextualized (blackness is not emphasized or even mentioned to any great extent) approach to Christianity, which seemed light years away from the radical, countercultural roots of diasporan black Christianity some five centuries ago.

Black Theology and Practical Engagement with the Needs of Black (Young) People— The Mandate for the Black Church

The black church at its best has possessed an ability to harness its own resources, in addition to lobbying state-sponsored bodies, in order that it might respond to the existential crises in many black communities.[99] One of the primary areas of concern continues to be the education of our youth.

As far back as the early 1970s, writers such as Coard spoke about the dangers of white dominated British society and the corrosive effects it was exerting upon African Caribbean children.[100] More recent work by the likes of Gillborn[101] and Sewell[102] has charted the turbulent relationship between schooling and black children of African descent in Britain. The literature pertaining to the overarching experiences of black people in Britain is too numerous to cite at this juncture. It will come as no surprise that in response to the seemingly ever expanding acreage of column inches detailing the problematic nature of these ethnic minorities, often in the most lurid and vituperative terms, a counter deluge of antiracist texts have emerged in opposition to this prevailing tide of racialized negativity.[103]

My work as an educator and theologian has been a committed attempt to create models of learning and theological reflection that enable poor and oppressed black people to find hope beyond the immediacy of the circumstances in which they find themselves. Unlike the works of Beckford and Aldred (and to a lesser extent, Lartey), my work has been directly funded and supported by the ecclesial body of which I am a member. In this regard, I remain grateful to the Methodist Church for enabling me to have the space and the necessary time in which to undertake this work. The need to empower and affirm our young people is of vital importance in both contexts.

Tony Campolo, the popular American sociologist and Baptist preacher, once remarked that people who have no hope and nothing to lose are dangerous.[104] Similarly, the distinguished African American philosopher, Cornel West, has written extensively on the rampant nihilism that is at the core of contemporary American life. West writes,

> In January 1998, President Bill Clinton informed the nation that it was good times for America . . . Perhaps good times should be gauged by the depth of spirituality needed to keep keeping on in the midst of material poverty, and also in the spiritual poverty of brothers and sisters disproportionately White in vanilla suburbs. These sisters and brothers are dealing with existential emptiness and spiritual malnutrition . . . Furthermore, what kind of good times can this be when suicide rates are increasing among young people?[105]

The sense of hopelessness and the vacuum at the heart of contemporary youth experience represents one of the most serious challenges facing Britain and the United States in the twenty-first century. For many black young people, the promises of material progress, societal belonging, and affirmation have proved to be illusory. Some have managed to prosper, but others have not been so lucky.[106] As I reflect upon my formative development, recounted at the forefront of the first chapter, I am reminded that for every Anthony Reddie, there are countless black young people, and those not so young anymore, who have not found their way through the maze of entrapment that is poverty, marginalization, disaffection, and disillusionment.

For many, this ongoing malaise begins in early childhood. The seeds of dissatisfaction and displacement begin to emerge from the moment they perceive that the wider environment beyond their immediate confines is one that is not to be trusted.[107]

It was the need to provide a practical theological framework that might speak to the existential condition of black young people in Britain, which provided the thematic and methodological impetus for my doctoral studies in the late 1990s. My research was concerned with developing an approach to black theology through transformative pedagogy.

Reassessing *Growing into Hope*—A Practical Black Theological and Educational Program

Growing into Hope, a two-volume program of Christian education, was first published in 1998. Black theology provided the substantive resource for the content of the curriculum. Reading and researching the writings of black theologians, I began to appreciate more fully the hermeneutical enterprise of rereading biblical texts and recontextualizing them in light of black experience.

This process of rereading and recontextualization that was essential to the content and process of the curriculum owed much to the pioneering work of the renowned African American biblical scholar Cain Hope Felder. Felder in an important article commenting on this crucial hermeneutical process writes,

> The implication is that, whatever one may wish to say about the Bible, there is a need for a disciplined scepticism regarding western appropriations.[108]

This hermeneutic of suspicion of which Felder speaks not only challenges and critiques the normative theologizing of white Eurocentric scholars, but also posits an alternative discourse that recognizes and affirms black experience. Felder highlights particular texts that attest to the significance of Africa and people of African ancestry.[109] The texts that Felder highlights illustrate the central place of black people in the ongoing story of God's interaction with God's people. Grant Shockley has detailed the emotional and psychological impact this form of knowledge can have on black youth.[110]

The importance of black biblical interpretation is highlighted to greater effect by Felder et al. in a 1991 publication that has proved highly influential to a number of theologians and Christian educators on both sides of the Atlantic.[111] As I began to create the first section of the Christian education curriculum, I was mindful of the work of Thomas Hoyt Jr.,[112] William H. Myers,[113] Renita Weems,[114] Randall Bailey,[115] and Cain Hope Felder.[116] These important contributions to biblical studies, and the advancement of a black hermeneutic, have opened up the Bible for people of African descent. It was through the influence of these writers amongst many others that I gained the confidence to engage in black theological reflection. This confidence is displayed in the opening reflections at the beginning of each new section of the curriculum. These short theological treatises were, in effect, worked examples of black hermeneutics linked to the generative theme in question.[117]

Within this two-volume curriculum were 12 generative themes or perspectives on the Christian faith that constituted the substantive content of this practical approach to black theology. In the first volume of Growing into Hope, the theme was of Hope (containing an eschatological dimension, grounded in the incarnation of Christ), for the first week in Advent, which became the overarching framework for the two volumes. Over the next 18 months of the research, there followed five sections of black Christian education material, which was piloted amongst 26 inner city, black majority churches in Birmingham.

Volume one of the curriculum includes the themes of Hope (Advent week 1), Words and Stories (black narrative approaches to theology—Advent week 2), Heroes (the work of John Baptist and the prophets—Advent week 3), and Obedience and Responsibility (the role of Mary, the Mother of Jesus—Advent week 4). This section of the curriculum was followed by two single-week sessions, entitled Promises and Agreements (The Old Covenant and the New Covenant—the contract between God and human kind) and Variety of Gifts (God's creation, appreciated through harvest).

Volume Two includes six themes, split into two sections. First, there are four weeks of material covering Lent and Easter. The first section incorporates the themes of Wisdom (looking at proverbial wisdom amongst African people, especially mothers, and worked through the prism of womanist theology), "Paying the Price" (Christ's passion and struggle), "Journeying" (Palm Sunday and Jesus' new model of Kingship), and "Freedom" (Easter Sunday and the decisive act of liberation). The second section relates to the events of Pentecost and concludes with two sessions entitled "All Change" (Pneumatology) and "All Together" (ecclesial communities inspired by the Holy Spirit).

These sessions, written primarily for black children and young people, but used across the age range in predominantly inner city black majority churches, are practical attempts to teach the central ideas of black Theology through the medium of Christian education.

In *Growing into Hope*, I wanted to create a practical and accessible approach to sharing some of the central insights of black theology for predominantly black children and young people living in Britain. In order to demonstrate both the theological intent and the educational method at play in these two books, I want to recount a true story from the initial piloting period that preceded the publication of these volumes.

In late 1997, I was undertaking some fieldwork with an inner city Anglican church in north Birmingham, in the West Midlands of Britain. I was in the midst of piloting some of the Christian education materials that would later become *Growing into Hope*. The theme for this section of the curriculum was "Heroes," which corresponded to the third week in Advent, looking at the role and the importance of prophets, both within the Hebrew Scriptures and in the life and death of John the Baptist.

In order to assist these children to make the necessary link between biblical characters and more contemporary figures, I devised an exercise that offered them an opportunity to explore some of these issues in a humorous and participatory way.[118] In the initial draft, I had juxtaposed black heroes or heroines with a number of their white counterparts. Some of these people were sporting heroes or icons from popular culture, such as music or the entertainment industry. Others were traditional authority figures such as politicians, ministers of religion, or educationists.

In this initial piloting, I was struck by the reactions of these black children. In a mixed list of black and white people, these black children assumed that while all the people on the list could be seen as representative heroes, the small number of white figures present, however, were naturally more important. When I subsequently interviewed a cross section of this group, I was informed that these white people must be the most important, or why else would I have included them in a black Christian education text?

Notionally, I had wanted to stress the blindingly obvious maxim that in the sight of God, we are all heroes and have the potential to do seemingly extraordinary things. The reality, however, was somewhat different. In a world governed by white hegemony, the claims of black people and their achievements are rarely accorded parity with those who hold power and control the media. The insertion of great figures such as Martin Luther King or Nelson Mandela only serves to reinforce this disparity rather than dissipate it—in effect, to be noticed as a black person, you have to be almost superhuman!

Hence, ordinariness in some contexts is not a virtue but a curse. It is the curse of those who do not possess special talents or qualities to move them beyond the nameless, faceless mass of the many who are considered, at best, an unfortunate cross a white dominated society has to bear, and at worst, a demonic presence that should be exorcised. Victor Anderson notes aspects of this heroic mythology around the extra-ordinary-ness of genius in his withering critique of North American religiocultural criticism.[119]

Such is the generic, universal power of whiteness that it proved difficult for these black children and young people to perceive black authority figures as having parity with white ones. The curriculum, therefore, carried the declared intentionality of affirming and empowering black youth by means of a black prophetic, liberative approach to the Gospel, in which black cultural aesthetics and production were presented as normative and from which white practices or examples were absent.

It was this desire to redress the unwieldy balance toward those who are special or extraordinary,[120] that led me to undertake my subsequent research on black elders, detailed in a later book.[121] In *Faith, Stories and the Experience of Black Elders*, I was anxious to find the means to record and reflect upon the narratives of my parents' generation, the people who have made my progress possible, the people whose faith and vibrant expression of it challenged and guided me into a faithful relationship with Christ. There is nothing extraordinary about my parents or their countless compatriots, yet this country would be immeasurably poorer without them.[122] Indeed, the greater majority of inner city churches in Britain would not and could not exist without such individuals.

What is significant about *Growing into Hope* is that, unlike the work of Beckford or Aldred, it arises directly from the institutional support of my church and was owned by a significant number of black Christians within the denomination. I have known a number of ministers (both black and white) who have used these texts as the bases for their preaching and orientating the educational and liturgical life of the church.

The weaknesses in these texts are many. As they were developed by means of an action–reflection heuristic, it is difficult to detect a consistent, overarching theological method within the two books. Also, as the curriculum was written originally for children, often as young as six, the theology is sometimes oblique and simplified (in order to be accessible). The two books are not densely thought through theological treatises, but rather, accessible approaches to convert the central insights of black theology into an accessible educative medium for black youth.

The development of these texts and much of my subsequent work is reflective of the wider community from which I have emerged, namely black British Methodism. In the next section I want to assess the contribution of black Methodism in Britain to the development of black theology in my context.

I have to confess at the outset that my comments are partisan and are informed by my own sense of estrangement from certain forms of discourse that have emerged in Britain around the nature and intent of black theology.

For many years, particularly following the important work of Gerloff[123] and McRobert,[124] it was assumed that the natural repository for the incubation of black theology in Britain lay within the black-led Pentecostal churches. Particularly, within Gerloff's work, scant regard is given to the role of black people within white majority historic churches.

In much of the anecdotal conversations that ensued in the late 1980s and early 1990s, black Christians in white majority churches were often made to feel like second-class black people—we were viewed as not being particularly black.[125] In many respects, things have changed over the course of time. We now live in an era when we are much more nuanced in our discourse around what constitutes the nature of blackness and how it should be articulated and interpreted. And yet, within certain popular publications, it is still the case that one's perceptions of what constitutes black Christian religious identities in Britain is still predicated upon Pentecostalism, despite the fact that two-thirds of black Christian adherents belong to white majority denominations.[126]

The following section is an attempt to offer an alternative perspective for the development of black theology in Britain. In this section, I want to look at black Methodism in Britain as a microcosm or case study for the development of black theology in this context. I believe that the basic default theology and ecclesiology of Methodism provides an important context and corporate framework for the development of black theology within the British context.

I am not arguing for a form of Methodist supremacist epistemology. Rather, I simply want to assert that of all the institutional churches in Britain, Methodism remains the one most able to accommodate black theological thinking within her system. This is not to suggest, however, that Methodism is not without her major systemic and structural problems. I am not suggesting, for example, that corporate British Methodism accepts or agrees with the substantive content of black theology as it is undertaken in Britain. Neither am I suggesting that British Methodism wishes to incorporate or deal with black theology. In this analysis, I am at pains to differentiate between institutional (white-run) Methodism and the subversive and prophetic presence of black people within the corporate whole.

The Development of Black Methodism in Britain—A Pragmatic Radicalism?

I have chosen to highlight the black presence in British Methodism for a number of reasons. First, my own religious socialization, as I have detailed it in the first chapter, was shaped by my induction in British Wesleyan Methodism. That nurture has been both the fuel and the object of opposition that has driven my scholarly work since its inception, in the mid-1990s.

Second, I believe that the distinctive features of black Methodism in Britain, which emerged from the fiery furnace of racism and marginalization, offers some interesting counterpoints to the more familiar and often repeated narrative of generic, pandenominationalist African American religious developments in the United States.[127]

I believe this often hidden narrative offers an important corrective to the seeming orthodoxy of black British Christian religious discourse in Britain. This highly selective narrative asserts that black Pentecostalism is the summit of the black British Christian religious experience and that this particular tradition has provided the most significant resources for the development of black theology in Britain.[128]

This alternative narrative is built upon often hidden presence of black people in white majority historic churches. The greater majority of black people to be found within these churches come from the

Caribbean.[129] Heather Walton, in detailing the historic mainline links Methodism has had with the West Indian islands, contends that almost three quarters of black Methodists trace their recent ancestry to the Caribbean,[130] although this assumption is being challenged in recent times by the explosion of black Methodism in Britain with its roots in West Africa. Increasing numbers of black Methodists, particularly in London, now trace their roots to countries such as Ghana, Nigeria, and Sierre Leone.

The influx of black people from the New Commonwealth in the post–World War II migration of the last century led to serious upheaval and pressure within the body politic of these churches. The historic formulations of theology, custom, and practice were now called into question.

The aforementioned events has led to myriad reports trying to make sense of this sociocultural and political phenomenon.[131] In Methodist terms, the two most significant documents have been *A Tree God Planted* published in 1985 and *Faithful and Equal* in 1987. The former affirmed the place of black people within the British Methodist Church and the latter sought to provide a theological and structural means for denouncing and challenging racism. Recently, Robinson Milwood's[132] work and that of Naboth Muchopa[133] have continued to press for a more honest church that can deal with racism and notions of exclusion.

Black people stayed in British Methodism due to issues pertaining to identity and also by conviction and temperament. Added to this are questions of theology, history, and an oral tradition that told them that church could be more than the pain they were currently experiencing.[134] Finally, there is the determination not to be forced out of "their church."

Black Methodism in Britain—An Example of Black Theology in Britain in Practice

What is black British Methodism? At the risk of sounding immodest, I assert that my own writings have done more than most to define the theological and structural identities of black Methodism within the British Methodist church as a whole. In *Growing into Hope*[135] and *Legacy*[136] I have attempted to outline an educational and theological rationale for black people remaining within what are often (although ameliorated by history) discriminatory and racist institutions. There are a plethora of reasons that inform black Methodist's desire to remain within the main body of white dominated British Methodism.

In the first instance, there is the prophetic stance of Methodism. This is a reminder of what was once, and to a lesser extent is still, an important characteristic of Methodism, namely, social justice and a commitment to the poor. It was through the agitation of black Methodists that the British Methodist church created the first national Racial Justice Officer in 1984 when Mr. Ivan Weekes was appointed.

Second, there is a holding together of a synthesized spirituality that is dialectical in the best of traditions of black Christianity whether in the United States,[137] the Caribbean,[138] or Britain.[139] In effect, it is "this wordly" and "other wordly." It is committed to personal and corporate transformation. This view is one that asserts that education is an essential ingredient in holiness and sanctification.[140] In this light, the development of black Christian education[141] is of crucial importance. Black British Methodism is connected to a radical form of ecclesiology that moves beyond the blinkered dichotomy between liberal and evangelical.[142] It incorporates an inherent hermeneutic of suspicion regarding the usual ills of the world, particularly, ones that perceive blackness, black people, and the poor as the problem.

Inderjit Bhogal's essay on citizenship in *Legacy* is a classic example of a type of spirituality that reaches out toward the wider world and rejects a privatized notion of salvation and God.[143] Hence, it is able (as is Black Christianity at its best) to hold in tension orthodoxy and orthopraxis.

The Contribution of Black Methodism to Black Theology in Britain

This can be summarized in four parts. First, black Methodism is strongly allied to social justice movements in Britain, such as the "Make Poverty History" campaign. The Multiracial Projects Fund, which operates within British Methodism dispenses approximately £100,000 every year to voluntary-run projects (of all denominations) that are committed to promoting and working for racial justice. The British Methodist input and commitment to black theology in Britain can be seen in the manner in which the multiracial project fund continues to make significant financial contributions toward the development of this discipline. Recent examples include monies to host black theology conferences (often paying for flights and expenses of radical African American scholars who otherwise may not get invited to Britain) and providing development grants for publications, such as the black theology journal and the forthcoming reader in black theology in Britain. Particular thanks and recognition are due to Naboth Muchopa, the full-time racial justice officer for the Methodist church, who is responsible for overseeing the fund. This approach comes directly from John Wesley, the founder of Methodism, who argued there was no holiness except social holiness. His doctrine of Scriptural holiness argued for a notion of salvation that went beyond the claims made by the individual.[144] Black Methodism reminds black theology in Britain (in addition to her own church) that salvation is corporate, not wholly individual (as understood in Judaism), and that the transformation of all society is our ultimate goal.

What undergirds this social justice orientation to missiology is the strong emphasis given by Methodism (especially black people in Methodism) to an embodied theology. There is a high doctrine of the Incarnation within black Methodism.[145] This speaks against a spiritualized notion of God and transformation that characterizes the worst excesses of some examples of Pentecostalism. "The Word became flesh and dwelt among us" (John 1:14). Hence, the flesh matters, context, social location, and geography matters. Jesus dwelt amongst the landless poor of Galilee.[146] His movement located itself amongst the artisans far removed from the theocratic center of Jerusalem.[147]

Black Methodism (potentially, at its best) can align itself against the structural and systemic concerns that stalk this world, and not relegate them to a brief prelude before the "Eschaton," which will usher in the next world. Doreen and Neville Lawrence, Black prophets, to whom reference is made in chapter 4, are black Methodists. Spiritualizing hardship and struggle was not an option for them,[148] following the brutal racist attack on and the subsequent murder of their son Stephen, on April 18, 1993, in the South-East London borough of Eltham.

Following Stephen Lawrence's death, his parents led a vigilant and prolonged antiracist campaign in their efforts to attain justice for their murdered son. This faith-based campaign, in conjunction with those of other black-led social and cultural organizations, challenged the might of the British establishment: the Metropolitan Police force.[149]

In the area of ecclesiology, black Methodism offers a loose, dare one say low view of church, in which those who are social outcasts or deemed undesirables can find a place. Unmarried mothers are not turned out or turned away. Babies born out of wedlock are baptised (baptism is a corporate means of grace, not solely a privatized profession of faith).

People belong before they believe. A liberal approach to ecclesiology and a socially related theology means that black women have easier access to positions of power in the church. Biblical injunctions around the necessity for male headship are not invoked, as Methodist doctrine holds that *all positions* in the church are open to both genders.

The present chair of the Black Methodists for Unity and Liberation (BMLU),[150] the national caucus group for black people in British Methodism, is a woman. There are currently more black women training for ministry in Methodism than men.

As a corollary to the previous point, black Methodism, through having to deal head-on with white hegemony within its own ranks, has been forced to develop a theological hermeneutic that forces it to look at the structural injustice meted out to all people. Neoconservatism that constructs reactionary models of theological reflection becomes patently less attractive when one is dealing with ongoing realities of marginalization and oppression from white people in one's own church. This is often not the case in some branches of black-led Pentecostalism in Britain.[151] It is interesting to note that according to Cone, it would appear that in the area of social ethics and inclusivity, black people in the white majority United Methodist Church (UMC) are more progressive in challenging many of the age-old strictures around acknowledging and dealing with blackness, racism, sexism, and patriarchy than their peers in the black majority Methodist ones.[152] Cone's reflections share many of the insights I have just made in my comparative analysis of black Methodism in Britain.

Black Methodism, true to its heritage, remains a significant player in formal and informal education. Black Methodism continues to offer a strong commitment to the development of black Christian education (which can be construed as the applied or practical wing of black theology—see chapter 4).

For black British Methodism, this world matters, not just the one to come. The pioneering works of such unheralded black women as Sybil Phoenix[153] and Syble Morgan[154] are testimony to the grassroots activism of ordinary black Methodists. For people such as Sybil Phoenix and Syble Morgan, the world belongs to God, not to white men with power. Black theology, in partnership with all our churches, remains committed to working in partnership with God in order that God's creation can be redeemed and transformed for God, in and through the life, death, and resurrection of Jesus and in the power of the Holy Spirit. Black people in Methodism have played an important part in that development and continue to do so.

My focus on black Methodism in Britain has been written in order to draw attention to the wider context that has nurtured me and to which I owe a great debt. Whilst I am of the opinion that this framework provides the most hospitable space in which black theology in Britain can develop, I do not believe that it remains the only context by any means. What has been instructive, as I have undertaken this research, is the extent to which many of the defining features of black British Methodism, as I have outlined them, are reflected across the whole spectrum of black ecclesiology in the United States.

Undoubtedly, one can highlight the reactionary forces of conservatism in the Unites States, which have blunted and stunted the radical intent of the black church. The strict adherence to white evangelicalism is a direct case in point. Although one must add that this phenomenon is not limited to either Britain or the United States, it is, in many respects, now the default position of black Christianity across the whole world. And yet, in spite of these challenges and concerns, there remains, within much that is the black church, whether in the United States or in Britain and across every denomination, the seeds for a radical resurgence. This resurgence is one that will challenge the systematic and systemic roots of injustice that continue to plague the consciousness and potentiality of black people across the world.

In both the contexts, one can point to the work of courageous black theologians, who, although residing outside of the black church, remain no less committed to it—committed to its reform, redevelopment, and reawakening. The black church has produced the bulk of the black theologians who are presently undertaking their work in the many contexts in which their scholarly and pastoral ministry is located.

The black church continues to infuriate and anger me, often, to the point of distraction. Yet, I remain committed to it. For, it remains, by the grace and inspiration of God, the best example of collective work and corporate institutional development black folk have managed thus far. It may not be perfect—in fact, it may be so far from perfection as to warrant a swift call to the pastor and the doctor to first pray for, and then perhaps write out the death certificate—and yet I feel that God is not finished with her yet. There is life in the ecclesial mother yet! To quote my mother, "half the story is yet to be told."

3
Bring on the Sistas

This chapter draws on the work of Womanist theologians in Britain and in the United States. Like the previous chapters, this chapter does not purport to be an exhaustive and systematically argued overview of the respective developments of Womanist thought on either side of the Atlantic. Rather, it is a more subjective and personal reading of this movement from the vantage-point of a black British male theologian whose work and thought has been influenced by this burgeoning arena of black theological discourse. Clearly, as a black male, it is not my place to tell black women what to do and how they should do it. What I offer instead are some personal reflections on womanist theology, comparing and contrasting the significant themes and approaches between the United States and Britain.

What is Womanist Theology?

Without wishing to overextend our thinking through a prolonged period of theorizing, one might, in heuristic terms, describe Womanist theology as a related branch of black theology.[1] It is an approach to theology that begins with the experiences of black women as its point of departure in talking about God and the ways in which God-talk is undertaken.

Womanist theology utilizes the experience of black women to challenge the tripartite ills of racism, sexism, and classism. This discipline has been influenced by Feminist thought and, on occasions, has been inaccurately labelled as black feminism.[2] Womanist theology is both a method and a conceptual approach to theology that arises from the experience of black women.

In many introductory texts on womanist theology, reference is made to Alice Walker, for it is her work and thought that gave rise to the term "Womanish."[3] Walker identifies many of the formative notions of womanism. These include self-determination, self-definition, the love of oneself, a commitment to holistic living, solidarity with other women, and a respect for the experience and knowledge claims that arise from the reality of being a black woman.[4]

Womanist theology emerged as a necessary corrective to the andro-centric myopia of much that was black theology, which emerged in the late 1960s and the 1970s. It was not uncommon to find black male writers referring to man when wishing to talk about the plight of all black people. In effect, their androcentric thinking was no better than the white male theologians they were often critiquing.

Learning to Appreciate Womanist Theology—Insights from the United States

I have to confess that when I first read James Cone's *A Black Theology of Liberation* this glaring oversight did not register on my conscious-ness. It seemed perfectly natural, even as late as the 1990s, to witness writers speak about men as a means of encapsulating the whole of humanity.

Growing up within a white majority conservative evangelical setting, it was quite natural, indeed, normative to speak of God in solely male terms. Whilst the language of worshipping God in "Spirit and in truth" (John 4:23) was an accepted liturgical norm, the working thesis of the church was one that saw theology in male terms, resulting in the corollary of male leadership and headship. It was only upon reaching the final chapters of the twentieth anniversary edition of *A Black Theology of Liberation*[5] and the critical response of Delores S. Williams[6] that I realized the inherent flaws in Cone's initial work (and those of his contemporaries).

It was not until my own exposure to black theology grew and I became familiar with the work of that first generation of black theologians that I began to reassess the limitations of their work. I remember being excited and thrilled as I engaged with the articulacy and the bravery of that first generation of pastors and scholars blazing a prophetic trail across the consciousness of the United States in the late 1960s.

As a fledgling black British scholar funded by and operating within my own white dominated church, to read of African Americans denouncing racism and white hegemony in the most visceral and polemical of terms, I was struck by the parallel between this movement and the actions of Peter on the day Pentecost (Acts 2:14–42). I was reminded of my temerity and diffidence when challenged to name the sin of racism and white supremacy in my context.

Yet, amidst this holy prophetic Crusade of Christian truth-telling, I became cognizant of the parochial nature of this strident and righteous movement. As an example of this form of myopia, I want to highlight a brief section from the *Statement by the National Committee of Black Churchmen, June 13, 1969*.[7] The conclusion of the statement reads thus:

> As black theologians address themselves to the issues of the black revolution, it is incumbent upon them to say that the black community will not be turned from its course, but will seek complete fulfilment of the promises of the Gospel . . . We do this as black men and as Christians. This is the message of Black Theology. In the words of Eldridge Cleaver: "We shall have our manhood. We shall have it or the earth will levelled by our efforts to gain it."[8]

It can be argued that in selecting this particular passage from that 1969 statement, I have been unfair to the authors. In many respects, this is undoubtedly true. There is a real sense that the time period in which this statement was made was radically different from that in which we are living. In an age prior to the burgeoning of the women's movement and feminism, male centered language and models of speech were, of course, the norm. I am also aware that the carelessness and oversight in the use of language should not dissipate the importance and the power of this and other statements from that time. Those early black theologians and pastors got more right than they did wrong.

It needs to be stated, however, that despite their vigilance in challenging the horrors and absurd incongruity of white supremacy within a so-called Christian nation, these and many other men singularly failed to notice the ways in which their theological discourse continued to marginalize women. It would appear that some causes are inherently more important than others—because some people are inherently more important than others.

Part of my own journey in appreciating the privileges accrued to me by my maleness and the ways in which I have often unwittingly colluded in the gender oppression of women within a patriarchal system have been detailed in a previous piece of work.[9]

My own sense of development and growth has meant having to learn to speak out against the natural consequences of my own self-interest.

Namely, that part of the reason why so many black male theologians (whether they are theologians who happen to be black or whether they name themselves as black theologians) find it conveniently easy to separate racism from sexism is due to the fact that the latter does not affect them directly or in the same way as the former. As I have stated in the first chapter of this work, the old Caribbean aphorism says "Who feels it, knows it." Clearly, what black women have felt has been seen as being of lesser importance (and in some cases of no importance at all) when assessed from within the experience of some black men.

My growing self-awareness of the importance of black women to the development of black theology (and the church as a whole) and the necessity of womanist theology as a vital corrective to the overall movement find echoes in the recent work of Demetrius Williams. Williams has written about the numerous ways in which black religious scholars have adopted a variety of reading strategies of Scripture in order to create alternative models of liberation.[10]

Of particular import, in the context of this chapter, is Williams's reading of Galatians 3:38, in which he outlines the different ways in which this passage has been interpreted from within the African American tradition.[11] It is interesting to note that a cultural and religious community has learnt to read critically *against* the text in order to create a potentially radical hermeneutic from what is potentially dehumanizing theological discourses (it is notable that black people have learnt to read *against* Ephesians 6:5 and Colossians 3:22). Yet, that self-same community still possesses the facility to read *with* the text when it so chooses.

This tendency can be seen in the ways in which black Christian communities can read *against* Paul's injunction for slaves to obey masters (Colossians 3:22) but wives *should be* subject to their husbands (Colossians 3:18). These two injunctions come from the same section of writing, but there exists radically different ways of reading the text. Williams challenges many of these contradictory tendencies when he mounts a more expansive investigation into the ways in which black churches in the United States have read and sought to use Galatians 3:28 in the context of gender equality.[12]

In an illuminating opening section, Williams shares an experience of being damned as an indoctrinated secular liberal by a group of older black pastors for daring to suggest that black women can and should preach in the church.[13] These older pastors use biblical texts from the Pauline canon to justify their sexism—the same canon that they would clearly and cleverly read against in order to construct an antiracist, counterhegemonic hermeneutic. I have shared these observations at this juncture for I feel it incumbent upon me as a black male theologian to detail the extent to which I have undergone a "conversation" experience of sorts in order to unlearn the fallacies of patriarchy. This has been undertaken in order that I can more fully appreciate the challenges of Womanist theology. Like my African American peers, in the shape of Dwight Hopkins[14] and Garth Baker-Fletcher,[15] I have attempted to undergo a spiritual and psychological rebirth in order to be in solidarity with my black sisters.

Just as black people per se need to undergo some form of conscientizing process so that they can unlearn the distortions of white supremacist thought in order that they can relearn affirmative African-centered forms of thinking, *all* black men need to undertake a similar intellectual and spiritual process in terms of gender awareness. I share a little more of my own journey when assessing the publication of *Legacy*[16] at a later point in this chapter. *Legacy* was an edited volume of largely womanist prose and poetry (10 of the 15 contributors were black British Women) that was published in Britain in 2000.

Until black male theologians make a point of challenging patriarchy and sexism with the same energy and vigor they have used in their attempts to overcome racism, the black church will remain a context of missed potential, as the important voice of black women will be dissipated or even lost.[17] Black male theologians need to retune their radar in order that they become sensitized to the multidimensional threats that stalk our airwaves, which include patriarchy.

Are All Black Women Womanists?

I have posed this question because from my observation of the development of womanist theology, particularly, in the United States, I have sensed that the designation "womanist" seems to occupy a more organic and representative space in terms of its relationship to black women than is the case with the more generic nomenclature of black theology for all black people. In some cases, it might appear that womanist appears to be a more natural term or designation for all black women because its existence is linked less to an alleged ideological or political conceptualization and is attuned more to the natural biological identification of gender. Whilst not all black people will necessarily want to think of themselves in terms that would be consonant with black theology, if womanist theology is predicated on the basis of black women's experiences, then is it not the case that to be a womanist, you simply have to be a black woman?

Returning to the defining work of Alice Walker in outlining the basic building blocks of womanism, I have attempted to make sense of the essentials that comprise this growing movement. Are there particular core components or elements that constitute womanism and her more specialized offspring, womanist theology? Walker's initial definition continues to serve as an important point of departure for a description of womanism. Rereading Walker's definition, I am struck by how wonderfully elusive, elastic, and inclusive are the combination of images and themes she uses in order to delineate her understanding of this phrase womanist.[18]

Walker derives the term "Womanist" from an intergenerational rebuke from older Black women to their younger charges not to get ahead of themselves and to act too "womanish"—too grown up.[19] It is interesting to note that what was once a reproof has now become a term that is imbued with positive and defiant connotations in similar terms to the reconceptualization of the generic term black[20] or in the British context, Beckford's reworking of African Caribbean terms such as Dread[21] and Rahtid.[22]

From my reading of Walker's definition of womanist, I do not detect an overt or explicit ideological grounding for what might or might not be considered as womanist. In fact, it might well be argued that Walker eschews the kind of rigid categorizations that seem to bedevil male centered forms of conceptual discourse. Walker's definition seems to leave the gate open to the conceptual field in which womanist discourse might be held.

Later generations of womanist scholars, particularly within the arena of theological discourse, have sought to redefine and expand the range of meanings within this term, especially when it is used within a self-consciously defined Christian religious context. These developments in our understanding of the term have broadened the parameters whilst remaining true to Walker's vision and basic conception.

Mitchem, in detailing the development of womanist theology in the United States, cites the work of such scholars as Delores Williams, Emilie Townes, Katie Cannon, and Kelly Brown Douglas who have sought to redefine and broaden Walker's definition in order to construct the basic template for the articulation of a discipline called womanist theology (as opposed to the broader term of womanism).[23]

In the British context, Kate Coleman has argued that the term womanist, which is largely synonymous with African American women's experiences (a point I deal with at a later juncture in this chapter), has been used by black British women, but is beginning to be infused with new meanings as it responds to the particularity of the British context.[24]

Coleman, like her U.S. counterparts, does not attempt to trap herself within a tortuous, semantic maze of meaning and countermeaning in terms of who is, or is not, a womanist. It would appear that womanists have attempted to move beyond the limited and constricted boundaries of who is or can be a member of the movement. So are all women womanists then?

Well, not quite! My self-avowed "get out clause" emerges from my many encounters with both older black women in general and those (older or younger) whose own philosophical and theological outlook might be considered to be somewhat conservative. In conversation with such women in the course of my work as a religious educator, I have been struck by the reluctance of many of them to own the term womanist when it is applied to such individuals as themselves. Can one be a womanist even if one rejects the term itself?

I am aware of the constricting and regulating tendencies of essentialist thought that wants to herd all black people (in this case, women) into particular self-identified and carefully defined groups. Failure to "join the gang" leads to the epithet of "sell out," or "not black enough" or even more damning "Not being a true black woman!"[25] Can or should all black women be womanists?

The definitions attributed to womanism appear to be somewhat open-ended and inclusive and seem to be grounded within a generic appreciation of the multiple ways in which black women's experiences can be detailed. These definitions do not seem to carry any overt essentialized ideological strictures; nevertheless, the resulting theological constructions attributed to womanist theology do appear to be ideologically determined.

For example, womanist theology privileges the experience of black women as a point of departure in the methodological construction of this approach to black God-talk. British womanist theologian, Maxine Howell-Baker, in her articulation of "Womanist Pneumatological pedagogy"[26] stresses that her study

> without apology takes a subjective stance regarding its treatment of ideas, concepts and theories, in line with the key epistemological (how we know what we know to be true) precept in Black and subjugated thought systems that makes lived experience accompanied by concrete

illustrations indispensable to the process of constructing and representing meaning.[27]

The priority given to experience as a key hermeneutical device for interpreting and reinterpreting the Scriptures and the traditions that arise from these foundational texts is a central tenet of womanist theology.[28] The privileging and prioritizing of Black women's experience becomes a powerful mechanism for affirming the subjectivity of those who are marginalized and oppressed and providing a means by which traditionally patriarchal structures and Androcentric dominant discourses can be reread and even subverted.[29]

This important emphasis within womanist theology is not without its critics or internal difficulties. In terms of the latter, Howell-Baker states,

> Nor is such an experience-centred approach without risk of mirroring the very dominant thought structures it is designed to challenge, by elevating the Black woman's experience to a supreme position, or by refusing to engage in dialogue with other experiences.[30]

In terms of the latter, Victor Anderson has critiqued womanist theology for its predilection for highlighting the exceptional qualities of black women, particularly those whose subjectivity can be cited in literary output, such as autobiographies, poetry, and fiction.[31] To what extent are these women representative of the common experience of ordinary black women? Does womanist theology fall into the trap of highlighting the exceptional in order to illuminate the role and importance of ordinary black women?[32]

My reason for raising the question of women's experience as a crucial point of departure for womanist theology is due to the fact that this methodology assumes an ideological presupposition for appreciating the sources and norms for undertaking theological inquiry. In this regard, womanist theology shares much with her older sibling, black theology, insofar as both disciplines (whether they are indeed separate disciplines or one is a subset of the other is investigated at a later point in the chapter) use black experience as an important point of departure in theological inquiry.[33]

In fairness to both black and womanist theologians, the Bible remains an indispensable resource, alongside experience, as an essential text by which God's revealed presence is discerned.[34] Whilst many womanist theologians will want to assert that there is a dialectical tension between the authority of Scripture and the realities of black women's experience,[35] there are others who would see such a tension as an erroneous one. Namely, that the Bible, for all its alleged faults (this point itself would be regarded as illegitimate by many conservative black women and men), remains the only substantive text by which we can begin to undertake *any* talk about God and what might be construed as truth.

In an earlier piece of research, I witnessed, first hand, the determination and the tenacity by which many older African Caribbean women in Britain remained steadfastly wedded to the Bible. For them, there was no question that the Bible could or should be reread in light of one's experience.[36] I still remember one woman reproaching me after an interactive Bible study I had led, in which I had encouraged the group to engage in some role-play in order to unlock the Scriptures. Eyeing me with a spirited look, she said, "That's the problem with you youngsters. You spend all your time trying to interpret the Bible. You see me and these women (the other members of the research focus group), we simply believe it."

Now I should hasten to add that the woman's words were said with a wry smile, for the session had patently revealed that these women were much smarter and more subversive in their readings of the Bible than the façade of the biblically literalist approach would seem to suggest. But the point I want to assert is this: to what extent can we use the term womanist to encompass the positionality of these older black women? Anderson, in critiquing Jacklyn Grant's approach to womanist theology, argues that one of the problems with prioritizing black women's experiences within a paradigm of ontological blackness is that one then

> reduces the logic or Womanist exceptionalism formally to the recuctio ad absurdum that every black woman is also a Womanist.[37]

The dangers of trying to create an overarching framework into which all black women of faith can be deposited becomes even more fraught and problematic, when one considers the thorny and vexed question of sexuality within womanist theology. Whilst Delores Williams offers an inclusive definition of a womanist that supports the notion of same-gender loving relations,[38] other black women scholars, most notably Cheryl Sanders, reject this as being inconsistent with the tradition bequeathed to black woman from their forebears.[39] For many conservative black women (sociologically and theologically), the crucial question to be asked of womanist theology is summed up in Sanders' query

> In other words, what is the necessary condition for doing Womanist schol-
> arship? To be a black, a woman? A black feminist? A black lesbian?[40]

After much reflection I am of the mind to suggest that whilst womanist theology offers a more open and less ideologically driven paradigm than the overarching discipline of black theology, which enables it to potentially embrace all black women within its orbit, there is no doubt in my mind that being a womanist, nevertheless, necessitates a particular consciousness of self, the Bible, and the whole Christian tradition that is not the common ground on which necessarily all black women walk. I think all black women can *potentially* be womanists (as is the case for all black people in terms of being black theologians), but not all will necessarily either feel comfortable or wish to be grouped in such a category.

Womanist versus Feminist?

A crucial component in the make-up of womanist theology is the invocation of the very name itself. The term womanist has gained an important and necessary potency for the way in which it has become clearly identified with the needs and aspirations of black women. The term is both descriptive and normative. It not only seeks to embrace important characteristics of what it means to be a black woman, but also contains an ideological component in that it stakes a claim for what black women can and should be, juxtaposed alongside the need to reject those things that have traditionally constricted their life choices.

The term womanist has become an almost iconic one and is now used in an interdisciplinary fashion across a range of disciplines. As we have seen in the previous section, the seemingly generic nature of the enterprise has caused some problems and even controversy for some black women. Clearly, not all black women are necessarily womanist. But should all black women named themselves as such? And most crucially, can (and should) all black women call themselves feminists?

Within the British context, Kate Coleman, a black Baptist minister, is one of the leading black British women theologians who has written at length on the development of her spirituality and liberating consciousness and that of the overarching movement of womanist theology in

Britain.[41] Commenting on the use of the term womanist, Coleman writes,

> It is said that Alice Walker, who coined the phrase Womanist, had grown weary of having to use the qualifying words whenever she described herself as a feminist, such as "Well, I'm a Black Feminist," and then having to explain what she did and did not mean by that. This has often been the case for many Black women who have wanted to express allegiance to certain feminist themes without necessarily having to identify themselves with it in its entirety. In addition there are many Black women who, perceiving feminism as anti-black and anti-men, have not wanted to be identified with it at all.[42]

Is womanist theology, then, simply just "Feminism" under an alternative guise that black women can live with? Alternatively, are there substantive themes, concerns, and methods of engagement that differentiate womanism from feminism? I attempt to partly answer these questions (recognizing that each in itself could sustain a Ph.D. study) through four examples. I look at four key texts (*Sisters with Power* and *Legacy* from the British context, and *White Women's Christ* and *Black Women's Jesus* and *Kattie's Canon* from the United States) in order to discern a sense of where womanism stands in relation to feminism. In taking this particular approach, I am acutely aware of the obvious and, in some sense, alarming fault lines.

First, there is the all too obvious danger of using work that cannot hope to represent the wide and diverse tradition that is now womanist scholarship. The texts I have chosen are not meant to serve as microcosms for womanist theology. In fact, it would be true to report that in Britain there is no one single book that might be described as a womanist text as such. I have chosen these texts because, in many respects, they have had an important influence on me, a black male educator and theologian and have assisted in shaping my own consciousness. So, these texts tell you more about me than they necessarily do about the ongoing development of womanist theology in Britain and in the United States.

Second, in seeking to compare womanism with feminism, one runs the risk of devaluing the innate individuality and uniqueness of each tradition on the notoriously slippery altar of comparative studies. Such approaches often result in collapsing important distinctive features in either tradition, resulting in an unhappy comparative mishmash[43] that pleases no one.[44] I have chosen to take this potentially dangerous route of comparing womanism with reference to feminism in order to do justice to the complexity of self-naming and establishing identities. As black folk, we know the importance of being able to name ourselves and construct a language in order to give expression to our existential experiences. All black people will know the folly and the deceit in the old aphorism "Sticks and stones may break my bones, but words will never harm me." Words do hurt and have even been known to kill. My parents went from being "colored" to being "Black" within their own lifetime. I still remembered being called a nice little "colored boy" at primary school and then gravitating to alternative nomenclatures like "Black" "African Caribbean," "African," "Black British" or, as is vogue in certain quarters, "Afro-Saxon." The names we employ and the terms we use to designate ourselves matter intensely.

In this section of the book, I am not proposing to delineate the central components of womanism and feminism in terms of their substantive content, rather, I am interested in a more limited sense, in charting when and how these words are used. To what extent is womanism a normative self-designated term for all black women? Are some more comfortable with feminism than with womanism and do some prefer neither term?

In keeping with the structure of the book I have chosen two texts from each context with which to dialogue. Within the British context, I have chosen Joe Aldred's edited book *Sisters with Power*[45] along with *Legacy: Anthology in Memory of Jillian Brown*.[46] I edited the latter in 2000.

The first and perhaps most obvious thing to remark about these two texts is that although the majority of the contributors are black women, the books are edited by black men. There are, undoubtedly, a number of ameliorating factors for this state of affairs. As one of the editors of these books, it would be very easy to use this opportunity to mount a spirited and serious defense of my role as the convener and coordinator of a text that is primarily about one black woman and a number of other black women writing in response to the death of the former.

Instead, I will simply say (not speaking for my colleague Joe Aldred) that the fact that black men edited both the texts is a telling observation (and perhaps indictment) of the paucity of black women in the theological academy in Britain and their lack of access to the levers of publishing. Certainly, in my own case, I am acutely aware that I was the individual in the most advantageous position to get the book project off the ground. I doubt whether any of the black women involved in the development of *Legacy* could have done so, not,

I hasten to add, due to any shortcomings in their own abilities, but rather, as a recognition of the largely patriarchal nature of theological book publishing in Britain.

Sisters with Power

Sisters with Power is an edited collection of autobiographical pieces by women, most, but not all of whom, are black. The various pieces in the book are drawn from a wide cross-section of women, each reflecting on some aspect of ministry, theology, faith, and spirituality. Within the text there are a mixture of names and personalities: from well-established writers and scholars, such as Kate Coleman,[47] Lorraine Dixon,[48] and Mukti Barton[49] to less well-known writers in the academic field, such as Christine Russell Lumby,[50] and Andrea Encinas-Meade.[51]

Aldred's aim in editing the book is to enable women to speak for themselves and to dispel the age-old notion of black people being oral people who, consequently, lack a literary tradition.[52] In his opening summation, Aldred writes,

> *Sisters with Power* brings together Black, Asian and White Christian reflections on a range of topics that these women writers have chosen. The book is topically thematic: its themes is women, mainly black women, speaking and writing for themselves. In a patriarchal society, it is matriarchal power at its best.[53]

Aldred's final comment is a touch overstated given that these essays by women are contained in a text overseen and edited by a man. It can hardly be called "matriarchal power at its best." What is interesting when rereading *Sisters with Power* in the context of our discussion around names and the naming processes of women, whether black or white is the paucity of references to womanism in the text. The term womanism is used explicitly on only a handful of occasions, most notably in Lorraine Dixon's piece,[54] whereas Dionne Lamont refers to ethics and feminist theology in her essay.[55]

I am at pains to stress that I am not seeking to make any form of judgment on the appropriateness or otherwise of the designations many of these women use in order to name and identify themselves. Many simply use the term Christian woman whilst others happily settle for black woman, white woman, or Asian woman. What is clear from this text is that a group of experienced and highly capable women have adopted a varying range of expressions with which to name themselves and womanism is just one.

Legacy: Anthology in Memory of Jillian Brown

Jillian Brown was a friend of mine. She was a talented polymath. Among her many interests was womanist theology. Jil (as she preferred to be called) was undertaking a Ph.D. in womanist approaches to death and dying when her own life was cruelly cut short by a brain haemorrhage in 1999 at the age of 31. *Legacy* was edited in her honor. The book consists of three sections. Section one includes many of Jil's own writings, in the form of poems, essays, and sermons. The second section is a brief response by members of her family, and section three consists of work by many of her friends (a number of whom were members of the black theology in Britain movement), a majority of whom are black women.

Legacy was my attempt, as the editor, to enable a number of budding black scholars to write and share their thoughts and feelings in response to the tragic death of an individual who was one of us. Priority was given to those whose opportunities to get their work published, thus far, had been limited thinking especially of black women. Despite my best attempts, I am aware, I belong to the grand tradition of paternalistic males who create space for black women to do their work. I have to confess that it did not occur to me (or Aldred perhaps?) to hand over the reigns of the project to a black woman, who would have been eminently more suited to the task of overseeing the project than I was. Such is the tyranny of egoism!

Not all contributors in *Legacy* are women. In this respect it is different from *Sisters with Power*. Ten of the fifteen contributors in *Legacy* are black women. I know that comparisons are invidious, so I do not intend to make any like-for-like responses between these two British texts. In many respects, they are different. While *Sisters with Power* is an eclectic, self-defined, cross-cultural text with no immediate or obvious ideological intent, *Legacy* is a more self-conscious black theological piece of work, written in response to one who named herself as a womanist.

Legacy is also notable for the apparent absence of the term "Womanist," whilst the substantive context of the book is largely steeped in both methodological and thematic concerns that are commonplace in this tradition. Established black British women scholars such as Lorraine Dixon[56] and Valentina Alexander[57] do not invoke the term on many occasions, even though the subjects on which they are writing are those that resonate with the wider contours of womanist thought. Interestingly, even Jil's own work is not replete with references to womanism.[58]

Neither womanism nor feminism is mentioned extensively within *Legacy*. In rereading these British texts I have speculated on the reasons for the absence of particular terms or designations in the writing of many of the black women. I feel there are, perhaps, two pointers or insights one can offer at this juncture for this absence. One is what I will term pragmatic appropriateness and the other perhaps is of a more philosophical nature. In terms of the former, pragmatic appropriateness, it should be noted that neither text is an explicit academic tome.

Although both books are well written and the contributors are of the highest quality, neither is intended to be a grand statement in terms of women's approaches to theology and scholarship. Undoubtedly, both have been used as source material for accessing aspects of black women's spiritualities and theological disposition but they should not be construed as fully fledged, self-determined pieces of academic scholarship.

Had these two texts been conceived in an academic context then we may have seen a very different set of writing from an alternative cast of players. Perhaps it is the context of writing for a more accessible audience that has led many of these women to eschew the use of seemingly ideological terms like womanism and feminism, even when, as in the case of *Legacy*, the substantive content of the work contains many of the inherent building blocks of womanist thought and practice.

On a more philosophical note, one can point to the developing work of Caribbean and British scholars such as Marjorie Lewis,[59] Diane Watt,[60] and Maxine Howell,[61] whose work with and amongst black women is challenging many of the commonly held assumptions around appropriate naming strategies for black women. Lewis's work has been most instructive for the way in which she is searching for a nomenclature for Jamaican and British women that goes beyond the designation of womanist or feminist. Lewis has constructed a Jamaican-inspired notion of theology that is built upon the contextual experiences of black women.[62] Lewis writes of her particular construction of theology:

> I am of the view that the appropriate term is "nannyish t'eology," an expression couched in the Jamaican language, which clearly suggests its derivation from Nanny the icon and prototype. I offer this as the appropriate nomenclature for a contextualized Jamaican Womanist theology, because it embodies a consensus about the valued understanding of women's roles in Jamaican society.[63]

Watts, on the other hand, prefers feminist for her particular naming strategy,[64] whilst Howell uses womanist in her work.[65]

It would seem, from this albeit very limited sample of black theological work undertaken by black women in Britain that there is an ease and a plethora of naming strategies and designations that black women are employing in order to identify their experiences and the thematic and methodological approaches at play in their work. The multiperspective and eclectic nature of British identities, drawing upon black Atlantic,[66] postcolonial, and Diasporan routes[67] and critical theories have enabled black women in Britain to remain remarkably fluid in their use of terms with which to name themselves.

This is, perhaps, part of the reason (in addition to the aforementioned question of pragmatic appropriateness) for black women, even when writing in a self-conscious manner about their own experiences, willingly deploy a variety of labels with which to name themselves, labels that move from generic Christian woman to feminist and womanist.

White Women's Christ and Black Women's Jesus

Jacquelyn Grant's *White Women's Christ and Black Women's Jesus*[68] was the first womanist theology text I read. I came across Grant's work soon after having devoured the black anthologies of Cone and Wilmore and Cone's early triumvirate of texts, *Black Theology and Black Power*,[69] *A Black Theology of Liberation*,[70] and *God of the Oppressed*.[71] Grant's book was significant for alerting me to the hitherto unrecognized strains of patriarchy and androcentrism that were very much (and still are, if truth be told) a part of my make-up.

The Christianity into which I had been socialized was one that had been heavily influenced by the eighteenth- and nineteenth-century holiness movements.[72] Within this intense pietistic movement, the centrality and preoccupation with Jesus was the dominant theme in the liturgical and discipleship life of the church. The Jesus I learnt to love was a blue-eyed, blond-haired Bjorn Borg-like* individual who, in every respect, was the antithesis of myself.[73] This Jesus was not only white, but also a very masculine male, complete with rugged good looks and a manly (and yet tastefully styled) beard! Both Josiah Young[74] and Cham Kaur-Mann[75] have addressed the centrality of Jesus' identity in cultural and ethnic terms, when outlining their varying and yet complementary approaches to Christology.

---

* Former five times Wimbledon champion.

In the context of my own religious development, Grant's book was like a thunderbolt from the sky. A recent rereading of Grant's seminal text reminded me of the thought that first came into my mind when I first encountered this work, namely, that the bulk of the text is concerned principally with rebutting the limited claims of feminism. It would appear that the white women's Christ gets more of a hearing than the black women's Jesus.

It is not my intention to mount any substantive critique of Grant's book, as there are others who are singularly better equipped to undertake that role than I am, but I make the previous comments simply to highlight the tension that seems to reside in this text. Unlike many of her British counterparts, Grant can be plainly identified as a womanist from this text. Although many black writers in *Legacy* use womanist ideas and themes for their work without necessarily invoking the term to name their own experiences or methodological or thematic concerns, Grant is brilliantly and self-consciously clear in this regard.

Grant utilizes black women's experiences as the methodological underscoring of her work. *White Women's Christ and Black Women's Jesus* is organized around an explicit womanist agenda; in that the author foregrounds the often submerged and overlooked contributions of black women to the task of doing theology, which arise out of their corporate experiences of struggle and oppression.[76]

As I have stated previously in my assessment of the naming tendencies of black women scholars, it would be invidious to seek to make any generic comparisons between the different texts, as Grant's work is not only self-consciously an academic text, but also written within a social, cultural, and political milieu in which the originator of the term womanist was also located. Grant and Walker share similarities in experiences and outlooks, without attempting to collapse their respective works into an unhelpful synonymous whole. Clearly, black women in Britain and in the Caribbean (in the case of Lewis, who can be termed a "come and go"[77] black Atlantic woman) are working in differing contexts, in which new terms and designations are beginning to emerge in order to name black women's experiences.

Throughout the work, Grant juxtaposes the limitations of white feminism with the more inclusive and expansive vision of womanist theology, with particular reference to Christology. I wonder, to what extent Grant's theological method betrays a debt to her mentor James Cone; like Cone, her work is adept at juxtaposing womanist theologies in a comparative analysis with normative white, Euro-American theological expressions. Just as Cone's early work uses twentieth-century giants such as Barth and Tillich as comparative resources from which he can express his own notions of a black theology of liberation, Grant makes use of such scholars as Letty Russell, Mary Daly and Rosemary Ruether.

Whilst Grant is undoubtedly a womanist and calls herself one, there is the sense that like early Cone, she may be charged with offering a purely reactive form of analysis, given her reliance on critiquing the failures of feminism in order to delineate what is necessary and vital about womanist theology.

Katie's Canon

In many respects, Katie Cannon's 1995 text *Katie's Canon*[78] is the easiest of the four texts to assess in terms of how the writer positions herself vis-à-vis, womanist and feminist thought. Like Grant, Cannon is an unashamedly womanist who names herself as such in her text. Like Grant, her book is replete with personal and theological references to womanist themes and concerns and in her use of black women's experiences, particularly, literary sources she employs accepted womanist methodologies in the development of her work.

Unlike Grant's work, *Katie's Canon* does not offer any extensive comparative analysis with feminism. This may be due to a number of reasons. First, this is an edited retrospective, not an original defining text like that of Grant's. Second, given that it is written at a later juncture to Grant's text, Cannon's work may reflect the growing self-confidence of womanist theology to determine and mine its own sources, being less concerned with a systematic comparative analysis with white traditions and canons.

In this respect, Cannon's work is easier to locate as a self-confessed womanist text insofar as it operates mainly within an African American contextual framework and is not seeking to draw on sources or norms from outside of that tradition. This is not to criticize Grant's work by comparison; it is simply to suggest that these two books are different in terms of their methodological intent.

What complicates matters in terms of *Katie's Canon* is that chapter three is entitled "The Emergence of Black Feminist Consciousness."[79] Canon uses the term "Black feminist" to describe a conscientizing process amongst African American women in the black Church. Why is it black feminist, not womanist? It would appear that Canon is using the term black feminist partly in a historic sense to detail the development of black women's antihegemonic practices in the black church. But this still does not answer the question why the term womanist is not used. This becomes all the more striking when one sees that the final section of the chapter is entitled "Black womanist

Consciousness."[80] Toward the end of the section and the chapter, Canon writes,

> Black Feminist consciousness may be more accurately identified as Black Womanist consciousness to use Alice Walker's concept and definition.[81]

The clue to this apparent ambiguity may be found in the foundational definitions of womanism as outlined by Alice Walker.[82] The fourth tenet of Walker's definition states that "Womanism is to feminism as purple to lavender."[83] Essentially, Walker is stating that the two traditions are not entirely unconnected, for within the seismic cavern that often separates womanism from feminism is the shared experience of being a woman in a world of male hegemony.

More recently, African American Womanist scholar Stacey Floyd-Thomas has collaborated with Laura Gillman, a white feminist scholar in order to create an interdisciplinary dialogical methodology for bringing the experiences of black and white women together.[84]

The work of African American women in disciplines other than theology would seem to offer an interesting point of contrast in a manner similar to that of nontheological black women in Britain. Whereas in the latter context, Heidi Safia Mirza[85] and Amina Mama[86] use the designation of feminist. In the U.S. setting, the work of such scholars as Audre Lorde[87] and Patricia Hill Collins[88] are equally comfortable using the term "Feminist" in order to describe themselves.

So, is it feminism or womanism? For some women, it is neither. For others, particularly for African American women working within theological disciplines, womanism has become the designation of choice. In Britain, black women are not always prone to invoke the term womanist, partly for pragmatic accessible reasons, particularly if they are not located wholly within the academy, but are still involved in pastoral ministry in local churches. For many black women, there is also the question of their multiple identities and location outside of North America, which makes the term womanist not a wholly comfortable one. In both the contexts, black women outside of the traditional theological disciplines seem more able and likely to embrace the term feminism.

As I stated in a previous section in this chapter, essentially the process of naming oneself is an act of existential liberation and as such, is an intensely personal, cultural, political, sociological, and theological statement. It is one that is bound up with broader macrosystemic ways of thinking and operating, but it remains an individual response that should be beyond the overarching strictures of the sociological and cultural essentialists who want to police such naming activities.

Is Womanist Theology a separate discipline from Black Theology?

When I was first introduced to black theology in the early 1990s, the need for the articulation of theology, from the perspective of black women, was something of an after thought. The truth was, generic black God-talk was simply androcentric black theology. The idea that women might have something to contribute or that they had been badly served by the myopic tendencies of those first and second generation of black theologians in the United States did not cross my mind.

When I first read Jacquelyn Grant's *White Women's Christ and Black Women's Jesus*,[89] the visceral shock of that moment was a profound one. The growth of womanist theology over the past decade has been a necessary and impressive development. As this development has continued a pace, the question has arisen about the relationship of this discipline to that of its close sibling, black theology. In effect, is womanist theology a vital subset of black theology, or is it an important discipline in its own right?

In order to answer this question as both an insider and an outsider, I want to analyze womanist theology in a British and U.S. context. Is womanist theology a separate discipline? Should it be so? If it is separate, to what extent is that a temporary tactical move in order to construct a necessary experiential space in which the specific needs of women can be addressed away from the harsh glare of patriarchy? Are there substantive differences between Black theology and Womanist theology?

Womanist Theology and Black Theology in Britain

Womanist theology within the British context is a more fledgling enterprise than her counterpart in the United States. The number of scholarly womanist theologians is in single figures and there are, at the time of writing, no substantive sole-authored Womanist theological texts in the country. This is not to suggest that black women have not been writing. Individuals such as Valentina Alexander,[90] Carol Tomlin,[91] and Elaine Foster[92] have made significant contributions to black women's theological development in Britain, but for a variety of reasons, none has gone on to make a distinctive, ongoing scholarly impact. Alexander is believed to be the first black British woman to gain a doctorate in theology. Her groundbreaking thesis has, at the time of writing, remained unpublished[93] and she has decided to concentrate her efforts in community development work and grassroots activism and not in the academy. Tomlin has since developed a successful career within education rather than in theological studies, whilst Elaine Foster has left Britain to live and work in the Caribbean.

The absence of black Women theological scholars in Britain has, like the more generic enterprise of black theology, led to a lack of specialist scholarly development in this discipline. For pragmatic and perhaps more philosophical reasons (which I deal with shortly), womanist theology in Britain has been seen more as a subset within the overarching branch of black religious studies, particularly, black theology, than as a specialist discipline in its own right. In order to demonstrate this perception, I highlight my work and that of my colleagues Mukti Barton and Robert Beckford. I must acknowledge that this assessment predates Beckford's move from theology to cultural studies. These reflections are written concerning his former oversight of the MA in black theology in the School of Historical studies at the University of Birmingham.

Mukti Barton is, at the time of writing, tutor in black and Asian theology at the Queens Foundation (for Ecumenical Theological Education in Birmingham). She stepped into this post after the aforementioned Robert Beckford left in 1998. Barton is an Anglican laywoman, who was born and brought up in India. Her self-designation as an Indian woman who belongs to the wider network of black theology in Britain is testament to the more plural and political identification of the term black than the more ontological and cultural perspective that exists in the United States (reference to this point has been made in the opening chapter).

Barton's background is Asian and feminist theology. Her two most significant works are *Scripture as Empowerment for Liberation and Justice: The Experience of Christian and Muslim Women in Bangladesh*[94] and *Rejection, Resistance and Resurrection*.[95] Earlier, I remarked that there were (at the time of writing) no sole-authored womanist theological texts in Britain. I made this remark cognizant of Barton's work and her publications on the empowerment of Christian and Muslim women and addressing racism, the latter, principally, in the Church of England. My reason for not assessing this work as an example of womanist theological discourse is due to the self-designation of these texts, which lies very much at the nexus of feminist and Asian theologies rather than womanist theology.

In the crafting of her teaching in black and Asian theology at the Queen's Foundation, and similarly, in the MA course at the University of Birmingham, womanist theology is situated within the overarching framework of black theology. To the best of my knowledge, I am not aware of any specialist-taught courses or modules in womanist theology (as opposed to research ones) as a stand-alone discipline at undergraduate or postgraduate level, in any college or University in Britain. This is not to suggest that there are no courses in black women's studies or gender studies, which might not have a component that includes the religious sensibilities of black women, but this, to my mind, is not the same as a specialist, particular approach to the theologizing of black women arising from their experiences of multidimensional oppression.

Womanist Theology and Black Theology in Britain—An Exercise in Pragmatism?

The Centre for Black Theology in the school of Historical Studies at the University Birmingham and the Queen's Foundation (for Ecumenical Theological Education) are both situated in Birmingham less than a mile apart. These two institutions represent, to the best of my knowledge are the only academic agencies in Britain in which the teaching of black theology is normative and operates on a basis that goes beyond the tokenistic one guest lecture at the end of a standard (white) generic course mentality, which is the usual standpoint in most other bodies (assuming they even acknowledge the existence of black theology).

The credit for the development of these differing but complimentary traditions rests on the shoulders of many of the people I have named in chapter 1 (Aldred, Beckford, Wilkinson, Lartey, and others). In both the institutions, womanist theology has never existed as a completely stand-alone course.

The pragmatism of which I speak lies, perhaps, in the realization that in a country where the theological landscape remains steadfastly white, male, and largely clerical, to get black theology onto the academic agenda represents a momentous achievement in itself, without the added difficulty of attempting to diversify that marginal voice with the inclusion of womanist theology.

I make these comments without being sure of the extent to which these considerations have ever been construed in conscious terms.

I have not come across any policy document or manifesto that has made any reference (explicit or otherwise) to the aforementioned contention.

Given the paucity of black women theologians, one is forced to ask the question concerning the possibility and viability of constructing specialist, particular stand-alone courses in womanist theology, aside from the more substantive philosophical point of whether this a good thing in itself. In Britain, there simply are not (at the time of writing) sufficient number of womanist scholars to create specialist stand-alone courses in womanist theology. The growing number of black women currently undertaking postgraduate studies in Birmingham (principally) will, in time I am sure, rectify the state of affairs I am presently describing.

In making this analysis, I am forced to acknowledge the role played by predominantly black male theologians, including myself, in this regard. To what extent have black male theologians in Britain been content to simply reserve a discreet space for womanist theology within their courses (in my own case for a guest woman lecturer to come and provide the Womanist input), content in the knowledge that the rest of the space remains a largely androcentric one? Perhaps the dearth of black women scholars should not prevent black males scholars such as myself from collaborating with black women whenever possible in order to jointly craft courses in which the perspectives of black women will permeate the entirety of what are often generic black theological curricula. This approach has been undertaken by Dwight Hopkins and Linda Thomas in their highly creative and challenging approach to dealing with gender issues and related perspectives in black theology in Chicago.[96]

In the defense of the present situation, vis-à-vis womanist theology and Black theology in Britain, it should be added that the alarmingly small number of black religious scholars as a whole has led to the sense of wanting to cover all bases in terms of the overall development of black theology in Britain. As mentioned in the chapter 1, most black theologians in Britain have developed as omnicompetent practitioners whose expertise cover a number of disciplines within the academy.

Given the dearth of scholars available and the critical spaces in which black theological discourse can take place, the development of black theology in Britain has operated largely at the generic level, in which womanist theology has existed as an important subset.

Whilst many black male scholars and their female counterparts are constantly endeavoring to ensure that womanist perspectives permeate the whole of the syllabi of their teaching (I, for example, would never dream of teaching Christology without juxtaposing womanist perspectives alongside androcentric ones), it would be naive to believe that this approach represents an ideal state of affairs. Just as black theology in Britain could benefit from the degree of specialization that exists in the United States, the move to more specialized courses and programs in womanist theology would be of immense benefit to the development of this discipline in my context.

Womanist Theology and Black Theology in Britain—A Principle Response

The lack of specialized courses or programs in womanist theology represents, it might be argued, an attempt to provide a solidified and united front by black people against the overarching edifice of white supremacist thought. As womanist theology has largely eschewed the separatist and antimale perspectives that have characterized parts of militant feminism,[97] it could be argued that womanist theology in Britain has been content to play its part within the more generic and unified whole of Black theology in order to counter the worst excesses of white dominated ethnocentrism in the theological academy within Britain.[98]

The glaring weakness with this tentative contention is that it is proposed by a privileged black male whose voice is heard within the theological academy and who is not required to make inconspicuous (often unrecognized and unrewarded) sacrifices in order that the corporate whole can continue. Black British women scholars such Elaine Foster[99] and Yvette Hutchinson[100] have critiqued the ways in which traditional, patriarchal readings of the suffering of Jesus have led many black women to adopt pietistic, passive suffering roles in order that others can flourish, often at the expense of their own selfhood and development.

The failure to develop specialist courses and programs in womanist theology may have been, at some level, an implicit, principled position, but I remain unconvinced by the logic of this contention. The need to provide a unified presence in the face of the often imposing edifice that is white hegemony may have its historical antecedents, particularly in terms of the black church,[101] but as my own work,[102] and that of Doreen Morrison[103] and Victor Anderson[104] can attest, this simply leads to forms of legitimation for the existing ills within black communities. This, in turn, leads to the homogenizing of experiences that finds particular groups of people being marginalized at the expense of the corporate whole.

In short, whether working within a pragmatic or a principled framework, there can be no excuse for not seeking to develop specialist courses or programs in womanist theology. I want to eschew the potentially corrosive binaries of "being a part of black theology" and "being separate from black theology."

As I hopefully, demonstrate shortly, the strength of womanist theology in the United States has been its close but distinct relationship to the mainstream of black theology. It has been sufficiently close to be in solidarity with black theology and yet at a critical distance to critique and challenge it. As I have stated in a previous piece of work,[105] it is only the most marginalized who possess the power, accrued from the God who sides with "the least of these," to liberate themselves and those whose collusion with the oppressive structures oppress them. Black women and womanist theology have a unique prophetic role to call all others, including black male theologians and black theology to account.

Womanist Theology and Black Theology in the United States

Unlike her counterpart in Britain, womanist theology in the United States suffers neither from a lack of exponents in the field or in terms of specialized courses or programs. On the contrary, from my observations, womanist scholars seem to be aplenty across the range of disciplines, except perhaps biblical studies. African American women are making significant strides in developing the content, range, depth, and methods by which they undertake their work. In this section, I want to make a few tentative observations on the development of womanist theology in relationship to black theology in the United States.

In the previous section of this chapter, I remarked on the way in which many African American women within the theological academy seemed comfortable using the designation of womanist to describe themselves. This designation is one that is located around the experiences of black women as its initial point of departure, and as such, is not limited to any particular discipline, whether inside or outside the theological academy. Womanist scholarship can be found in systematic and constructive theology, ethics, sociology of religion, biblical studies, religious education, pastoral theology, homiletics, religion and society, and worship and liturgy.

This overarching designation is important as it provides a thematic and methodological framework in which African American women can locate their scholarly commitments and personal, subjective agency.

In an arena that is undoubtedly patriarchal and inherently conservative, Walker's multifaceted designation and descriptor provides an important framework around which African American women can coalesce. Whilst one should be rightly wary of the dangers of essentializing the experiences of all black women, as I have highlighted in a previous section in this chapter, this designation, nonetheless, provides ample room in which to manoeuvre for black women in their efforts to challenge the mountainous edifice of patriarchy.

African American ethicist Enoch Oglesby uses the metaphor of the mountain in his attempt to develop a model of Christian ethics that can surmount the seemingly invincible peaks of racism and white hegemony that have blighted the subjectivity and personhood of black people in the United States.[106]

I want to argue, like Oglesby, that black women have used the frameworks provided by womanism to create a means by which they can conceptualize the multidimensional systems and levers that dehumanize, repress, and constrict them. Using the old adage "you can't fight what you cannot see," womanist scholars have adopted a multidimensional form of analysis[107] in order to unmask the multifarious ills that plague them. When I was undertaking my doctoral studies back in the 1990s, I was inspired by the work of womanist religious educator Evelyn Parker, who uses personal experiences in the form of narratives drawn from archetypal black women as a means of engendering critical moral reasoning within African American adolescents.[108] This work provides black youths with a means of interrogating contemporary and historical experience as a means of ensuring that they are able to be critical, progressive agents in their ongoing lives. Parker's work assists these young people to name, unmask, and challenge the threats that confront them.

Womanist theological scholarship has also provided an important broader context in which individual black women can become empowered to undertake work that once upon a time would have been dismissed as anecdotal, "folksy," and lacking in intellectual rigor. In another piece of work, I have drawn upon the scholarship of womanist ethicist Emilie Townes[109] and womanist religious educator Lynne Westfield[110] in my quest to locate alternative methodologies for undertaking participative grassroots theological work with ordinary black people.[111] Townes's poems[112] and Westfield's "Kitchen Table Banter"[113] provide important insights into the ways in which black women have used womanist methodologies for constructing new and creative approaches to undertaking theological discourse.

Womanist Theology and Black Theology
in the United States—Supportive Siblings

Womanist theology in the United States has developed a distinct set of ethical, methodological, and substantive theological practices to render it a significant complimentary set of disciplines in its own right, alongside its older sibling black theology. In actual fact, the language of sibling is a helpful analogy on which to make the distinctions and commonalities between black and womanist theology in the United States. Womanist theology has now gained its individual identity as a "person" in its own right. She is playful, but can be stern, is earnest but also light hearted, is generous but can and will protect her space, she is loyal but not to the point of allowing herself to be exploited.

The rapidly maturing woman, that is, womanist theology has much in common with her older sibling black theology. People often remark on how similar they are in the way they speak and act. Yet, in the midst of their similarities, their parent, the divine self in whose image both siblings have been created can see the differences. Womanist theology is different from and yet intensely engaged with and committed to her older sibling black theology. Not to recognize the difference that exists within the younger sibling is to fail to take seriously the separate identity of black women and their experiences.

Womanist Theology and Black Theology
in the United States—A Diunital Relationship

Karen Baker-Fletcher asserts that Womanist theologians and ethicists have long argued for a form of discourse that eschews the binaries of either/or in favor of a dialectical both/and approach to theorizing.[114] A diunital form of analysis is one that can live with the inherent tensions and seemingly contradictory notions of things being similar and yet quite distinct and different at the same time. Such is the case with womanist and black theology. This difference should not be construed as being oppositional or as rivalry. Black theology needs the insights of the younger sibling in order to correct the presumed arrogance that can emerge when older male children are often indulged and privileged, in many cases, at the expense of their younger female siblings. As an eldest male child, I speak out of personal experience at this point! Black theology has needed the insights of womanist theology to remind it of its own blind spots and oversights. James Cone responded to the corrections offered him by the development of womanist theology:

> Contrary to what many black men say (especially preachers), sexism is not merely a problem for white women. Rather it is a problem of the human condition . . . If we black male theologians do not take seriously the need to incorporate into our theology a critique of sexist practices in the black community, then we have no right to complain when white theologians snub black theology.[115]

Womanist theology is a separate set of disciplines but remains committed to black theology for both siblings are concerned with essentially the same issues and struggles for self-determination, respect, and freedom in the widest possible sense of the term. Unlike particular articulations of feminism, womanism has never seen black men as being "the problem." Like a supportive but challenging sister, womanist theology remains committed to work alongside her older sibling in the supportive task of seeking to make a way out of no way. In this respect, the work of Karen and Garth Baker-Fletcher offers us a critical, important methodology for appreciating the similarities and differences between womanist theology and black theology.[116] Their methodology for collaborating on the joint project of bringing womanist and Xodus theologies together is one that is not antagonistic, jealous, grudging, or oppositional. Talking of their methodology, the authors write

> We take seriously the notion that theology is God-talk. God-talk is a dialogical encounter. Here, it is dialogical in a literal sense because we are two voices—one Womanist and one XODUS . . . . We are *only two voices*, bringing our distinctive perspectives as a womanist and a black male theologian. We hope that more Womanist and Black male theologians will engage in this kind of dialogue. Such dialogue is important because it values the ongoing process of theological reflection. It neither pits ideas against one another, nor gives token nods to each other. Genuine engagement is necessary in the academy, church and community. (Emphasis in the original)[117]

Womanist Theology and Black Theology in the United States—Offering New Ways of Being!

One of the important facets of womanist theology is the attention given to participation and interaction. In many respects, my own development as a theologian and educator, in more recent times, has been influenced most profoundly by womanist theology. These developments in my thinking and action have supplemented my previous adherence to the work of male scholars such as James Cone and Grant Shockley.

Womanist theology has challenged black male theologians to think about new ways of undertaking their work. In my work, I have been enabled to draw upon my formative skills as a dramatist in order to create an artistic and participative approach to the task of doing black theology.[118] It is interesting to note that the work of the early generation of academic male black theologians such as James Cone,[119] Major Jones,[120] Deotis Roberts,[121] and Preston Williams[122] is very traditional in terms of the methods they employ in undertaking their systematic theological discourse.

Amongst a newer generation of black theologians, I have noted a significant change, both in emphasis and in theological method. In this newer generation of male black theologians, there has been a movement away from doctrinal or systematic concerns into more interdisciplinary avenues. The works of Pinn,[123] Hopkins,[124] and Beckford,[125] for example, have alighted on the area of black popular culture as an arena for pursuing black theological discourse. I wonder whether these younger black male theologians could have undertaken this kind of work were it not for the pioneering work of the likes of Katie Cannon in her use of literature, particularly in her engagement with the poetic and prose output of Zora Neal Hurston,[126] and Emilie Townes and her use of poetry.[127] Both women, I would submit, have transformed the whole arena of theological ethics.

Womanist theology has been able to maintain its critical distance from black male theology whilst remaining committed to the cause of naming often unnamed forms of structural oppression that have dehumanized and trivialized black people for centuries.

Like a critical sibling, womanist theology has challenged her older counterpart to be more of what they should always have been had not the older child refused to acknowledge the wider needs of others. I am sure that there are many black male theologians who remain indignant at the challenge thrown out to them by their sisters. Demetrius Williams's observations at the binarism of some black pastors in challenging racism while defending sexism through an appeal to biblical texts[128] has been echoed in my work when having engaged with some black male ministers from both Pentecostal and Anglo-Catholic traditions. The Pentecostals, like the older men in Williams' encounter proof-text Pauline passages from Scripture, whilst the Anglo-Catholics point to church history and tradition.

Speaking on a personal note, as I draw this chapter to a close, I am reminded of my one and only attendance (at the time of writing) at a national grassroots caucus meeting for Black clergy in Britain, in the late 1990s. What was most instructive at this meeting of largely older African, Caribbean, and Asian men (I was one of the handful of nonordained people present) was that the necessity to fight racism in the structures of our respective churches went unchallenged; yet, when one black woman curate dared to mention sexism and patriarchy, she was sharply reminded that this was contrary to Scripture.

I reminded that speaker that nowhere in Scripture is slavery repudiated in explicit terms for non-Jews and yet black Christian experience, whether in its more passive folk-orientated guise,[129] or in the more polemical form of black liberation theology has created an ingenious means of "reading against the text."[130] Part of the creative genius of black people has been their ability to manoeuvre the text in order that it might serve the wider purpose of black liberation.[131] My presumptuous retort was met with a stony silence.

In answer to the question posed in the title of this chapter (*What Are the Sistas Saying?*), my response is "They are saying a great deal." They are reminding black theology of its prophetic calling to proclaim the Kingdom of God—a kingdom in which racism, sexism, and patriarchy are no more, a place where there is wholeness, peace and equity, a place where men and women will work together in partnership and mutuality, a place where every voice will be heard and no one will be silenced. The sistas are challenging the brothers, indeed challenging all of us to be more than we dared dream were possible and to believe that this vision begins now, in this very moment as we speak. Thank God for the sistas!

4

Education, Education, Education

Black Christian Education: The
Practical and Applied Arm of Black Theology

From our vantage of some 30 years on from its inception, one can be mistaken for assuming that the development of black theology has been not unlike those of other comparable disciplines within the theological academy. Namely, that the discipline of black theology is purely an intellectual exercise located solely within universities and seminaries, with little connection or relationship with the lives of ordinary people in the world outside the academy.

As one surveys the development of black theology in recent years, the range of methodological approaches and sophistry of argumentation is most impressive.[1] What remains at issue is the extent to which black theology has developed as a grassroots movement, in which the central ideas of the discipline have been rooted in and connected with the realities of ordinary black people in local churches and other communities of faith. This ongoing struggle has been the concern of a number of black theologians.[2]

In many respects, black theology has been aided in her efforts to connect with ordinary black Christians in local churches, and so become a grassroots movement of conscientization through black Christian education. Black Christian education is the practical, educational outworking of black liberation theology, and seeks to distil the central ideas of this liberative movement into teaching and learning strategies for the emancipation of all black people.

Black Christian education arises from the development of black theology. The rise, development, and growth of black theology have offered a significant challenge to the mainstream hinterland of the academy. Black men and women have increasingly populated what was once perceived as the sole domain of white, middle-class men. These are more than capable scholars who are not content with simply being grateful to be at the academic party but have begun to reconceptualize the very task of doing theology itself. Taking their cue from the great James Cone,[3] two generations of black scholars have begun to develop their own approaches to the task of doing black theology.

The prophetic nature of James Cone's work has not only given rise to newer generations of black theologians but also inspired a wholesale reappraisal of the task of Christian education. James Cone's landmark *Black Theology and Black Power* offered a new impetus and an ideological charge to a generation of black religious educators.

Black Theology and Christian Education—A New Relationship

In the development of Christian education by and for black people, many scholars have used the seemingly more acceptable term of Christian Education and/of/for the Black/African American Church.[4] I have rejected this term (the black church) in my work for I feel it fails to make explicit the black hermeneutical dimensions of liberative change that is the central theological motif of black theology. Whilst the black church remains the single most important social institution within African American life,[5] the ambiguous, almost schizophrenic nature of this body in the United States (dangerously conservative and wonderfully prophetic, often in the same breath)[6] means that Christian education for black people cannot be left solely in the custodianship of the church. Also, I find this particular designation much too ecclesial for my liking. The liberative dimensions of black theology are for all people and extend way beyond the sometimes limited praxis of the black church even if the church has been the most important repository in which this liberative movement has been incubated.[7] I have chosen to use the term Black Christian Education (often adding the words "of liberation" at the end to emphasize the point) in order to assert the clear, unambiguous relationship between black theology and black Christian education. Both disciplines are linked in their desire to take the black experience seriously and to use that as their initial points of departure. Both are unashamedly proud and unapologetic about their use of the term black,[8] prefixing it before the other terms, in any form of designation.

Asserting that Christian education is related solely to or with the black church is to circumscribe the nature of the discipline in ways that are highly suggestive but not always attested by experience. That the black church should be a liberative and prophetic institution in the life of black people on both sides of the Atlantic is beyond argument, in theory, but to assume that this is the case is not always borne out by practice. Although black Christian education is a form of Christian ministry that one would expect to find within the church, its agency for transformation extends way beyond ecclesial bodies.

By linking Christian education almost axiomatically to the black church, one fails to recognize that in the multiplicity of black ecclesial bodies on both sides of the Atlantic, there is much that is termed the Black Church that is now light years removed from the historic legacy of black Christianity. One only has to observe the rise of the Prosperity Gospel[9] movement to see the sad truth of this contention. I believe that the best nomenclature for the teaching and learning of the liberative truths of the Gospel, which arise from the realities of the black experience, is that of black Christian education.

The development of appropriate Christian education curriculum materials for black people owes much to the pioneering work of Olivia Pearl Stokes. In the late 1960s and early 1970s, Stokes argued for the need for Christian education within the black church in the United States of America to be informed by the discipline of black theology.[10]

To argue the apologetic for a liberative, black Christian education theory and practice, one first needs to understand the nature and discipline of black theology.

As we have seen in previous chapters of this book, black theology as a discipline owes a good deal of its existence to the seminal work of James Cone. Cone used the contemporary struggle of the civil rights movement of the 1960s and the burgeoning growth of the notion of black power in the latter half of that decade as resources for undertaking theological discourse.

These two contrasting poles in the black American experience, argued Cone, were the twin foci that stimulated his consciousness toward the creation of a black theology of liberation. The combination of the ideological tenets of black power and Christian theology enabled Cone to construct a theology that attempted to reconcile two differing but united goals: the desire for black self-determination, juxtaposed with the notion of black existential self-affirmation and validation, in relation to the ultimate reality of God.[11]

Arising out of Cone's intellectual struggle to understand the contextual experiences of African Americans within that civil rights era and the ferment of the black power movement was the emergence of black theology. James Cone describes the exercise of black theology thus:

> Black theology is a theology of and for Black people, an examination of their stories, tales, and sayings. It is an investigation of the mind into the raw materials of our pilgrimage, telling the story of "how we got over."[12]

Cone in an earlier book contends that the central force of black theology is its concern with the essential striving of black people to understand their existential experiences in a hostile, racist world.[13] James Cone argues that black theology is a theology of liberation. It is a mechanism by which black people can explore their individual existence in light of their experience and their historical relationship with the God who would desire them to be free. Cone writes

> The task of Black theology, then, is to analyze the nature of the gospel of Jesus Christ in the light of oppressed Blacks so they will see the gospel as inseparable from humiliated condition, and as bestowing on them the necessary power to break the chains of oppression.[14]

When Olivia Pearl Stokes argued for the necessity of black theology to be the first point of departure for black Christian education, she was making recourse to a basic conviction of black existential experience. Namely, that central to the development of a Christian religious experience is the ontological reality of blackness.

The Necessity for Black Christian Education

The rationale and import for black Christian education has arisen, in part, due to the encounter between white Europeans and black Africans some five centuries ago. The emergence and development of the Atlantic slave trade unleashed a terrible legacy of oppression and exploitation upon the African self. Some ten million Africans were transported from continental Africa to the "New World" for profit. The major historic denominations of the West were involved directly and indirectly in this pernicious and violent assault upon African people.[15] Prior to the development of this movement in capitalistic greed and economic expediency,[16] there had been in existence a philosophical belief in the inherent superiority of European peoples over and against those of African descent.[17]

Dubois as early as 1915 argued against the falsification of African history and the attempts by European historians to distort and discredit Africa.[18] Similarly, Rodney makes it clear that efforts to discredit Africa have their roots in the fifteenth century when Europeans made the concerted attempt to construct images of Africa as "other."[19]

One of the chief pernicious legacies of the epoch of slavery was the rationalization of the economic machinery of captivity. This was achieved through a rigid ideology that asserted the inferior status and subhuman nature of the African slave.[20] This form of insidious indoctrination was so pernicious that to quote the notable reggae singer Bob Marley, it was a form of "mental slavery."[21]

The remedy of societal and global ills such as racism, exclusivism, sexism, classism, world poverty, and economic exploitation are tasks that a liberative approach to education can attempt to counter and challenge. This approach to education is one that is not born out of economic advantage, material gain, vested interests, or political and economic power.

Rather, it is an approach that in its very weakness, the weakness of marginalization and denigration, has drawn directly upon the life and teachings of Jesus and the liberative, transformative power of the Gospel, in order to grant freedom to both the oppressed and the oppressor. When Jesus reverses the social norms in the Sermon on the Mount,[22] the new principles he advocates are ones that cannot be obtained by the powerful. It is the poor, the marginalized, and the oppressed who, in the process of their transformation and liberation, possess the power to gain the insights and the vision to look beyond the immediate and the temporal, to transform the existing norms and challenge the status quo.

Black Christian education harnesses the power of God's spirit to transform the lives, experiences, thinking and action of people of African descent. It can assist them to discover their authentic selfhood.

Contemporary Approaches to Christian Education in the African American Experience

In my work as an educator and theologian, I have attempted to work at the nexus between black theology and Christian education.[23] This has often led to intense feelings of scholarly schizophrenia, as one is perceived as not belonging to any particular camp or movement. Often, I am perceived as being *too* practical for the theologians and *too* theological for the educators. These feelings are always exacerbated when I am in the company of African Americans, for whom the specialization around distinct disciplines, as I have outlined in the first chapter, makes the policing of such parameters much more commonplace than in Britain. Yet, despite the sense of being a confusing conundrum, I remain indebted to African religious educational thought for providing the substantive backdrop by which I have been enabled to undertake my doctoral and postdoctoral studies in Britain.

In short, were it not for the progressive and pronounced developments amongst African American Christian educators, I would have been singularly unable to construct an interdisciplinary pathways between black theology and Christian education for the British context.

In order to assess the significant developments of black Christian education in the United States, I want to highlight three approaches, as case studies. I am not suggesting that these texts are in any way exemplary of the totality of African American religious educational thought. Rather, I have chosen them because of the influence they have exerted on me and the extent to which I have been able to draw on their ideas in order to create a link between pedagogy and black theology.

I have also chosen these texts because of their attempts to engage with black theological themes as the substantive content of their pedagogical approaches to black conscientization. For, whilst there has been a long, honorable tradition in black Christian education in the United States in its engagement with explicit, deconstructionist liberative themes, not all of it has been prepared to engage explicitly with the central tenets of black theology. For, the works of scholars such as Joseph Crockett,[24] Anne Wimberly,[25] and Jonathan Jackson,[26] though exemplary, have not made explicit the radical reinterpretation of Christianity by black people in order that the Gospel of Christ might speak to their ongoing experiences of humiliation and suffering. In highlighting the following texts, I want to suggest that they offer helpful insights into the dynamic relationship between black theology and Christian education.

Yolanda Smith's Reclaiming the Spirits

Yolanda Smith's *Reclaiming the Spirits*[27] is an important contribution to the burgeoning literature emerging from a new generation of

African American religious educators. Smith's approach to Christian education, like that of her predecessors such as Grant Shockley, Olivia Pearl Stokes, James Tyms, and Anne Wimberly, operates within the normative frameworks of faith provided by the black church traditions in the United States. Her approach to black Christian education is by means of an investigation into the ongoing legacy of the spirituals in black religiocultural contexts. Smith writes,

> The African American experience of slavery gave birth to the spirituals through the secret religious meetings, the work environment, and the harsh realities of bondage.[28]

The author asserts that the spirituals are an important hermeneutical device for Americans of African descent as they signify a "triple heritage" for black people in the United States. The author states,

> by exploring the spirituals, then, African Americans can gain insights into their African roots, their African American history, and their Christian faith.[29]

Using the spirituals as a central theological motif, Smith explores the various dimensions of this religiocultural musical tradition through a variety of categories and approaches. In chapters 1 and 2 of the book,[30] the spirituals are analyzed through the lens of historical analysis. The spirituals are shown to be an important conduit for analyzing the three components of the "triple heritage." The African, African American, and Christian dimensions of the black identity in the United States can be discerned by reflecting on both the content and the developmental process by which the spirituals came into existence. Smith argues that each element of the "triple heritage" must be explored throughout the educational process.

Later chapters deal with textual and thematic analysis,[31] black and womanist theologies in dialogue with Christian education,[32] and systematic theology.[33] The section on black and womanist theologies is of particular interest to me, given my attempts to use these forms of liberative praxis as the basis of my approach to Christian education. Smith provides a helpful summary of the central tenets of both disciplines, and outlines some helpful, if rudimentary, in which they can serve the educational ministries of the church.

The chapter that encompasses what might be termed a systematic theological examination of the spirituals is helpful as it locates this phenomenon within a broader theological and confessional context. This is one in which themes or categories such as "God," "Jesus," "The Church," "Sin," and "Eschatology" are addressed from the perspective of historical and contemporary expressions of faith of ordinary African Americans.[34]

By reflecting upon the deep resonance of the spirituals in African American religiocultural life, Smith is able to offer a rich constructive pedagogical tapestry for utilizing this phenomenon in affirming the contemporary religious nurture and socialization of black people in the United States.

The weaknesses of the book are of a broader nature and concern the more generic enterprise of African American theological and religious discourse than simply a reflection of this text in and of itself. Given the brutalities of and the implications and effects of the epoch of slavery on the psyche of all Americans (black and white), it is not surprising that so much of the African American religious discourse that emerges from the academy uses slavery as its initial point of departure. Indeed, as an outsider (an advantage and a weakness in terms of making any analysis of this kind), I have often thought that the slave epoch represents a kind of emotional touchstone for an authentic rendering of blackness as relates to issues of identity and belonging for many African Americans.

In short, slavery represents the absurdities of one's existence in the United States and that supreme sense of satisfaction at what one has achieved.[35] I think this legacy provides a powerful mythic sensibility around which one can mobilize, and an overarching sense of romanticism of the relevance of the past to the realities of one's present situation. Neither of these facets is in existence in Britain where the black presence lacks the sheer emotional and visceral sweep of the African American experience.

I make these comments in humility for I sense that this book represents so much of what is vitally relevant and perhaps vacuously rhetorical about African American religious discourse. As one reads this text, one is forced to ask: to what extent can the spirituals really function in an operative way in Christian education and in the ongoing life of the black church in the twenty-first century? Is this not simply a mass exercise in educational and theological romanticism? It is interesting to note that the part of the book I have found the least satisfying is the last one, and the attempts by the author to put this educational methodology into a practical framework and context within the black church in the United States.

I am at pains to add, however, that these comments should in no way detract from what is a very important piece of work that contributes to the ongoing development of African American Christian Education—or as I would say, black Christian education.

Reassessing the Legacy of Grant S. Shockley

My introduction to the work of Grant S. Shockley came whilst undertaking my doctoral studies at the University of Birmingham. Through the usual process of following the trail of citations in the published work of one's scholarly forebears, I came across a book coedited by Shockley, in the late 1980s.[36] *Working With Black Youth* that Shockley coedited with Charles R. Foster enabled me to make a significant philosophical breakthrough in my doctoral work, as Shockley provided me with a wonderful historical analysis of the development of black Christian approaches to affirming and empowering black young people in the United States.[37]

These reflections offered me a substantive paradigm by which I might conceive my own scholarly work in the British context. Detailing the growth of black Christian education in the United States, Shockley charts the significant development in the ideological underpinning of the practice as evidenced in black churches, as they occurred in the 1960s.[38] Commenting on the developments in Christian education prior to the 1960s and the civil rights movement, Shockley writes,

> Those programs that did exist were conventional, imitative of white models, poorly attended, and were, for the most part, socially marginal. Historically, black and white youth programs had developed separately, but most black youth programs were indistinguishable from their white counterparts in educational philosophy, goals, strategy, program, and leadership style.[39]

Whilst Shockley's words were directed at the specific enterprise of Christian education, his comments remain apposite in the present era, as they speak to much of the contemporary development of black churches on either of the Atlantic, particularly, in Britain. For many black churches, despite their development from white churches, their present structure and modus operandi are often distinguishable from their white counterparts. Grant Shockley has been, alongside James Cone, perhaps the most important influence on my scholarly pilgrimage to date.

In an attempt to place the legacy of Grant Shockley into a broader sociopolitical and theological context, Charles R. Foster and Fred Smith have edited a collection of his work, in a more recent publication.[40] *Black Religious Experience* by Charles R. Foster and Fred Smith is an important text for the twenty-first century for it uncovers a hidden, forgotten legacy, and rediscovers a salient voice that created a corpus of work and scholarship that continues to inspire and challenge. In *Black Religious Experience*, Foster and Smith provide a telling overview and a critical assessment of the work and legacy of Shockley, tracing the development of his scholarly output over a long and impressive career.

This is a timely volume because it brings to our attention a much neglected voice in the theological academy. Grant Shockley was a pioneering African American religious educator and an ordained United Methodist Church minister. I have juxtaposed these two descriptors of Shockley, not as binary opposites, but in order to hold together the scholarly, pastoral, and ecclesial underpinnings of his work. As a black minister within a white majority church, Shockley sat outside of the seemingly essentialized identity of black religious expression that is often identified with the historic black church denominations in the United States.

The tension of holding together a sense of his black identity within a white dominated context was a mission (if not a crusade) he was to pursue for the whole of his life. The subtitle of this book, *Conversations on Double Consciousness*, reflects on the central concerns of Shockley's scholarly work within the field of Christian religious education.

In this respect, as a black theologian and educator working within the context of the British Methodist Church (the British equivalent of the United Methodist Church), I share with Shockley, this dichotomous existence: how to be black in white majority settings? How do we effect dialogue and mutuality within ourselves (with the different aspects of ourselves), and with others?[41]

The two authors, both of whom were personal friends and colleagues of Shockley, return to the published work (Shockley, sadly, never wrote a major book that encapsulated his ideas), and in a conversational format, begin to reassess the major emphases and themes in the work. This reassessment covers areas such as the Black religious education experience,[42] sources for a liberative religious education,[43] and the process toward Martin Luther King's notion of the beloved community.[44] This process of analyzing and reflecting on the major concerns of Shockley's work bring to our attention a number of fascinating insights. I am reminded, for example, that Shockley, although preceding James Cone by a generation, was, nonetheless, one of the first African American religious educators to engage with and indeed embrace black theology.[45] The authors citing Shockley's interest in black theology devote several sections of the book to his ongoing dialogue with the challenging ideas and rationale for this burgeoning practice and academic discipline. Shockley writes

> Black theology has caused the black church to see religious education from an entirely new perspective. Black theology suggests that there is now "a felt need to reconstruct a worldview as it concerns an entire people."[46]

Charting the development of Shockley's work through the book has given rise to a number of fascinating questions, such as to what extent did Grant Shockley's engagement with the ideas of black theology lead him to a complete reconceptualization of the nature and the intent of Christianity? Did black theology become the normative content for his approach to religious education?

As I pondered these questions, a number of potential fault lines have emerged in this text. Clearly, any book that is based on the thinking and output of an individual, and which uses fragments of his work in order to elucidate the development of his ideas, will always be deficient to some degree or the other. Extracts are helpful in giving us insights and snapshots of the scholar, but the danger remains that without any extensive narrative underpinning, we may be seeing pieces of work out of context or without the sufficiently nuance familial and societal backdrop that a conventional theological biography might have provided.

In this respect, the alternating conversational model of the book is both a strength and a weakness. Its strength lies in the sheer compassion, warmth, and love the authors bring to this project. Clearly, the authors knew Shockley and had a profound respect and love for the man. Shockley's scholarly contributions to the field of religious education are placed within the wider context of his own personal credo and his commitment to the church. This is not a dry academic tome.

Yet, the very conversational style tells us much about the authors' perspectives on Shockley, but not enough about Shockley the man. In this respect, a theological biography might have been more illuminating in displaying the personal and subjective vistas that informed his work (a la James Cone's For My People[47]).

After James Cone, Grant Shockley was my scholarly hero. Sadly, Shockley who had greatly inspired my own doctoral studies died a few years before I could make it to Atlanta, where he was living in retirement. At a time when I was told that it was neither legitimate nor desirable to combine the substantive content of black theology with pedagogical concerns of Christian religious education, Shockley demonstrated a commitment and desire to undertake such a cause. Whilst Cone gave me the substantive content for a form of Christianity that is empowering and transformative for black people, Shockley provided me with the educational philosophy by which this radical version of the Gospel could be brought to life in order to empower, predominantly, black youth in the British context.

Nancy Lynne Westfield and Dear Sisters

Nancy Lynne Westfield is a religious educator at the theological and the graduate school of Drew University in Madison, New Jersey. Westfield has become, in recent times, one of the most creative and eclectic of African American religious educators and womanist scholars. Westfield's most significant work to date is entitled *Dear Sisters: A Womanist Practice of Hospitality*.[48] Since discovering Westfield's work,[49] particularly, her creative and eclectic methodologies for undertaking practical/pastoral scholarship with African American women, I have been emboldened to develop my own creative work as a dramatist in order to undertake black theological work.*

Westfield's commitment to undertaking womanist theology by means of a reflexive, participative, eclectic, and creative methodology can be seen in the following extract where she writes,

> My mode of writing and reasoning is a reflective narrative with other voices interwoven. . . . As a womanist, I lean heavily upon personal narrative in order to relate black women's history and religious experience . . . My style is narrative in a poetic genre which emerges from a community deeply rooted in the language, imagery, rhythms of the King James version of the Bible.[50]

Westfield utilizes poetry and creative literary writing as a primary means of undertaking black theological work with African American women. In 1995, she formed the Dear Sisters' Literary Group.[51] This group

---

* The influence of Lynne Westfield's work on my own scholarship can be found in my previous book, in which, inspired by Westfield's use of poetry as a means of undertaking black theological discourse, I revived my long interest in drama. See Anthony G. Reddie *Dramatizing Theologies* (London: Equinox, 2006), pp. 150–153.

consisted of a number of African American women meeting together in each other's homes, on a Friday night in order to do womanist theology.[52]

Her Dear Sisters group is an attempt to create a means of engaging in the teaching and learning process so that

> Christian education must move towards practices that bring the sharing of story and the breaking of bread into the classroom if we are to invoke sacramental encounters for and with our learners.

Westfield's approach to Christian education, informed by womanist reflections, is an attempt to move the discipline from beyond the often arid teaching of abstract doctrine and creedal assertions toward a more holistic envisioning of nurture, in which hospitality and relationships are of primary importance.[53]

In order to effect this form of transformative knowledge, advocated by scholars such as bell hooks,[54] Westfield uses poetry as a methodological tool for the doing of womanist theology.[55] Westfield's utilization of poetry in order to undertake theological reflection has been influenced by womanist ethicist Emilie Townes, whose writings is replete with poetic verse, written as a means of exploring black theological concerns in an alternative construct.[56] Westfield's work is rooted within a womanist theological paradigm and uses personal experience as the initial point of departure in the collaborative process of doing theology. Westfield has spoken of her own positionality as the underscoring of her scholarly work as an educator and theologian.[57]

Unlike her older compatriots, such as Anne Wimberly,[58] Westfield identifies herself in unambiguous terms as a womanist and is comfortable using womanist themes and concepts to inform her work.

I have highlighted Westfield's work for I feel it is one of the best attempts to construct an approach to the teaching and learning of the Christian faith from within a womanist paradigm. At the time of writing, British womanist scholar Maxine Howell is attempting to use womanist concepts in her approach to juxtaposing pedagogical concerns with black liberative theological themes and norms.[59]

Reflecting on My Own Practice in Britain

In order to bring a more contextual British perspective to much of what I have written hitherto, I would like to outline a practical, black

British theological approach to undertaking Christian education with black people, particularly, black youth. This work utilizes the central tenets of black theology, in order to bring the innate radicalism of black theological thought into conversation with the realities of the black experience of youth. I have chosen to reflect upon Pentecost as the basis for this practical, educational exercise in black theological exploration, as the pneumotological insights of the Holy Spirit are crucial to diasporan African peoples, in both the United States and Britain—many Pentecostals often invoke the Holy Spirit as a means of asserting an abstract, "color-blind," spiritualized and apolitical theology that is inimical to black theology. A Christian educational hermeneutic of this event offers a radical rereading of Pentecost for black people.

Black Christian Education in the Service of Black Youth—An Example from the British Context: A Case Study

In this section, I want to outline an approach to undertaking youth ministry, using the insights of black theology, in order to empower black young people in Britain (and to a lesser extent, in the North America). This case study builds on some previous work that was undertaken a number of years ago, which is detailed in a previous publication.[60]

In order to show the experiential dimensions of this work, I have included the script of a short drama that was written as part of the research, which gave rise to this approach to a black theologically driven version of youth ministry. At the center of this piece of work is a script entitled "Survivors." I would invite you to read the script first, and then consider the black theological reflections that follow.

The "Survivors" was written a number of years ago for a Christian youth group with whom I was working. This piece was inspired by my engagement with a group of young black people in the north Birmingham[61] area of Handsworth. Handsworth is one of the most deprived areas of the city, and it was the scene of two large-scale urban riots (or "rebellions" as some activist prefer to call them) in the early 1980s. In my interactions with these young people, I witnessed at first hand their struggles to become part of the wider mainstream society of modern, late twentieth-century Britain.

These young people were constantly under pressure from a British state that policed and pathologized them in a fashion that would have garnered the sobriquet of human rights abuses had the context been a so-called Third World country, and not Britain.

I was recently looking over this sketch again, as I was preparing to write this section of the book. The title "Survivors" refers to a brilliant song written and performed by Bob Marley.[62] "Survivors" speaks to the ongoing struggle of black people, particularly young people, to find their redemption in a seemingly all-pervasive sea of racialized oppression. But, before I begin to wax too lyrical, I shall leave you to read "Survivors." Perhaps, with a group of young people, you might want to perform this piece yourselves? Drama always comes alive when it is performed.

Survivors

By Anthony Reddie

We see a circle of chairs five in all. They are all empty. After a few seconds, enter two people. The setting is a restaurant. Bob Marley's track, "survivors" is playing in the background. After a few seconds it subsides.

WAITER: (*Showing other person to one of the seats*) Please take a seat Madam. I trust the rest of your party will follow shortly.

Waiter walks away. Woman 1 takes a seat. She takes out a mirror and begins to adjust her hair and appearance.

CAROL: (*Looking around*) They never can tell the time. There's nothing like B.M.T. . . . Black Man's Time. If a black man says he's going to arrive at such and such a time, you can always guarantee he'll arrive half an hour late. Funny how black man never seem to own watches.

Reenter the waiter, this time with a man.

WAITER: (*Showing Man 1 to a seat*) Would Sir care to take a seat next to the Lady?
BRIAN: Sure ting . . . (*Taking a seat*) . . . So wha'appen sister?

CAROL: You're late, that's what's happened. You don't own a watch? You got lost on the way here? Don't tell me, you went to wrong restaurant?

BRIAN: (*Beginning to laugh*) So wah wrong wi yu?

CAROL: You haven't got time enough to hear it . . . How are things?

BRIAN: Sweet and nice. I've just released my firs album. Mostly self-written, but there are a few cover versions. You remember that time back in Sunday school?

CAROL: What time?

BRIAN: The time you said I would never be a musician.

CAROL: When did I say that?

BRIAN: That time the minister had us out at the front, talking to us about our future hopes. You laughed. So did everyone else. But here I am. One fully fledged musician.

CAROL: Modest as well I see.

BRIAN: And what about you sister?

CAROL: I still do a bit of singing. A little session work, but I'm into psychology these days. I went for training and graduated with honors. I've been practicing for ten years now.

BRIAN: (*Laughing*) My, we really is in the high life these days. The sister's done good.

Reenter waiter with another woman

WAITER: Would Madam care to sit here?

SUSAN: (*Sitting down*) Hi ya guys. I haven't seen you lot for years.

BRIAN: Long time no see sister! You still a nurse?

SUSAN: If not, then the guy I was tending to half an hour ago is in serious trouble.

BRIAN: Still a fiesti gal hi?

SUSAN: Don't you forget it. How are you Carol?

CAROL: Can't complain. Well I could, but it wouldn't change anything, so I won't bother.

SUSAN: Still the same old cheerful Carol I remember from Sunday school? You're not still a miserable wretch, are you?

CAROL: Are you still loud and noisy?

BRIAN: (*Trying to break it up*) Sisters, let's not start bad mouthing each other. This is meant to be a reunion dinner. A chance to see how the sisters and brothers are making out after all years.

Reenter waiter again with two more guests, a man and woman

WAITER: (*Showing them to their seats*) If sir and madam would kindly take a seat.

MARY: (*Sitting down*) Look who I dragged along with me?

ANTHONY: (Also sitting down) Cars! I hate them. A work of the Devil. Well my car is anyway. I don't know why I bother with that old scrap heap. I'd junk it at a scrap yard, only they'd probably charge me to take it away. I think God punished me with this car. The Egyptians were sent frogs, Jonah was thrown inside a whale, God sent me this car. Thanks a lot God. (Looking to Mary). No disrespect intended Mary. You being a Vicar and all that.

CAROL: (To Anthony) You never did have any respect. I can remember your Mother wetting your behind with her leather belt when you wouldn't behave in church.

ANTHONY: Somethings don't change. Still the same old Carol. Or should I say caustic Carol?

MARY: I don't mind Anthony.

WAITER: Are we ready to order?

MARY: Give us a few minutes.

WAITER: That will be fine Madam.

Exit waiter.

MARY: (*Standing up*) Let me have a look at you all. Brian! I read about you in the newspaper the other day. How many copies has your album sold?

BRIAN: Only half a million. Not bad if I say so myself.

CAROL: And if you didn't say it, nobody else would. Modest huh?

MARY: And what about you Carol? Still looking into people's minds and thoughts?

CAROL: Yep, that's me. Dirty business looking into people's brains. You never know what you'll find in there when you look. I usually wear gloves myself.

MARY: Still the same old Carol. Caustic Carol. (To Susan) Matron Hall I believe.

ANTHONY: Forced any bed pans under sick patients lately?

SUSAN: You've been watching too many carry-on films.

MARY: And Anthony. The lippy boy with the fast tongue and sharp pen.

BRIAN: Not to mention the bal' head.

ANTHONY: Women find balding men attractive.

CAROL: Women with dark glasses and Guide Dogs.

MARY: And so here we are. The five of us together again. After all these years. Grown up and respectable.

ANTHONY: You speak for yourself. Once upon a time, I was young and foolish. Now I'm older, but I'm still foolish. Only, now I'm a bal' head. And to think, I use to have an afro when I was a yout'.

MARY: Who would have thought? All five of us would grow up and do things with our lives?

BRIAN: You hear the preacher? (*To Mary*) Getting in some practice for tomorrow?

MARY: No. I'm strictly off duty tonight.

ANTHONY: Well that's a relief. So I can cuss and talk raw tonight, can I?

SUSAN: I'll tell your Mum if you do. She'll wet your behind like in the old days. Remember those licks?

ANTHONY: Remember them? I can still feel them. My behind is still giving me pain even now.

CAROL: I guess they meant well. Spare the rod and spoil the child as Mum used to always say.

BRIAN: Well, my Dad never spared it on me. Thanks a lot Pops.

SUSAN: (Standing up) Let's drink a toast. To the five of us.

MARY: What are we toasting?

SUSAN: Survival. We're the survivors, aren't we? Our parents came to this country to give us chance. They wanted us to be successful and make them proud. And here we are. Successful! We've done it.

MARY: If a Black person manages to stay out of prison, out of a mental institution and out of the grave, then they have survived. And there are plenty of us who haven't made it.

ANTHONY: Well, I'll drink to that. In fact, I'll drink to anything.

CAROL: So I've heard. They don't call you Alcoholic Anthony for nothing.

ANTHONY: Bwoy, she is a hard woman.

MARY: But we are the survivors. Our parents raised us well and here we are, a living testimony to that. Let's drink.

All five raise their glasses and drink. Brian begins to choke. Susan runs across and begins to slap him across the back very roughly.

SUSAN: Don't worry, I'm just clearing your wind pipe. You'll be alright in a minute.

MARY: Is Brian alright?

CAROL: That's Brian. His eyes were always bigger than his mouth.

BRIAN: (*Coughing*) I think I'm OK.

SUSAN: (*Still slapping Brian*) You'll be alright in a minute.

BRIAN: You don't have to handle me so rough you know. Do you rough up all your patients like this?

SUSAN: Yu ungrateful wretch. Mi should ah let yu choke.

MARY: Come on now, let's not fall out. We're all family.

ANTHONY: As the Lord says. Where two or three Black people are gathered in my name, an argument will always break out.

CAROL: Have you ever seen that waiter anywhere? Taking his time.

BRIAN: (*Snapping fingers*) Garcon. Garcon. Boy (*Looking around*) Whey 'im dey?

ANTHONY: (*Also looking around*) Nope, I don't see him anywhere. Could be one long hungry evening. Pass me some more of that wine. I feel another toast coming on.

MARY: Spoken like a good Methodist.

CAROL: Less of the good.

Brian gets to his feet and walks to the front. He looks around.

BRIAN: We made it guys. Our forebears started the journey back in the days of slavery. Others followed. Then our parents continued with the journey. And now they've passed the baton onto us. Just like the preacher in Sunday school said, "We're the ones who will continue on with journey to the end, wherever that is going to be." Before you know it, we'll be passing it on to our children and the next generation.

ANTHONY: Heaven forbid. I'm too young and handsome for children.

CAROL: Too bald more like.

MARY: The same caustic Carol, right to the end.

SUSAN: (*Looking at Congregation*) We made it. We've all made it. We are all the survivors, all of us. The family will survive.

MARY: The family always will. We are blessed by the Lord. God loves all of us. Tonight we are all here as testament to that. Testament to God's love.

CAROL: That was a very nice preacher, but here comes the waiter.

Reenter the waiter.

WAITER: Sorry for the delay, ladies and gentlemen. Would you care to order now?

SUSAN: (*Looking at the Waiter closely*) Wait a minute, I've seen you before. Aren't you? You're the fiesti teacher who once said I would never amount to anything. (*Looking at the waiter closely*) Not so big now are we? Not so big at all.

WAITER: (*Embarrassed*) Hmmmm . . . I think I should be going.

EVERYONE: Go!

SUSAN: After all, this is a family affair.

MARY: And only survivors are allowed to sit at this table.

EVERYONE: The survivors.

A Black Rereading of Pentecost—A Paradigm for Black Transformation in the Twenty-First Century

Rereading Texts

I am sure that this passage is hugely familiar to many, if not all of us. Once upon a time, in a now seemingly dim and distant past, I was once able to read this passage in an allegedly neutral way. I say "allegedly neutral" because such a way of reading and interpreting any text is impossible. We all, as readers, bring our subjective bias and personal, ethnic, class-based, or societal concerns to the text with which we are engaging.[63] I suppose I have always engaged in such a reading.

In more recent times, as a black theologian, I am more honest with how I read and engage with biblical texts. I am no longer pretending to be neutral. I am a black male in his early forties. My parents are from the Caribbean. My ancestors were brought in chains to that part of the world by rapacious Europeans from the continent of Africa. As I began to reflect upon this script, written at the dawn of my burgeoning consciousness, as a black theologian and Christian educator, it occurred to me that I must reassess this passage. These formative influences inform the hermeneutical process in my engagement with Scripture and Christian tradition.

In the course of my previous research with black children and young people in Britain, I have seen at first hand the way in which an overarching Eurocentric mindset has captured the Gospel of Christ and held it hostage. The mercantilist and capitalistic exploits of the West and the racist ideology of superiority, all propagated from within a Christian subculture, were used to subjugate and enslave black people and people of color across the four corners of the world.[64]

The tendentious teaching of Christianity to people of African descent has been an important facet in the historical development of the Christian faith in Africa, the Americas, and the Caribbean. Grant Shockley believes that the historic agents of the Christian missionary enterprises in the Americas and the Caribbean had specific intentions for the propagation of the Christian faith. The Christian faith was intended to legitimate white hegemony and reinforce black inferiority.[65]

The Pentecost Narrative from a
Black Theological Perspective

Reflecting upon "Survivors" and the experiences of black young people, incorporating their struggles and triumphs made me reread this text in another light. The people being transformed in the text are black people. The characters at that first Pentecost event were black! Now, I know there will be many who will want to challenge the historical basis of such a contention. Black people? In this story? Surely that is wishful thinking on my part? As dubious an enterprise as the historically inaccurate Anglo-Saxon Arianization of Jesus in more recent times?[66]

In answer to this question, I would point to the work of Cain Hope Felder. In his commentary on the Pentecost narrative, he identifies the references to Mesopotamia, Pamphylia, Egypt, and parts of Libya near Crete[67] as being places connected with Africa. Felder states thus:

> Indeed, the physiognomy of the Elamites of Mesopotamian archaeological reliefs shows them to have been a dark-skinned people with hair of tight curls. The modern academy has unfortunately zealously sought to "whitewash" all inhabitants of the ancient "Near East" in the vicinity of the Tigris and the Euphrates rivers.[68]

So far from reinventing a spurious form of counterhegemony, Felder and others.[69] are asserting both a black presence in, and a black, African-centered form of hermeneutics for reading the Bible. Recourse to these resources has informed my reading of this passage and the resultant reflections.

My assertion that the people at the center of this narrative are black is not made solely on anthropological or archeological grounds, but is referenced to a number of wider concerns. "Black," in the modern lexicon of Euro-American ethnocentric epistemologies, denotes "oppression," "marginalization," and "demonization." As black has become virtually synonymous with evil (the only positive term with which I am familiar is "being in the Black" in Britain means that you have money in the bank), many black theologians have sought to invert the term, in order to invest it with positive connotations.[70]

If being black is to be poor, oppressed, ill-educated, downtrodden, and marginalized, then being identified as black locates such individuals within the very heart of God's purposes for human kind. In Luke 4:18,

Jesus' words state thus:

> The Spirit of the Lord is upon me, because he has anointed me to preach good news to the poor. He has sent me to proclaim the captives and recovery of sight to the blind, to set at liberty those who are oppressed, to proclaim the acceptable year of the Lord.

Our attempts to spiritualize these words of Jesus have had the effect of muting the radicalism of such pronouncements. The poor are not simply those who are poor in spirit but those who are literally poor— those who have been the traditional losers of the worst excesses of global capitalism and free market exploitation.[71] Similarly, recovery of sight to the blind should not lead us into the erroneous belief that Jesus is directing his concerns solely at those who are spiritually blind. In the continent of Africa, for the want of the most rudimentary of sanitation systems and fresh water supplies (that would cost a minuscule of monies spent on consumer luxuries in the West), the high incidence of cataracts and blindness could be dramatically reduced. What of them? Surely Jesus had these black people in mind?

In terms of "set at liberty those who are oppressed," I want to bring us back to my script, Survivors. The characters in the play, all of whom are black, have returned for a reunion. After many of years of struggle, they have returned, to be with one another again. The title of the sketch refers to the ongoing struggle of black people to survive in a "polite" and "civilized" society, where "fair play" holds sway, and "the decency of Englishness" precludes any notion of racialized oppression in this fair "Sceptred Isle," to quote a good white Englishman, William Shakespeare.

In this pristine nation of tolerance and understanding, bad things rarely happen (that is reserved for Johnny Foreigner), and if they do, they most certainly are never racist in intent.[72] Try telling that to the Lawrence family? Try telling that to the family of Cherie Groce, Joy Gardner, Blair Peach, and others. These individuals are all high profile names who have either died whilst in the process of being arrested by the police or in police custody. The litany of black people who have died in police custody or at the hands of invisible and "still be found" assailants makes for depressing reading.[73]

For the black characters in my sketch, part of their celebration is the sheer relief that they have not succumbed to the seemingly all-pervasive threat of dubious arrest, punitive incarceration, mental ill health (accompanied by more punitive incarceration), and suicide.[74]

The incidence for all the aforementioned within Black communities in Britain is alarming. The characters in "Survivors" have endured, but by what means? When the character called Brian in the sketch proclaims,

> We made it guys . . . Our fore fathers started the journey back in the days of slavery. Others followed. Then our parents continued with the journey. And now they've passed the baton onto us,

he is making recourse to the survival ethic that has been ground within the life experiences and the very fabric of black existence since the epoch of slavery. African peoples have been passing on stories of survival and overcoming since our earliest times.

Janice Hale commenting on the importance of African stories of experience says,

> These stories transmit the message to Black children that there is a great deal of quicksand and many land mines on the road to becoming a Black achiever . . . They also transmit the message that it is possible to overcome these obstacles. These stories help Black children de-personalise oppression when they encounter it and enable them to place their personal difficulties into the context of the overall Black liberation struggle.[75]

Black Christian Education, Informed by Black Theology, As a Means of Resistance

Alongside the importance of African-centered stories of experience is the utilization of Scripture as a resource for surviving and resisting. Black theology has sought to connect black people with the empowering and affirming nature of the Gospel of Jesus Christ.[76] In responding to the Gospel, black people have used the study of and their interaction with Scripture as a means of attempting to ascertain answers to the most basic, existential questions pertaining to life in the post–Enlightenment era.[77] Harold Dean Trulear surmises this critical, emotional, and intellectual dilemma most succinctly. When writing of the importance of Christian religious education to black people, he states,

> Rather (Religious education) it has carried upon its broad shoulders the heavy responsibility of helping African Americans find answers for the following question: What does it mean to be Black and Christian in a

society where many people are hostile to the former while claiming allegiance to the latter?[78]

Whilst Trulear's comments are directed at the United States, they resonate with, and have relevance for every community of African people, whether on the continent of Africa, or within the varied locations of the Diaspora.

The Pentecost Narrative: A Paradigm for Transformation

In Acts 2:1–47, we see a depressed, frightened, and dispirited group of individuals transformed by the spirit of God into a forceful, dynamic, and vibrant community. Throughout the long turbulent struggles of black people, particularly on our diasporan journeys, we have been sustained, strengthened, and transformed by the dynamic power of God, manifested in the form of the Holy Spirit.[79] Be it my ancestors who suffered from the indignities and the corruption of the human spirit that was slavery, or the first generation of black migrants who came to Britain as part of the Windrush generation,[80] black people have survived. We have not survived, however, by our own strength alone, but by the grace of God.

Doreen and Neville Lawrence: Prophets of Our Age

Returning to the text, once again, I am constantly intrigued by the boldness of Peter. Peter testifies to the personal experience and reality of Jesus, and the energizing nature of the Holy Spirit. Similarly, within historic and contemporary black experience, black people have felt compelled and have been empowered to challenge the status quo and proclaim the prophetic Gospel of Christ. In our present age, within the British context, we have been given the presence of Neville and Doreen Lawrence. Lawrence's son, Stephen, was brutally murdered on April 18, 1993, in the South-East London borough of Eltham.

This was a horrific racist assault by a group of white youths. Two of the suspects—Neil Acourt, then 17, and Luke Knight, who was 16—were initially charged with the murder, but the Crown Prosecution Service (equivalent of the District Attorney in the United States) dropped the case citing insufficient evidence.

Following Stephen Lawrence's death, his parents led a vigilant and prolonged antiracist campaign in their efforts to attain justice for their murdered son. This faith-based campaign (both parents were Methodists), in conjunction with other black-led social and cultural organizations, challenged the might of the British establishment. The Metropolitan Police force[81] was specifically targeted due to their role in the initial investigation.

Stephen Lawrence's close friend, another young black British youth, had initially phoned for the police, after Stephen and himself had been attacked. The lengthy (and largely unexplained) delay in arriving at the scene of the crime, coupled with their decision to initially arrest the young black victim, was cited as being instrumental in the later failure of the case in court. Monumental mistakes were made in this case, as a largely white-run and staffed police force displayed inherent racist practices in their investigation. Crucial pieces of evidence were overlooked and key people not interviewed.

The ongoing political agitation of the Lawrence's family finally led to a government commissioned inquiry, which was overseen by a notable member of the establishment Sir William MacPherson, a retired High Court Judge. MacPherson's report, in February 1999,[82] was a landmark publication because it enshrined in the British lexicon the term "institutional racism." The British police and other members of the white-controlled establishment (including the British Broadcasting Corporation—The BBC and other public state-run bodies) were forced to concede that systemic and systematic racialized practices were endemic to their corporate ways of working. The MacPherson report curtailed, once and for all, the commonsense subterfuge and denial of white authority to their complicity in terms of racial injustice as it collides with black people in Britain.[83]

Neville and Doreen Lawrence have been the prophets of our age. I believe that through the unrelenting pain and grief at the murder of their son, Stephen, the Lawrences have been inspired, at great personal cost, to proclaim the liberative and prophetic challenge of the Gospel.

For many in Britain, Stephen Lawrence's death has become an iconic and paradigmatic moment not unlike the death of Emmett Till in the United States in 1955. The death of Stephen Lawrence galvanized the black community in Britain like never before. It brought into existence a radical and relevant form of black theology that has forced major concessions and apologies from the white-run power structures in Britain. The redemptive forces of God's prophetic word, coursing through the bruised and emotionally battered lives of the Lawrences, have given rise to a seismic change within the body politic of this country and her relationship to black people. In colloquial terms, the "cat is now out of the bag." White hegemony can no longer deny the existence of institutional racism in this country.

So What of the Future?

Rereading the narrative of Acts chapter two, I feel that the dreams and visions for our present age that emerge from these reflections are bound up, inextricably, with the death of Stephen Lawrence. In verses 22–25, Peter speaks of the means by which Jesus was released from the chains of death, in order that a new humanity could emerge, and it is my belief that Stephen's death is the catalyst that can bring about the possibility of a new Britain.

Can my country, like that of the United States, which still carries the scarlet stains of sin and oppression that is the collective blood of the faceless millions who were butchered in the name of Christ, move onto a higher plane, to renounce that past and embrace a new paradigm for the future? Are we willing to acknowledge the sins of the past? Is Britain and America willing to admit its faults, in respect of its treatment of black young people, such as the ones in "Survivors?"

In the sketch, the characters speak of the many black people who have not survived in Britain. However, these characters have survived. A growing number of black young people are doing increasingly well in Britain. The professions, the world of commerce, the music industry, the media, and the sports fields are finding their ranks being swelled by the growing numbers of talented black young people making great strides in their chosen areas of endeavor.[84]

Despite these important successes, however, there remain a substantial number of black people who have not received a significant opportunity to realize their dreams. Many have become so demoralized that they have never developed the self-esteem to create any worthwhile dreams of their own.[85]

Within the Pentecost narrative, we witness a number of people being transformed and energized by the power of the Holy Spirit. In verse 17, Peter, quoting the words from the prophet Joel (Joel 2:28–32), states,

Your young men shall see visions and your old men shall dream dreams.

I assume, of course, that this includes young women and old women! The dreams and visions that seem to abound within the Acts text are ones that are not the exclusive preserve of any particular group of people. The ability to be transformed and to prophesy, and to see visions and dream dreams, is not restricted to any one ethnic or cultural group.[86] The Jerusalem that hosted pilgrims, following the festivals of Passover and the Feast of Weeks, were cosmopolitan affairs. The emphasis that is given to the list of peoples and locations in verses 5–13 indicates the diverse, pluralistic nature of the Pentecost event. Pentecost was a multicultural event, as indicated by the evidence of different languages. This disproves the often invoked "color blind" theologies of some Pentecostals who assert that in "the Spirit" there are no cultural or ethnic differences, or that God does not see color.

At the very heart of the God-inspired transformation of human persons is the clear sense of God's love and commitment to diversity and difference. In the account, we hear of people speaking in their mother tongue. There is no presumption of preeminence in terms of language, culture, or expression. To put it bluntly, the class-based notions of high European scholasticism that seems to pervade Western Christianity[87] cannot be justified on scriptural grounds. These are cultural appropriations (which, of course, have their value if we do not become slaves to them, or if they are not used to enslave and diminish others) that are human constructs, not divine precepts.

The ability to have visions and dream dreams are the preserve of all human kind. The God of all, in Christ, has called all humanity into an unconditional relationship with the divine. The need to be inspired, coupled with the possibility of transformation, is the potential that resides within every human being.[88] Any society that prevents or precludes certain members of its citizens from realizing the true extent of these possibilities will have to answer God.[89]

A society that has constricted and restricted the opportunities afforded to Black people is one that needs to acknowledge its faults and be redeemed by the power of God. As the twenty-first century begins to take shape, we need, more than ever before, an affirming and respectful society. Not one that tolerates people who are perceived as different or other.[90]

This new century should be one where all societies and nations acknowledge difference and understand the ways in which one's own individual identity can be enhanced through an engagement with others.[91] We need societies and nations in which all people are recognized and acknowledged as possessing the spark of genius and which comprises the raw materials from which brilliance can be mined.[92]

The visions and dreams of Pentecost remind us that God is bigger and beyond the inherent bias, prejudice, clan, or ethnic loyalties that bedevil this and previous eras. The visions and dreams that arise from my reading of Pentecost are related to the concerns and hopes I carry, as a black person of African descent.[93] They are inseparable from my existence, and those of my forebears. It is my hope that the Spirit of God, as manifested in Acts chapter two, will enable black young people, like those depicted in "Survivors," to realize their innate, God-given talent, for the benefit of all peoples, in this and every nation in God's creation. In the final analysis, it is nothing less than a hope in the fuller realization of the Kingdom of God.

Black Christian education has always been a practical discipline that has enabled black people to learn and rehearse the language of freedom.[94] It has been concerned with helping us to learn more about ourselves and about the God who created us to be free.[95]

What does it mean to be within the "Body of Christ" within a so-called Christian nation that still possesses the ability to casually discriminate against people who are not white, levelling its vituperation with particular savagery at black people?[96] Black Christian education has been and continues to be, at its best, the practical theological discipline that attempts to offer black people in the United States and in Britain pedagogical resources and strategies for courageous and prophetic living.[97]

I am and will remain, to some extent, a black Christian educator at heart. My work sits at the nexus between education and theology. I am committed to a form of black Christian education that takes black theology as its essential default position. Black people need to constantly learn and relearn the liberating truths of the Gospel. We cannot assume that historic truths will continue to be learnt by osmosis.[98] Black communities must be intentional in their desire to ensure that those on the margins—that is individuals and groups who are the most vulnerable in our midst—are enabled to learn to read the values of the wider society and to critique them for their veracity.[99]

As black folk, we know from bitter experience that all glitters is most definitely not gold. We must continue to be vigilant in educating our youth to be wary of the blandishments of rampart capitalism, consumerism and the globalized culture. We have experienced at first hand the ways in which the Gospel of Christ has been used against us, nevertheless, we have been inspired to take that which was oppressive and subvert it in order that it might be the means of liberation. We have demonstrated that the slave masters tools can, if not overthrow the slave master's house, can certainly do it some serious damage.

Black Christian education, allied by the substantive concerns of black and womanist theology must continue to provide the pedagogical tools that will continue to damage the slave master's house, thereby, making it inhabitable. Freedom for black people has never been given—rather it has always been hard won. Black Christian education must become the grassroots movement that converts the radical insights of black theology into an accessible format that galvanizes all black people to fight for the continued freedoms that have been ours from birth. We must continue the struggle to ensure that all of us, from the last to the least, are able to declare with pride to succeeding generations, "This is the story of how we 'got over' and are continuing to do so."

5

Published and Be Damned—Reassessing the Role and Development of the Black Theology Journal

In this chapter, I want to make a critical reassessment of the journals *Black Theology in Britain: A Journal of Contextual Praxis* (hereafter referred to as BTIB)[1] and its successor *Black Theology: An International Journal*.[2] At the time of writing, *Black Theology: An International Journal* (hereafter referred to as BTIJ) remains the only academic publication dedicated to the articulation of black theology in the world. With the demise of the *Journal for Black Theology* in Southern Africa, *Black Theology: An International Journal* has assumed added importance for the furtherance of the critical conversation regarding the development of black theology across the many contours of continental Africa and the African Diaspora.

Clearly, as has been the case in the entirety of this book, my perspective on the development of BTIJ is a highly subjective, and perhaps, a selective one. I write as the current editor of the journal and in that respect, offer a subjective-insider perspective on this publication and its development over several years.

Black Theology in Britain Journal: Making Black Theology Visible in the British Context

The first issue of the journal was published in October 1998. It was launched at the George Cadbury Hall, in Selly Oak, Birmingham, on October 10, 1998. This was approximately six months after Robert Beckford's groundbreaking *Jesus is Dread*.

BTIB emerged as a direct response to the desire to locate a repository that would harness the burgeoning developments of this discipline and ongoing practice in Britain. BTIB was an important means of making black theology in Britain a more visible and respected academic discipline within the theological academy in Britain. Prior to the emergence of the journal, there was little, if any, explicit mention of black theology within academic publishing in Britain. In many respects, one is tempted to posit the rather simplistic notion of there being a pre–JiD and a post–JiD epoch—pre–*Jesus is Dread* and post–*Jesus is Dread*. Although *Jesus is Dread* is the work of one visionary figure, the journal, in the long run, has proven to have affected the more substantive impact on the body politic of the theological academy in my context.

Prior to the emergence of the BTIB, there were few, if any, hospitable spaces in which black religious scholars could publish work that could explicitly address many of the taken-for-granted assumptions that govern the articulation of black theology, whether in the United States or in Britain. One of the noted exceptions was *Contact: The Interdisciplinary Journal of Pastoral Studies*[3] (now renamed *Contact: Practical Theology and Pastoral Care*[4]), in which articles by black scholars based in Britain at that time, such as Robert Beckford,[5] George Mulrain,[6] Jeffrey Brown,[7] Emmanuel Lartey,[8] and Lorraine Dixon[9] have featured. For the most part, most mainstream, generic theological journals (generic simply means white, Eurocentric in complexion and orientation) display no recognition even of the mere existence of black theology in Britain.

The truth is, as I have found from personal experience, it is possible to teach students training for ordained ministry, who have already gained considerable experience of studying and teaching in largely secular academic theology (at bachelors, masters, and doctoral levels) who have never been introduced to one black theological scholar.[10] The state of much that is academic theological publishing helps to make this form of myopia possible.

In making black theology in Britain visible, the BTIB journal established a platform from which budding black religious scholars could tentatively begin to stretch their academic wings and take flight into the sometimes (perhaps oftentimes) perilous skies of theological scholarship. In chapter 3 on womanist theology, I spoke of the metaphor, invoked by Oglesby, of the mountain[11] as a heuristic for naming the often invisible travail of racism. In making reference to this text once again, I want to suggest that for black British scholars, BTIB became the essential resource that enabled many of them to give voice to that which had formerly been hidden, in a manner not inconsistent with Oglesby's notion of the mountain.

Black theology in Britain, which had formerly been a relatively hidden and not overly scholarly enterprise, had a dedicated space in which black writers could articulate their work in a supportive, critical, and affirming context. As I demonstrate in a short while, many of the leading black British theologians, myself included, received their first academic validations as (post) graduate students through their initial forays into scholarly theological reflections by way of published work in BTIB—one of my earliest pieces first saw the light in issue one of the journal.[12]

Giving Birth to the Journal

From my reading of the archive material that has been passed on to me by the previous editor,[13] the birth of BTIB was a product of a three-way conversation between the Revd. Dr. Emmanuel Lartey, who subsequently became the first editor, Bishop Dr. Joe Aldred (the first Chair of the editorial board), and the Revd. Dr. Inderjit Bhogal (a founding member of the board, who remains a member of this body).[14] Before I proceed to offer an edited account of the journal's formation, I think it is important that I spend a few moments detailing something of the invaluable role played by Inderjit Bhogal to the development of Black theology in Britain.

In the first chapter, where I outlined the principal players in the development of Black theology in Britain, I made no mention of Inderjit Bhogal. This was not an unfortunate oversight on my part, but rather, a recognition that in a chapter that centered on the development of black theology through publications, Inderjit, whilst an invaluable and, in many respects, indispensable figure in that narrative, has nevertheless, written comparatively little in order to be included in that section of this work.

Bhogal's strengths do not lie in the articulation of black theology in written form, although he has written a number of important short contributions to black theology in Britain.[15] Rather, Bhogal's strengths lie in his advocacy and campaigning skills. Bhogal has the distinction of being the first black or Asian president of the British Methodist Conference, an annually elected post dating back to the late eighteenth century and John Wesley, the founder of Methodism.

In a previous chapter, I outlined the role played by black Methodism in the development of black theology in Britain. Methodism's normative ecclesiology and missiology makes it, perhaps the most adept of all the major churches in Britain at engaging with black theology. This can be seen in the fact that Methodism (at the time of writing) is the only church in Britain to fund a resident black theologian (namely myself) and to have elected as president and leader of the church,[16] one of the most radical liberation theologians in the country—Inderjit. In the inaugural address to the annual Methodist conference of 2000, Bhogal said the following:

> Centuries before John Wesley coined the word, Jesus Christ pointed to the "connexionality" of God's Kingdom or Commonwealth. He broke barriers and was "in-connexion" with those that others excluded, socially and spiritually. He welcomed the poor, the "unclean," "the sinners," the harlots and the publicans and ate with them.[17]

For Bhogal, a man of Asian descent, born in Kenya, who migrated to Britain in 1964, identification with the development of black theology in Britain and the needs of the marginalized and oppressed peoples at the grassroots of society has been total. Bhogal was a pivotal figure in the organization of the first ever conference in black theology in Sheffield (northern England) in 1994 (at which the renowned African American Hebrew Bible scholar Randall Bailey was present) and also in the development of the earlier publications (to which reference has been made) *A Time To Speak*[18] and *A Time To Act*.[19]

I offer this brief assessment of Bhogal's contribution to the development of black theology in Britain, in recognition of the pivotal role he played, alongside that of Lartey and Aldred, in enabling BTIB to be birthed in 1998.

The birth of BTIB was the result of lengthy negotiations between these three principal individuals in addition to a number of others on the fledgling editorial group. The journal was essentially a four-way partnership between the Centre for Black and White Christian Partnership, headed by Joe Aldred, the Department of Theology at the University of Birmingham, represented by Emmanuel Lartey, the Queen's College, represented by Robert Beckford and the Urban Theology Unit (an ecumenical, but largely Methodist-run theological institution) in Sheffield, headed by Inderjit Bhogal. Other significant players included Ron Nathan and Patricia Gowrie.[20]

Having identified the names associated with the birthing of this momentous undertaking, I think it is worth acknowledging, from the paperwork, the indefatigable work of Joe Aldred in the creation of the

journal. Whilst the minutes do not offer us an exhaustive or comprehensive account of the ongoing dynamic that led to the creation of the
journal (one has also to be attuned to what is not written in addition
to what is), one cannot deny the importance of Aldred's contributions
to the whole process. My reading of this process indicates that Bhogal
provided the memory and the vision for the undertaking, Aldred the
sheer momentum and organizational dynamism, and Lartey the academic expertise and intellectual know-how. Given that I was not present at these meetings and have only the printed minutes on which to
make these assessments, I am at pains to acknowledge that much of
the last sentence is speculative supposition on my part—no one's
exegetical skills are foolproof!

One of the main important subtexts for the creation of the journal
was provided by Joe Aldred who, writing a few years later in one of his
edited texts, states,

> A tragedy of our time is that some cultures, in particular black cultures,
> are pigeonholed, stigmatized even, as "oral"; while others, in particular
> white European cultures, are regarded as "literary." Clearly, all cultures
> enjoy both elements in their traditions to some extent. However, an
> unfortunate, if inevitable, result of this stereotyping is that black cul-
> tures in Britain are not encouraged to write: the literary cultures have
> traditionally written for them and about them. This collection
> challenges this paradigm.[21]

Although not stated in the minutes of those early editorial meetings,
the need for black people to document their experiences and so dis-
prove the spurious axiom that we are solely oral and do not write was
clearly embedded in the modus operandi of the journal. The additional
desire to ensure that our story is told by those who know it first hand
("who feels it, knows it" as defined in the first chapter) and can attest
to its veracity was also uppermost in the minds of the founding fathers
and mothers of the journal.

The creation of BTIB owes much to the indefatigable work of a
small group of people whose committed dream and energy to see black
theology in Britain come of age gave life to this seemingly impossible
undertaking.

Perhaps the hidden heroes/heroines in this narrative, however, are
that of the publisher of BTIB. From the minutes, it becomes patently
clear that Sheffield Academic Press' (SAP) commitment to publishing
this journal lay not in any expected financial reward. Rather, SAP, not
unlike their support of other radical and marginal theologically

contextual journals like feminist theology, lay in their identification with the intent and importance of black theology as a discipline in Britain. SAP's ability to see beyond the short term-isms of financial gain enabled them to possess a visionary attitude to support the journal. Any reservations of supporting, what would most likely in the short run, be a loss making venture is not recorded in the minutes. I am not so naive as to assume that these concerns were entirely absent from the resulting discourse surrounding the development of the journal. What is quite clear, however, is that these concerns did not prevent SAP from publishing BTIB. It is interesting to note that at the time of writing no major American publisher has shown the kind of brave, prophetic commitment of SAP (a relatively small operation in comparison to the likes of many such companies in the United States) to sponsor a black theology journal in America. SAP is to be congratulated for its foresight and convictions.

Trying to Bring the Academy and the Church Together

One of the important aims of the journal was the desire to create a forum in which academic and pastoral concerns could be juxtaposed in one setting. There was talk about encouraging contributors to write not only on a variety of themes and concerns but also to think more broadly on the various styles of writing that might be employed, in order to engage with an anticipated wide readership.[22] Consequently, there was much encouragement of the use of poetry, short stories, and even cartoons as a means of developing and articulating black religious discourse.

The desire to create a publication that would appeal to a wide variety of people, particularly those within the broader areas of Britain's black communities, can be seen in the minutes of the meeting held on the November 10, 1997 that stressed the need for the journal to be

accessible and informative for a wider community especially including those many groups and individuals concerned about the particularities of Black experience in Britain.[23]

In order to achieve the stated aims of being accessible and attuned to the needs of the wider black community, members of the editorial board, particularly Aldred, were assiduous in their efforts to establish contact with a wide variety of community organizations and individuals.[24] In my rereading of these notes, I sense a commendable and ambitious agenda at work; but one, which in hindsight, would not be overly successful. The agenda is certainly an ambitious one. The initiators of the journal were rightly determined to try and hold together the needs of the academy and the church—scholars and ordinary Christians. BTIB was not conceived as an elite academic undertaking. In a manner similar to the rallying cry of those pioneers in the United States in the late 1960s for black power and justice, BTIB was a response to a felt need, not simply an esoteric and abstract undertaking.[25]

The aims of the initial editorial committee were indeed laudable, but perhaps, over ambitious? I make this comment, not in a pious revisionist tone, seeking to offer a self-satisfied supercilious sneer from behind the barricades of history. Rather, my comments are, I hope, an honest reflection on the subsequent development of the journal since its inception in October 1998.

In attempting to create a delicate balance between the academy and the church—and scholars and ordinary Christians—the journal was attempting to mount a brave undertaking that has largely eluded Black religious scholarship since the late 1960s. James Harris[26] and later, Dale Andrews[27] have attempted to create a bridge between the academy and the church by utilizing the overarching backdrop of pastoral/practical theology.

The desire to create one publication in order to address two differing arenas was always going to be one that was fraught with innumerable difficulties. In the event, I believe that the need to provide a publication that possessed intellectual rigor and was academically credible outweighed the desire to reach a relatively benign and nondemanding "home" audience. In my analysis of black intellectual and communitarian leadership through drama, I have argued that black leaders are apt to take the mass of ordinary black people for granted in their efforts to challenge white hegemony.[28] Often, such individuals work on the assumption that one's own will support them no matter what the level of inaction or studied oversight may be, which then frees them to get on with the seemingly more important task of tackling white hegemony.[29]

I do not want to suggest any overriding sense of cynicism in the motives or intent of the people who helped to create BTIB. In making the aforementioned comments, I am arguing that the need to ensure that the journal found its rightful place in the theological academy within Britain was ultimately seen as more important than trying to gain a popular readership amongst ordinary black Christians.

One might well argue to what extent do established generic white journals garner a wide readership from amongst the ordinary church going public in Britain or in the United States? I do not think that the founder fathers and mothers of BTIB have any reason to berate themselves for the failure of this publication to attract a wide readership. Most mainstream journals are not read by ordinary white Christians.

My comments with regard to the journal have been made not only in terms of any analysis of the intentions of the originators but have also emerged from speaking with a number of grassroots black Christians, as I have shown them back issues of BTIB. A number of these individuals, upon looking at the front cover and the inside contents page of the journal, remarked "This was not aimed at people like me!" The sense of estrangement from the journal was summed up by one respondent who, upon looking at the front cover, remarked, "Black Theology in Britain: A Journal of Contextual Praxis . . . And what does Contextual praxis mean?"

For many ordinary black Christians, the inclusion of this phrase served as an obvious signifier that the journal was not aimed at people like them. The term "contextual praxis," whilst providing an important short-hand for those familiar with the lexicon of Liberation theologies, nevertheless, becomes an impenetrable barrier to those who have not been exposed to any significant form of theological education. A number of ordinary black Christians immediately identified in this term a symbolic marker that designated this journal as one that was beyond their sensibilities.

I am sure that for the creators of the journal, this result was the furthest thing from their mind. The realities, however, of trying to create a respected and legitimate academic publication outweighed the imagined sensibilities of those for whom a scholarly journal was already a frightening proposition, prior to their engagement with the formidable subtitle.

At a relatively early stage in the planning for the journal, the editorial committee began to assess the names of the group of international scholars that would assist in the ongoing development of the publication. From my reading of the working draft, a number of names were suggested to act in the capacity of international advisors to the British-based editorial committee and board.[30]

It is interesting to note that although these discussions regarding an international advisory board were taking place in 1998, there is no evidence of any such group being in existence when analyzing the subsequent composition of the first editorial committee and editorial advisory board. In fact, in the first four issues, from October 1998 to May 2000, there are no international figures represented in the editorial life of the journal. As there are no references in the paperwork at my disposal to shed light on this, it is perhaps prudent if I refrain from making any comment on this matter. It is not until the fifth issue, November 2000, that international names were added to the journal. In the fifth issue, the names included were luminaries such as Jacquelyn Grant, Dwight Hopkins, and George Mulrain from Jamaica (the latter had been resident in Britain for many years and had been a founder member of the monthly Black theology forum).

Topics, Themes and Areas of Concern in the Early Issues of *Black Theology in Britain*

In my analysis of the first half dozen issues of BTIB, I am struck by the broad range of topics, themes, and subject areas that were addressed by a number of writers. A clue to the largely British cast of writers in these issues can be found in a note from the minutes of one of the editorial committee meeting prior to the publication of the first issue. The minutes states:

> It was stressed that the focus (of the journal) must be the British context but the appeal should be broad.[31]

As I have stated in the first chapter (indeed the basic conceit of this work), the formative developments of black theology in the British context owed much to the comparative insights of African American black theology. Whilst this transatlantic input from the United States undoubtedly had a beneficial and profound effect upon Britain, there is a sense (as I have hinted at in the first chapter) that this constant drawing upon African American sources and approaches was indicative of a critical lack of confidence in contextual black British thinking.

My reading of the early issues of BTIB, in which there are no African American voices, perhaps speaks of a desire for black theology in Britain to come of age and to claim her own distinctive voice in and of itself, and not as a comparatively poorer cousin to her richer and more confident relative. In the first issue, there are pieces by six authors, all of whom have been and to some extent remain stalwarts in the development of black theology in Britain.

Valentina Alexander's piece is concerned with looking at the intersections between Afrocentric thought and traditional black Christian consciousness and spirituality,[32] in a manner not dissimilar to that offered by African American woman theologian Cheryl Sanders.[33] Ron Nathan's article looks at Caribbean youth identity in the United Kingdom and suggests a Pan-African theological framework in which these developments might be housed.[34] Like Alexander, Nathan's work is very much attuned to the needs of the British context, it, nevertheless, resonates with the work of African American scholars—in this case, that of Josiah Young.[35]

The remaining articles in that first issue include pieces by George Mulrain,[36] Kate Coleman[37]—one of the leading black women theologians in Britain—and myself.[38]

In many respects, the first issue of BTIB provides a useful microcosm for a number of the following volumes, in that many of the familiar and salient themes, which I have characterized in the first chapter as being distinctive of black theology in Britain, can be found, both in this single issue and in many of the subsequent ones. First, it is worth noting the eclectic nature of the first issue. Like the previous generation of black theological work in Britain, black theology is understood in a more generic fashion, rather than in a narrower sense to denote systematic/constructive theology and ethics. Like later issues, this first volume included a range of subjects, such as theology, musicology, education, and sociocultural analysis. Later issues of the journal continue in the same vein as the first volume and include topics such as political mobilization,[39] history,[40] musicology,[41] psychology,[42] and ecclesiology.[43]

This eclectic approach to black theological work was in keeping with the more generic conceptualization of the discipline in Britain, compared to the United States. This eclectic approach was also reflective of a desire to create a broad tent in which a number of people, often languishing in other largely all-white disciplines, could find a convivial home and an affirming space in which to articulate their work. By offering a broad definition of the nature of black theology, the journal welcomed contributions from a range of subjects, under the broad rubric that the space was for people who defined themselves as black (in the broadest of terms) and were engaging with issues of faith and practice as they affected black people.

One weakness of these early issues of the journal is the distinct lack of articles in the area of systematic or dogmatic theology. This omission is, in many respects, reflective of the general development of black theology in Britain, as I have highlighted in the first chapter.

One important role of the journal, in addition to offering a conducive space for black scholars across a wide range of disciplines, united by a commitment to faith and praxis, was its ability to nurture and empower new scholars. Whilst those early journals were very much committed to academic excellence, this desire was tempered by the need to identify, encourage, and support newer scholars.

A majority of the black British writers in those early issues were (post) graduate students, often studying at the University of Birmingham. I, for one, am a recipient of the kind and supportive attitude and nurturing tendencies of Emmanuel Lartey, the founding editor. Lartey possessed the priceless ability of being able to offer supportive and critical feedback of one's work, thereby enabling many fledgling scholars to learn the art of writing scholarly pieces for academic journals.

This unstated part of the remit is one that remains with the current editor and continues to be an important missiological task of the journal. Black religious scholars are rarely born into that role, but more likely grow into it, learning from their forebears. As I often tell my students, "We all had to start at some place and our first efforts rarely make for palatable reading!"

Black Theology in Britain Becomes *Black Theology: An International Journal*—A Broader Canvass!

The first article by an African American scholar in BTIB came in the fifth issue, in November 2000, with Diana L. Hayes's piece entitled, "Women's Rights are Human Rights."[44] What is most heartening to report, having recently reread Hayes's piece is that (and this is meant as no disrespect to Professor Hayes) it does not read as being inherently superior to the pieces in previous issues by black British writers. The previous writing of black British women compares favorably with that offered by a distinguished African American professor. The journal has provided a space that has enabled black theology in Britain the process of coming of age.

BTIB was principally concerned with trying to establish a critical space in which black British religious scholars could articulate their ideas. The minutes do not indicate whether African American scholars were turned away, they had simply not heard of the journal, or they were not encouraged to offer pieces, thinking that the journal was an entirely British-based affair.

Certainly, by the time Emmanuel Lartey handed over the editor's reigns to me, in the autumn of 2001, there was emerging within the editorial committee a sense that the journal was about to enter a new era, which might necessitate a name change. It is no coincidence that the change of name from BTIB to *Black Theology: An International Journal* (hereafter identified by the abbreviation BTIJ) resulted in many more submissions from African American scholars.

Prior to the name change, Dwight Hopkins, one of the more internationalist of African American black theologians published a piece entitled "New heterosexual Black male."[45] He is one of the relatively few African American scholars to have his work published under the old nomenclature. The arrival of North American writers in the shape of such scholars of note as Anthony Pinn,[46] Josiah Young,[47] Elaine Crawford,[48] and of course, the now legendary James H. Cone[49] has coincided with the broadening of the parameters of the new journal. Alongside the growing inclusion of African American scholars has been the augmenting of the international advisory board, which now includes such luminaries as Jacquelyn Grant, Randall Bailey, Dwight Hopkins, and Anthony Pinn. These individuals have offered their wealth of experience and breadth of scholarship in order that the journal should continue to grow and develop.

Having adopted an international title, this newer incarnation of the journal has now become one of the primary means by which black theologians across the globe can be in conversation, with one another. However, despite the growth of this publication, there remain a number of inherent tensions, which, as the current editor, one has to constantly monitor.

The primary concern remains that of balance, to which I eluded in the first chapter of this work. Given the huge disparities in black theology as practiced in the United States and that of her more fledgling cousin in Britain, there remains the fear that the overarching confident and dominant foliage that is the United States will simply overrun the relatively tender shoots of the British plant.

Within the U.S. context, the ongoing development of black theology has led to the emergence of a multiplicity of avenues in which black religious scholars can publish their work. In terms of book projects, one can point to such publishers as Orbis, Fortress, Pilgrim, Continuum, Westminster John Knox, Beacon, Mercer, and others. In Britain, by contrast, there is a paucity of publishers with whom black British scholars can get their work published. To date, the principal company that has been prepared to publish work by black British theologians has been Darton, Longman and Todd (DLT) who have supported the bulk of Robert Beckford's published work since the late 1990s.[50] Other notable exceptions to this seemingly all enveloping sea of whiteness include Methodist Publishing House (MPH)/Epworth Press and recently, Equinox, the publishers of BTIJ.

Having cited the plethora of publishers that are happy to support book projects by black scholars in the United States, one has to acknowledge that a different landscape may exist in terms of scholarly articles, which although the lifeblood of academic scholarship, is often seen as the unglamoros and less commercial end of the intellectual continuum. I will attempt to addres the role of BTIJ as a conduit toward the international development of black theology at a later juncture in this chapter.

Black Theology: An International Journal—An Inclusive Space?

Right from the outset, BTIB and its later offspring BTIJ were conceived as being privileged spaces for black scholars. The initial draft of the preamble to the journal reads thus:

> This new journal is designed to provide a forum for the articulation of the faith perspectives of Black people in Britain. Black theology, a term made popular by African-American theologians expresses an attempt to wrestle with matters of faith arising out of the situation of being created Black in a world dominated by structures put in place by White interests. The journal welcomes contributions from people reflecting on their faith in relation to African, Caribbean, American and/or Asian origins and contexts, which have relevance for Britain.[51]

As a declaration of intent, there can be no disguising the ideological nature of this undertaking. BTIB was a determined attempt to create a critical space in which black scholars, particularly those working within the British context, could get their work published. What made this undertaking a distinctly ideological one is the realization that a number of committed white scholars, some of whom I have cited in the first chapter, have made telling contributions to the development of black theology in Britain. Can black theology identify itself as being a paradigm for antiracist, antioppressive practice and still exclude others from its good offices on the grounds of race? Is this not the worst kind of reverse racism?

This ethical dilemma was not a new one. In the development of black theology in the United States in the late 1960s, the first generation of black theologians were confronted with a similar dilemma. The relationship of black theology, as articulated by black theologians, with that of liberal white scholars provides a fascinating subtext to the opening section of Wilmore and Cone's first volume of *Black Theology: A Documentary History*.[52]

BTIB and BTIJ remain determined to privilege the voices of those whose contributions to the theological landscape often go unheard. In a previous piece of work, I have argued that there is rarely any parity between the relative contributions of black and white scholars.[53] A number of years ago, I remember teaching a class in black theology to a group of white students and made the bold assertion (partly as a provocative gesture to stimulate conversation) that I could not think of any white person who had made a selfless act that had benefited black people. The students felt outraged at my universal swipe at all white people. In the ensuing discussion, I asked the group to tell me about the radical white people who had stood up against racism and white supremacy, having not first been convicted to act by black people, who initially had undertaken that action and not been recognized for doing so. There followed a deluge of silence. So I asked another question. "Tell me about any radical white Christian people at all?"

Without much hesitation, the conversation moved to Bonhoeffer. So I asked the group to tell me all about Dietrich Bonhoeffer. The silence was now broken by an excited cacophony of voices as the students with great enthusiasm sought to demonstrate the error of my previous words by showing me how "magnificent" an example Bonhoeffer had been, how insightful and challenging was his theology, how impassioned was his writing.

I asked the group as to how many of them had heard of Bonhoeffer before they commenced their theological studies. Some of them had heard of the name. I then asked the group how many had heard of Marcus Garvey or W.E.B. Dubois. None of them had. My concluding question was this: "Why is that when white people do heroic actions we never fail to hear about it, but when it's black people, unless they are Martin Luther King, we simply don't get a look in?"

The truth is, given the great disparities in power and esteem between white Euro-American epistemologies and those of black people, I feel it is fallacious to begin to think about operating an open-door policy, which simply reinscribes the normativity of white epistemologies at the expense of black notions of truth. As I have

demonstrated in the previous chapter on Christian education, such is
the power of white norms that when white contributions are juxtaposed alongside black ones, many black young people still assume the
superiority of the white presence.

In a previous work, I was able to show how many black young
people are unable to visually construct images of black people from
so-called generic and neutral forms of Christian learning materials.[54]
With reference to specific biblical material, I write thus:

> In their own imaginings, without any added stimuli and cultural frames
> of reference, these individuals were unable to think of biblical charac-
> ters in terms other than those associated with White Europeans.[55]

The power of Eurocentric norms is such that succeeding generations of
black young people are already struggling with the overarching
normativity of white hegemonic constructs. I feel that the privileged
visibility of whiteness does not need the collusion and assistance of
BTIJ by offering a designated black space to people who can easily
publish their work in other places, especially those publications that
will not accept the work of black scholars.

I am aware that many people will accuse me of being overly hard
and unsympathetic. But to my mind, white people are particularly
advantaged and privileged by the present world order to such an
extent that they do not need any help or support from largely disenfranchised black people. Neither am I going to go out of my way to
congratulate white people, for displaying the kinds of attitudes and
behavior they should be doing anyway, given the clear ethical
demands of the Gospel. As African American womanist scholar Lynne
Westfield reminds us, it can become all too easy for black people to
find themselves playing "nurse maid" to emotionally distraught and
guilty white people, when the world has already given them all of the
privileges and advantages for simply being white![56]

Having defended the past and present policy of privileging the voice
of black people, it is instructive to note the occasions when white
scholars have featured in the past issues of the journal.

One of the most significant pieces in the journal was that of Mark
Lewis Taylor, which was published in the sixth issue of the journal in
May 2001.[57] Taylor's article was not the first one by a white scholar to
be published in the journal. That honor was given to Roswith Gerloff,
who was formerly the director of the Centre for Black and White
Christian Partnership (BWCP).[58] Reference has been made to Gerloff's

contribution to black theology in Britain in the first chapter. Gerloff, a white Lutheran minister, was the first director of the CBWCP, based within the historic Selly Oak Mission colleges in Birmingham. Her defining contribution to the development of black theology in Britain was through her monumental two-volume study of black-led churches in Britain.[59]

Until more recent times this work was the most visible piece of scholarship on black-led Christianity in Britain. Her work, in many respects, has been superseded by a host of black British scholars, who have offered both an updating of and a critique of her work.[60]

I have chosen to highlight Taylor's contribution because I feel, in many respects, it offers a more ethically sound perspective for a contribution by a white scholar to a black theological journal. Although Gerloff's article is a well-argued, thoroughly researched piece, there remains a number of difficult questions regarding the efficacy of white people doing research on and articulating black theological discourse. In a previous piece of work, I have critiqued the relationship between white authority and black subjectivity, arguing as to whether white people can ever accurately assess the veracity of black theological discourse.[61]

Mark Lewis Taylor's article is an assessment of the *Dictionary of Third World Theologies*,[62] which begins with an analysis of the role and development of dictionaries in a generic sense. Taylor argues that these texts are not merely the accumulation of words and arid definitions. Rather, argues Taylor, dictionaries are

> sites of contestation, compiled sets of power negotiations, flexing the "archival" power for deciding what is included and omitted, what is mentioned and remembered.[63]

Taylor juxtaposes his more generic polemic around the ideological positionality of dictionaries alongside a particularized analysis of the *Dictionary of Third World Theologies*,[64] in which "we are celebrating one remarkable fruit of the movements and parties of resistance."[65]

Taylor's presence in the sixth issue of the journal is telling. Both the location of his article and the subject matter itself is highly instructive. In terms of the location of the article, it is important to note that a highly skilled and experienced author is allowed access to the journal, but only after a clear norm has been established, namely that prioritizes the authentic expression of black scholars. Whilst wanting to prioritize and privilege the voice of black scholars, the journal had, by the sixth issue, become increasingly more confident in the established norm to consider the merits of including work by sympathetic white Euro-American scholars. The fact that Taylor's work is sympathetic to the intent and ideological presuppositions of black theology offers us the second instructive point as to its inclusion in this issue of the journal.

Taylor's work, which includes such influential texts as *Reconstructing Christian Theologies*[66] and *The Executed God*[67] displays a firm commitment to naming those oppressive structures and theological constructs that have historically constricted and defined the worldview of those on the margins. The inclusion of this piece in the sixth issue sets a creative and inclusive precedent for the black theology journal. Namely, that assertive and radical work by sympathetic white scholars can be included in the journal on the proviso that first, their work is very firmly anchored within a liberationist framework, second, that their presence should never become the majority voice within any one issue, and third, that their work should not attempt to speak for black people. Unlike Gerloff's piece, Taylor's article does not seek to present or interpret black theological discourse. Rather, it offers a supportive and radical contribution that reflects upon the wider contours of oppression and marginalization as they affect the mass of voiceless black people in the world[68] without attempting to speak for them.

In the wake of Taylor's article, the journal has witnessed a further contribution from a white scholar, namely, Clive Marsh whose work on black Christologies in white majority contexts is a creative and challenging piece of writing.[69]

In conclusion, then, the black theology journal has remained a privileged space, in which the theological articulation of black people has been prioritized, and from which the dominant voice of white people has been largely excluded. At the time of writing, in over a dozen issues, dating back over a period of seven years and approaching a hundred articles or essays, only three white scholars have been published in the journal. The black theology journal remains a "Black thang!"

Nurturing New Voices

One of the important roles the journal has played in the development of black theology, particularly in Britain, is as a conduit for the emergence of new, important voices to the theological academy. For many first generation black British religious scholars, BTIB and BTIJ have proved an invaluable space in which they might learn the demands of theological scholarship and the skills of writing and articulating their work for a wider audience. To date, editors of both the journals have occupied a dual role of publishing the best available work by established black scholars whilst seeking to nurture and develop new voices to the academy.

The Relationship between the Journal and the Black Theology in Britain Forum—Some Personal Reflections

As I have mentioned earlier, the black theology journal has been important in providing an affirming space in which black British religious scholars might seek to articulate and publish their work. Prior to its emergence, there existed very few spaces (save for a pastoral theology journal) in which black British religious scholars could publish their work. The journal has offered a dedicated space in which the nascent developments of black theology in britain could begin to give expression to its distinctive voice.

Crucial in the development of black theology in Britain has been the role of the monthly black theology in Britain forum. Reference has been made to the forum in my assessment of the work of Emmanuel Lartey.[70] Lartey was a founding member of the monthly black theology forum in 1992. The forum has met in the evenings in the last week of the month since that time. The early leaders of the group were Emmanuel Lartey, George Mulrain, and Robert Beckford.

The format of the monthly black theology forum in Birmingham has changed very little since its inception in the early 1990s. Though the venues have changed over the years, moving from the Centre for Black and White Christian Partnership to the Graduate Centre for Theology and Religion, and now to the Queen's Foundation (for Ecumenical Theological Education), the forum remains committed to the articulation of black theological conversation.

In more recent times, there has been a proliferation of black theological forums, with established black scholars and those of more recent vintage meeting in the northern city of Sheffield and another group meeting in London—these are the ones of which I am aware and there may be others! Without wishing to appear blasé or arrogant, I think it is true to say that the Birmingham black theology forum is the "senior" venture in Britain and remains the main pastoral and academic space in which black theology in Britain is undertaken.

The Birmingham branch of the forum, at the time of writing, meets on the last Thursday of every month. From the outset, Lartey and others were adamant in ensuring that two primary conditions were fulfilled. First, that the forum should be a black only space. Black, as I have outlined in the first chapter, was (and remains) understood in more plural, political terms to denote nonwhite people of whatever ethnicity. Thus far, the forum has been sustained by people of African, Caribbean, and Asian descent. White people have not been permitted to attend.

Over the years, this policy has been challenged, by those within and also external to the monthly meeting. Some have felt that this policy, similar to the one adopted by the journal, is theologically and morally indefensible. The reasons for the forum remaining a black only space have already been given in my assessment of the similar policy of the journal, so I have no intention of rehearsing them once again.

It is interesting to note, however, that on the many occasions when white people have had the opportunity to engage with black people, particularly in inner city churches, many chose not to do so, often choosing to take the well-worn white flight to the suburbs.[71] The litany of largely all-white churches that then became multiethnic ones when the black folk moved in, and have now become black only enclaves, as the white folk have "made a hasty retreat for the white highlands" is too replete to mention at this juncture. The truth is (and remains) that for many white people, they want to have dialogue with black people on their own terms, on occasions that suit them.

The black theology forum remains a black only space in order that black people do not have to apologize for their discourse or explain it for the benefit of those who often want to relativize or trivialize our experiences by comparing it to other forms of oppression. In terms of the latter, I have lost count the number of occasions when white people have sought to compare their struggles with those of black people, sometimes even seeking to suggest that black people have gained a marked advantage over themselves. The black theology forum operates as a black only space in order that racism and white patrician arrogance is removed from the equation.

The second primary condition of the forum has been the insistence that we do not "do church." There are no devotions, prayers, hymn singing, or ecclesial niceties to the meeting. The meeting is perceived as a dedicated space to critical thinking and constructive theological work. From the outset, I believe that Lartey, followed by later chairs (Joe Aldred, Robert Beckford, and myself) have sought to ensure that the forum is a critical space in which black scholars (budding, or those more experienced) are enabled to think outside the box. Participants, whether they are undertaking formal scholarly work or occasional visitors seeking to be a part of a creative conversation outside of the usual rubric of Bible study or worship, are encouraged to think challenging and radical thoughts safe in the knowledge that there are no strictures surrounding orthodoxy in the meeting. In short, the golden rule is one of respect—there is no championing of denominational loyalties or reproof around what is permissible in terms of ideas or concerns. The forum has also resisted the call to meet at a "black church" in Britain in order to be more accessible to ordinary black people. The reason for not doing so are due not to any desire to exclude ordinary black Christians, but rather, to ensure an openness and inclusivity that might not be maintained if the meetings took place in a black church.

The decision not to "do church" has, I am sure, angered or concerned some people. But I remain unrepentant on this matter. As I have told members of the forum on occasions, particularly when newer members have joined, black people do not suffer from a shortage of churches—in fact, church is one of the few things for which we can cite almost unqualified success. What we lack, however, are the critical resources, both human and textual to support the continuing growth of black Christianity. The forum remains a critical space in which black theology can be undertaken in order to offer an insightful and much needed critique to the worst excesses of white Christianity and the failure of the black church to live out her prophetic mandate to be a sign for the reign of God.

As result of much of the above, the forum has remained a largely minority enterprise. For a brief period, in the mid-1990s, there did seem to be a certain novelty value attached to the notion of black theology in Britain. Numbers attending the forum approached 30–40 people on some evenings. Those years were, in many respects, the high water mark for the numerical success of the forum. In more recent times, numbers have been more modest, with 6–20 people attending, depending upon the nature of the topic under discussion and unforeseen variables such as the weather and other commitments, often domestic, which may impede attendance. Whilst the number has decreased, the depth of engagement and rigor of debate has increased.

The conduct of business at the forum has largely remained unchanged over the many years of its existence. Volunteers often offer papers (formal and academic or more informal and discursive), which in turn is followed by conversation and questions. Over the years, the forum has been augmented by the presence of high profile visitors principally from the United States. Guest speakers have included James Cone, Jacquelyn Grant, and Noel Erskine. The input of international scholars has not been limited, however, to high profile figures from the United States.

Given Birmingham's reputation as an international center for the study of mission and intercultural approaches to theology and ministry, many international students have traveled to the city, in order to study at the University of Birmingham. A number of these students have subsequently attended the forum and made invaluable contributions to the intellectual exchange of ideas and scholarly thinking, which has ultimately been of benefit to the largely black British membership. Individuals such as Maitland Evans[72] and Clarice Barnes[73] spring to mind.

The importance of the forum to the black theology journal lies in the preparatory role it plays in enabling largely inexperienced scholars to offer their developing work for critical, but most crucially, affirming conversation, prior to examination or publication. I remember all too clearly the sheer dread and trepidation when I volunteered to give my very first paper to the forum in the spring of 1996. The forum provided me with a benign space in which I could tentatively offer a few indicative thoughts on my research, safe in the knowledge that the critical feedback would be constructive and was not designed to destroy my confidence. It was in this challenging and yet pastorally sensitive space that I was able to amend my work and begin to shape it for possible publication in the journal.

Over the years, a succession of black British scholars has used the forum to develop their work, prior to offering it for publication in the journal. This is not to suggest that the sole purpose of the forum is to feed the needs of the journal or that all contributors to the journal have attended the forum. The relationship between the two is not a hard and fixed one. Rather, there exists between the journal and the forum a mutuality that is born of a common sense of purpose. The two arenas are committed to the development of black theology.

In the case of the forum, its sphere of operations is limited to Britain, largely around the West Midlands conurbation; the journal now has a more international scope, seeking to draw together a diverse range of scholars from all corners of the globe. The journal, particularly, in its early years, flourished, not least because of the existence of the forum in which many fledgling black theologians were enabled to learn and hone their craft, alongside their formal studies at the university. I remain committed to the continued existence of the forum as a means of nurturing and developing new generations of black theologians in Britain and elsewhere.

Future Developments

At the time of writing, I am pleased to report that BTIJ is in a healthy and confident state. From small, modest beginnings, the journal has grown and developed. The journal has now become a significant arena in which the international development of black theology in a published form is undertaken. From being a largely British only affair, it has grown to become a genuinely international operation, in which scholars from Africa, the United States, Britain, and the Caribbean are eager to have their work published. This growth in the reputation and coverage of the journal has, undoubtedly, made my role as the editor much easier than that which often faced my predecessor. And yet, as we bask in the well-deserved glare of our achievements and successes, there remain a number of important areas in which the journal needs to improve if it is to remain a vital, incisive, and liberative space for black theological scholarship.

Through my research on the development of the journal, I have been concerned about the comparative low number of published pieces by black British and African American women. This is not to suggest that black British or African American women have not written for journal or been encouraged to do so, but from my analysis, more needs to be done in this department.

Thus far, only one issue (Vol. 4, No. 1, November 2001) has failed to include an article by a black woman. I am eager to ensure that this is not repeated again. But the hard truth remains that as an editor you can only publish the material that is at your disposal. I am pleased to report that the journal continues to receive high quality submissions from brilliant black women from Britain and the United States and further afield. These pieces proceed through the usual academic refereeing process with no recourse to amending or massaging the criteria in order to achieve some semblance of gender balance.

The journal continues to receive high quality submissions from experienced luminaries as well as fledgling undergraduate and (post) graduate students alike. The standard of work is improving and the commitment of Equinox, the independent publishers who produce the journal, headed by Janet Joyce (managing director) in London is ensuring that more academic institutions across the world are subscribing them for their libraries. The journal is hopefully becoming a "must read" for those interested in the ongoing development of black theology across the world.

The journal has gone from strength to strength, but there remains much that can and needs to be done. We cannot and must not rest on our laurels. Yet, as I offer this challenge to all concerned with the journal, in order that this pioneering publication continues to grow and develop, my mind is brought back to the formal minutes of that first editorial committee, back in the early months of 1997. What vision and what foresight they had. What commitment and belief they must have possessed. Black theology in Britain barely existed in published form at the time of their deliberations and dreaming. How did they even conceive of a black theology journal when there appeared barely sufficient numbers of suitably qualified academic black theologians to fill a wardrobe? Yet, from such small acorns do mighty oaks grow!

I salute the indefatigable work of such pioneers as Joe Aldred, Inderjit Bhogal, Kate Coleman, Pat Gowrie, Paul Grant, Robert Beckford, Ron Nathan, Emmanuel Jacob, Glynne Gordon-Carter, Valentina Alexander, and of course, my excellent predecessor as editor, Emmanuel Lartey. *Black Theology: An International Journal* has grown from being a ridiculously impossible dream to become a vibrant and concrete reality. As my African American brothers and sisters have been known to exclaim, "God makes a way out of no way." Long may *Black Theology: An International Journal* continue to demonstrate the truth of this affirmation!

Where We Headed Now?

In this, the final chapter of this study, I want to outline a number of possibilities for the development of black theology, within the United States and in Britain. By definition, given that I am not a clairvoyant, this chapter will be much more speculative than the ones that precede it. There is a sense that every black theologian could mount an impassioned claim for what they feel should be the essential priorities to which black theology should attend if it is to progress in the future. In that respect, I am no less opinionated and biased in my assertions than are my many peers. So, this assessment about where we are headed now is very much my own idiosyncratic take on what black theology should be doing and in which direction it should be moving.

In order to write this chapter, I have attempted a significant gear change, in that I have adopted a rather different methodology than that employed thus far, in order to emphasize the alternative role black theology can undertake in the future. This new future is one that is beginning to display all the hallmarks of being a new epoch, somewhat divorced from the macrostructural certainties that have governed us thus far. This new thematic approach to and methodology for doing black theology will be somewhat removed from the roots from which this discipline emerged in the late 1960s. This thematic approach is one that is drawn from my previous work.[1]

Black theology since its inception in the theological academy in the late 1960s and early 1970s has sought to radically redefine the very notion of God and the resulting activity and enterprise of theology. The work of first generation scholars such as Cone,[2] Roberts,[3] Wilmore,[4] and others have been supplemented by a later generation of womanist theologians such as Grant,[5] Cannon,[6] and Townes[7] who have used the black experience as the initial point of departure in the construction and articulation of their respective approaches to black theological discourse.

These and many other developments have made a notable contribution to the corpus of literature relating to the religious experience of black people across the world. What has been somewhat surprising and indeed quite remarkable, given the radical intent of the plethora of black theological work that has emerged in the past 30 or so years is the extent to which this discipline has continued to work within the conventional modes of scholarly inquiry within the academy.

The roots of the academy lie within monastic scholasticism with its emphasis upon hierarchical individual disembodied knowledge production, often fashioned for an elite peer group. The form in which this discourse is expressed is almost exclusively within a rarefied text-based format, in which the conventions of writing (densely, linear argumentation, complete with citations) seem to make little concession for those outside this self-defined group.

What I am not suggesting in this chapter is that this form of theological discourse lacks either legitimacy or efficacy. Rather, this chapter seeks to offer alternative vistas for the production of black theological thought.

Jazz Music as a Heuristic for a Future Trajectory for Black Theology

In this chapter I want to outline a means of reimaging black theology drawing on the aesthetics of jazz music, and attempt to put into practice some of the developing theoretical conceptions of an improvisatory approach to this discipline.

My introduction to jazz music did not come through the traditional route of being exposed to African American culture—that was to come later. One of the seminal moments in my life emerged when raking through my father's old record collection. What first sparked my interest in the wonders that is jazz music was listening to a record by the premier instrumental group in Jamaica during the 1960s—the Skatelites.[8] The Skatelites perfected a style of music that was a fusion of North American R & B and Caribbean Calypso.

I am not a musician of any sort, let alone a jazz one. In my attempts to use jazz music as a heuristic for engaging in black theology, I have sought to operate from within an artistic discipline in which I seem to possess a modicum of talent. In previous books, I have outlined an approach to undertake theological reflection by means of drama.[9] In my creative, dramatic writing, I have attempted to approach the task of writing dialogue and developing characters using a jazz aesthetic. Using jazz music, I have approached the task of constructing an improvisational based approach to doing black theology in order to empower marginalized and oppressed peoples.[10] In effect, I have sought to write drama as if I were a jazz musician. I have tried to capture the rhythms and cadences of jazz music by creatively putting words and dialogues together on the page. In both *Acting in Solidarity*[11] and *Dramatizing Theologies*,[12] and to lesser extent in this text (see the sketch "survivors" in chapter 4), I have approached the task of doing theology through scripted dramatic material to conscientize ordinary black people of faith. In these dramatic pieces, I have invited marginalized and oppressed peoples to improvise and play with reality, so that they might be inspired by the Spirit of God to imagine a new future—a future that exists beyond the constricted and limited world in which they presently live.

My intention in this chapter is to outline an approach to the doing of theology (in terms, of articulation and pedagogy) by drama, which is infused by jazz, improvisatory sensibility, in order to outline a playful and creative future for black theology that attempts to surmount the multiple chasms that seem to exist in a number of competing arenas. This approach to black theology is one that is very much indicative of my own chameleon-like tendencies, which, in many respects, reflects the idiosyncrasies of the scholarly journey I have taken thus far.

I have attempted to conceive of a future for black theology that tackles the dialectical tension between the church and the academy. It is a thematic and methodological approach that attempts to traverse the tensions between lay and ordained, between the church and the academy; it is one that tries to surmount the divide between systematic and practical theologies, between theology and education.

The central motif in this particular conception of black theology is one that borrows from the practice of improvisation in jazz music. It is a way of conceiving black theology with a view to developing a more accessible method for engaging in God-talk that is reflective of the experiences of black people and their accompanying expressions of faith.

I have chosen jazz music because although it is principally a North American art form,[13] the Diasporan links in the movements of peoples and cultures across the black Atlantic offers black British scholars such as myself an opportunity to appropriate the aesthetics of its practice for another context, for my own purposes.[14] Black British musicians such as Courtney Pine and Andy Shepherd have developed ways of harnessing the inspiration of African American practices and infused them with contextual sensibilities from within Britain, in order to create a means of playing jazz that is at once part of here, and yet also belonging to somewhere else. I have attempted to use some of the practices and themes inherent within jazz as a means of outlining a playful, interdisciplinary approach, to black theology for the twenty-first century. This thematic approach is one that is eclectic, elusive, and sufficiently elastic to incorporate a plethora of perspectives and concerns, which can narrow the conceptual and practical divides I outlined a short while ago.

Jazz, as a black Atlantic art form, links black theology in Britain and in the United States. In this respect, this thematic approach to black theology mirrors some of the ideas used by Robert Beckford in his work with dub music.[15] In both cases, Beckford and I have sought to utilize black Diasporan cultures, often invoking black speech patterns and aesthetics, in order to fuse Caribbean, British, and American sensibilities into a composite framework through which black theological thought can be undertaken.

In this chapter, I have created a piece of drama, which draws upon the methodology of my previous work,[16] in order to highlight the means by which the jazz aesthetics of improvisation can be used to speak to and reflect aspects of black British identities and cultures.

A Jazz Hermeneutic for Black Theology

I have chosen to describe this conceptual approach as a "A Jazz Hermeneutic for Black Theology" because I want to use jazz as a heuristic to describe a means of conceiving this discipline in a way that offers fluidity and elasticity in both its theorizing and practical application. Whilst I am advocating a model for black theology, which transcends the black Atlantic, I am also acutely aware of my own subjectivity in the theologizing process. I am a British-born black theologian of Caribbean roots. My parents are of Jamaican birth, and the cultures and social mores of that Caribbean island have influenced and shaped me.[17] I am at once situating my own point of departure whilst also establishing the contextual nature of this particular conceptualization of black theology. I would like to suggest, however, that the efficacy of this approach is not limited to those who might describe themselves as of African Caribbean descent. As I show in a short while, many of the salient features of this notion of black theology are already in existence within African American religiocultural practices and traditions. I have adopted jazz as framework for engaging in black theology due to the creative methodology to be found in the practice and skill of improvisation. I speak more on this practice in a short while.

By using jazz music as a heuristic, I hope to bring to life many of the salient features of this emerging theory for articulating and undertaking theology with marginalized and oppressed peoples. Jazz music, particularly when allied to the practice of ministry, especially those elements that fall within the wider purview of practical theology, can become a demonstration for the dramatic and improvisatory possibilities of such disciplines as preaching or Christian education, for example.

I believe that this approach to thinking about and discussing God in the context of jazz ideals and practice can enliven some of the worst moribund conceptions of Christian praxis in the early twenty-first century.

It's a Jazz Thing!

So before I begin on the odyssey of imaginative leaps and postmodern game playing, I must say something about my notion of a jazz hermeneutic. One of my favorite pastime activities is listening to jazz. Sadly, I do not play, and my technical sophistication in musical terms does not extend much beyond "that sounds great" and "I know what I like." A good friend of mine plays in a jazz band in Birmingham, in the West Midlands, and he has patiently and gently schooled me in the intricacies of the music over the past ten years.

My favorite musician is the great John Coltrane. Coltrane was born in a small town of Hamlet in North Carolina in 1926. Coltrane was the master of the tenor and soprano saxophone. His seminal album, entitled *A Love Supreme*,[18] recorded in 1964, is cited along with Miles Davis's *A Kind of Blue*[19] as being one of the most influential jazz LPs of all time. Coltrane's journey from jobbing pro to almost literal God-like status[20] began with a mystical experience in the early 1960s.

Prior to his spiritual awakening Coltrane's biography reads like the stereotypical tortured genius of a particularly bad black and white 1940s' Hollywood film noir. In jazz history, there is a distinctly sad litany of depressed broken people whose mock tragic lives stain the collective memory of this inventive and creative art form. These are predominantly African American men and women who were geniuses on the stage and broken, beaten down wrecks off it, people who could create sublime art in the moment of one's mind eye, in the time it takes to blink, and yet were often deemed subhuman creatures the moment they stopped playing or singing.[21]

In an attempt to traverse the huge chasm between the incandescently sublime and the absurdly and sinfully ridiculous, many of these luminaries turned to drugs and other forms of stimulants to help them make sense of the painful contradictions of genius but also barely human. Billie Holiday, Charlie Parker, Art Tatum, Lester Young, Ma Rainey, and my personal hero, John Coltrane, all succumbed to the pernicious threat stalking them, namely humiliation and absurd nothingness—the plight of being black people in a world of pernicious racism.[22]

But Coltrane was different. In the early 1960s, Coltrane underwent a period of distinct personal change. He described this as a spiritual awakening. He emerged from this period of change a profoundly different man. He renounced drugs and alcohol and dedicated his music to discovering the spiritual realm that flourishes within human experience and is evident across the whole cosmos. I would urge all preachers to listen to *A Love Supreme* for it is indeed a transcendent and mystical experience.[23]

Coltrane, like all the great jazz musicians, is able to straddle that delicate balance between that which is given and the newness of each performance or individual encounter with the tradition, which, in turn, yields new insights and knowledge. In metaphorical terms, this delicate process of living with the tensions of creating the new from the already established has been likened to the art of standing on a high backed chair and pushing that object onto two legs and seeing how far one can push and retain balance before you lose control and fall onto the floor.

Jazz musicians are constantly reworking an established melody in order to create something new and spontaneous for that split moment in time. Duke Ellington once remarked that there has never existed a jazz musician who did not have some inclination of what he or she was going to play before they walked onto the stage.[24] One's improvisation is never totally created or made up on the spot. One does not create new art in a vacuum. All jazz improvisation is a negotiation between what has been conceived previously and what emerges in that specific moment, either on stage or in the recording studio.[25] All great jazz has its antecedents. To quote my musician friend, "it all comes from someplace, it isn't entirely yours to make it up as you like; you have a responsibility for this stuff."

Jazz music is a potentially rich paradigm for all people involved in the task of doing, reflecting upon, and writing theology. I make this claim with one principal thought in mind, namely, that jazz music represents both the best and worst in human nature. It straddles the contradictions between a group of intensely fierce individuals who, at the same time, come together to join forces to make music.[26]

In my research I have spoken with a number of jazz musicians. From my conversations with these persons and my reading of autobiographical and biographical literature,[27] I have seen the ways in which the collective that is the jazz ensemble represents all the challenges of being an individual, as is the case in our personal existential relationships with God, alongside the perennial tension of being an individual while in the company of others. The latter is the challenge of attempting to share the same space and time with others, with whom you are called to work with and live in cooperation and mutuality—the others you are called to love, but whose personality may drive you to distraction, to drinks, drugs, and even violence. One can see clear evidences of these tensions in the accounts of the early Christian communities in the Mediterranean.[28]

The litany of fistfights, feuds, vendettas, and sheer enmity within jazz bands is legendary.[29] This tension of being an individual with one's individual relationship to the Divine and the need to engage with others is summed up in Jesus' great injunction to "Love the Lord God and your neighbour."[30] Those twin injunctions sum up the working dilemma of every jazz group there has ever been. It is the working dilemma of every community on earth. It is the tension at the heart of the Kingdom of God.

Jazz music is a voluntary engagement, for jazz is a form that eschews rigid conventions or categorizations. It demands mutuality and community, and yet it has, since the early 1920s, been built around the searing geniuses and contradictions of brilliant soloists. It is free form and yet demands certain rules and conventions working alongside and with others—those with whom one might not possess any sense of empathy or love, save for the act of making music in that split moment of time.

Jazz represents the tension between time and eternity, between immanence and transcendence, between the sense that art is created within and through context, and yet it appears to carry within it the traces of inspiration and magic that comes from another space and time. When theologians investigate the contradictions of individuality and community, between being bound by conventions and yet being compelled to go beyond all that is known and accepted as given, one is dealing with the most fundamental of existential concerns.[31]

The questions jazz poses are concerns for Christian faith and for all humanity. What does it mean to improvise on a given melody? How far can one go before what you are creating is no longer faithful to the melody and sources that inspired the artist in the first instance? How inclusive can we be? Can anyone join, or do we have or need certain limits or boundaries to help define who or what the band or the community is meant to be and become?[32]

Scholars have shown that jazz music is not just an inconsequential art form, rather, it is a depiction of the most central concerns of human identity and existence in the twentieth century.[33] Jazz music is part of a rich musical heritage. Older black musical traditions, like the blues, reggae, dub, calypso, spirituals, hymns, and gospel music, have offered us a rich tapestry of cultural production through which the theologian can mine in order to discern the liberative impulse of God. Jazz music has become an integral part of this crucial matrix.

Using jazz as a metaphor for doing black theology with the marginalized is to be engaged in the serious task of creating a framework in which all people are enabled to become participants in a process of critical thinking, reflection, and then action. What I like about jazz music is the sense that at its best, everyone gets his/her chance to shine. In extensive improvisation, everyone gets his/her moment in the sun—even the drummer! I am sure many of you know the joke musicians often make about drummers? "What do you call a drummer? Someone who plays with a group of musicians."

Drummers, thinking especially of Ringo Starr of "The Beatles," for example, often get a bad press! In conventional white dominated rock music, the drummer is rarely lauded when compared to the lead guitarist or the vocalist. Yet, in jazz, not only are drummers the bedrock of the rhythm section, but also have the potential to become band leaders, as can be seen the in the case of the late great Art Blakey and before him Chic Web.

Jazz music at its best gives everyone a chance. In linking the aesthetics of jazz music to the practical discipline of drama in which participants are enabled to improvise upon a written text and then explore it for new meanings and theological connections, I have attempted to create a model of theological exploration in which all persons are active participants. It is a model of theological inquiry that draws on the best traditions of jazz music—namely improvisation.

Locating Jazz Improvisation within the Religiocultural Practices of Black Churches

If you have lived through my jazz fuelled rhetoric up to this point, you will, hopefully, see the obvious analogies for the practice of ministry, particularly, within the black church. In this respect, I want to highlight one of the most distinctive elements of black Christian cultural aesthetics and theological practice, namely the highly visible rhetorical traditions in black homiletics. I want to link aspects of this improvisatory practice in jazz to the practice of preaching, particularly, within what is often termed a postmodern epoch.[34] The preacher is a mediator who brings forth the established presence of God as revealed in the "Word" and attested through tradition, tempered by reason, and affirmed by experience. The preacher is not asked to simply mimic or replicate the established or agreed upon melody.

Just as the jazz musician is not limited by the thinking or the intentions of the composer, so the creative and responsible preacher is not bound, in a restricted fashion, by Scripture. The encounter that exists in worship is an engagement between the text and the context. The text that is Scripture is no more a fixed entity than the composition and the melody that inspires the musician. Whereas the jazz musician uses the creative environment of the stage and club as the setting for the inspirational changes that emerge between the artist, the audience, his/her fellow players, and the melodic and compositional text, the preacher stands in the pulpit in worship.

The preacher is a negotiator between that which stands in and of itself and that which is yet to be. The former is the "Word of God," the latter is the word that speaks to the moment. This is a movement from the established to the newly becoming. The driving force is not some vague notion of inspiration, but the mediated presence that lies within the God-head, namely the Holy Spirit. The preacher, like the best jazz musician, is attempting to bring to life all the exhaustive riches and resources that have inspired and challenged countless generations before them.[35]

Within Black liturgical traditions, particularly within African American religious culture, many scholars have spoken of the dynamic interchange that exists between the preacher, the congregation, and the Holy Spirit. The Spirit of God that mediates between the different parties enables both the preacher and the congregation to respond to the creative moment and space that exists within the sanctuary at that precise time in history.[36] The "Call and Response" tradition of African American worship is a time-honored means by which the congregation can engage and interchange with the preacher in order that the latter might be enabled to go beyond the written text of the prepared sermon.[37] Essentially, that which has been prepared (not unlike the established melody or composition, whether on paper or in the mind of the musician) is energized and given new meaning and expression through performance. The congregation or the audience (whether in the night club or in church) becomes an essential ingredient in the performative act of bringing new wisdom and knowledge to life.[38]

Scholars such as Theophus Smith have termed this interchange "conjuration."[39] Dale Andrews argues that black preaching and the use of Scripture has always been a multilayered engagement between preacher, congregation, the Bible, and the Holy Spirit.[40]

For those who think that the connection I am making between a secular enterprise that is jazz music and the godly inspired business of preaching is much too contrived, let me remind them of the seminal work of James Cone, who argued for such a link in the early 1970s.

In his now landmark book *The Spirituals and the Blues*,[41] Cone argued against the prevailing thought that there was a clear dichotomy between the secular expression of African Americans on a Saturday night (the blues) and that which was exhibited in worship on a Sunday morning (the spirituals). Cone emphasized the continuity and continuum between the spirituals and the blues in a manner not dissimilar to my contention, namely that the best preachers are in effect operating within a jazz hermeneutic. Preaching can be likened to the art of improvisation, in which the person delivering the "Word" is being inspired to create new meaning, understanding, and relevance within the context of worship, in mutuality with others.

Improvisation, Reciprocity, and "Call and Response"

Fielding Stewart,[42] Dale Andrews,[43] Carol Tomlin,[44] and James Harris[45] have outlined the differing facets of black preaching and the relationship between the preacher and the congregation. Within black orality, there exists a mutuality and a connectedness between the main or principal speaker and the wider audience or congregation. The meaning and truth of any encounter does not reside solely with the speaker nor does it lie with the audience. The speaker is not an active force and the congregation or audience a passive one. Conversely, there is an ongoing process of negotiation between the principle speaker and those who are in attendance. The congregation or audience is an active force. Their engagement with the preacher is integral to the successful enactment of the sermon.

Within black milieus in which aspects of black cultural and religious experiences are evident, it is not unusual to encounter explicit or implicit examples of a phenomenon many scholars have termed "Call and Response." Tomlin defines "Call and Response" thus:

> In Call-response, the audience responds to the performer, who, in turn, shapes his or her performance according to the audience response. A favourable response will encourage the performer to continue in the same or similar vein; a muted response may suggest a change of course or new strategies.[46]

Whilst black preaching comes in many forms and incorporates a wide variety of styles,[47] the expectations placed on black preachers by their congregations are always high. Preachers are expected to be socially engaged, linking the story of the negated and troubled black self with the ongoing narrative of redemption and transformation that comes from God's very own self.[48] Similarly, the relationship between the musician and the audience in jazz music is a symbiotic one. Both parties feed off one another. The context provides the unique meeting ground between the various vested interests—the musician, the audience, and the fixity of the melody.[49] The melody, the previously composed music, in the presence of the performers and the audience, will be refashioned and remade, but never disconnected from its source or the traditions that first gave rise to it.

The dramatic possibilities in black preaching and the wider context of worship offer comparative points of analysis with jazz music (a "jazz hermeneutic") and the wider framework of "A Jazz hermeneutic for Black theology." The role of the preacher in black worship is that of the dramatic focus for the performative qualities of all the accompanying players.

This approach to black theology is one that utilizes a jazz hermeneutic within the context of drama and performance. I have sought to take the central ideas of jazz improvisation and relocate them within the more accessible practice of drama and role play. After all, as I can testify from personal experience, some of us cannot sing or play an instrument. Most of us, however, can speak, act, and perform.

In a jazz hermeneutic for Black theology, the process of theological reflection is facilitated by a collaborative process of interaction and engagement. This takes place within a participative "Call and Response" dynamic between the various players in the drama. In jazz, this interaction takes place between the musicians and the audience; in black worship, it exists between the preacher and the congregation.

So, in effect, I am attempting to juxtapose three interrelated realities. I want to use the theory and practice of jazz to provide the overarching framework in which black theology can be undertaken by utilizing the aesthetics of improvisation. This framework is then informed by looking at the practice of improvisation in jazz music and also within the practical theological discipline of Black preaching.

Finally, this two-way dialectic is then distilled into a triangulated heuristic by introducing the third element, which is the practice of improvisation in terms of scripted drama. The third element is intended to earth the more elitist practices of the aforementioned two contexts (musical performance and preaching that are the preserve of only a few) within a more accessible setting. This setting consists of ordinary black people improvising around a piece of scripted drama that I have written.

This method for improvising around written texts gives rise to a process for both the articulation and the doing of theology, which involves the active involvement of marginalized and oppressed peoples. This process is termed "jazz Hermeneutic for black theology." I believe that this process, taken from the practice of jazz music and evidenced in the historic practices of Black preaching, can enable black Christianity to remain true to its eclectic and improvisatory nature. This can be seen in the way in which a jazz hermeneutic for black theology can assist black people in their reading strategies, particularly in relation to the Bible.

Getting beyond the Old Dichotomies of "Evangelical" versus "Liberal" in Biblical Interpretation Through Jazz Improvisation

The beauty of improvisation, as I have hopefully demonstrated, is the facility it possesses to get us beyond the traditional, and dare one say, sterility of the perennial arguments around evangelical and liberal approaches to the Bible.

Improvisation within jazz music is neither stuck with the seeming rigidity of past, as represented by tradition, or with the perceived relativism of late and postmodernity. At the heart of the debates surrounding evangelical and liberal approaches to the interpretation of Christianity is the often thorny problem of Biblical authority. Yet, as Vincent Wimbush has illustrated, until quite recently, black people have not been consumed by such arguments surrounding the literal or more allegorical interpretations of the Bible.[50]

Prior to the 1940s and 1950s, black peoples' engagement with the Bible was not characterized by the sometimes arcane arguments around doctrine and metaphysical postulations. Rather, the critical question was what was going to alleviate our suffering, and how the Bible attested to God's solidarity with poor black people in the past, in order that the future could be redeemed.[51] This point is amplified by Vincent when he writes,

> African Americans interpreted the Bible in light of their experiences . . . As the people of God in the Hebrew Bible were once delivered from enslavement, so in the future, the Africans sang and shouted, would they. As Jesus suffered unjustly but was raised from the dead to new life, so they sang, would they be "raised" from their "social death" to new life. So went the songs, sermons and testimonies.[52]

James Cone argues that central motif within the metanarrative of the Bible is that of God's revelation in human history, exemplified in Jesus Christ, in order to liberate from oppression all those who have been *denied a voice* (italicized words are my emphases).[53]

Many marginalized and oppressed peoples have read and interpreted the Bible in light of their own context and experience. They have done so in order to locate the overarching truth of God's revelation in history. This process has involved them looking within and behind the text in order to locate themes that attest to the reality of their existential condition. With reference to the exodus motif within the Bible that was an emblematic theme for black people in South Africa during the epoch of apartheid, Robert Beckford writes

> For Blacks it was a paradigm (Exodus) of how God was going to set them free from the political bondage . . . Given the dangers of bias, ideological approaches to the text require a high degree of self awareness and also sensitivity to the bias within the biblical text and the context of the reader. Greater awareness forms part of the checks and balances of reading a passage of Scripture ideologically.[54]

Within the context of jazz music, the musician as I have outlined previously, is not limited by the notation or the exactitude of the melody as he or she has received it. The art of improvisation is a challenge to find new meaning and phrases to transform an existing melody, without departing from the original to such an extent that the previous incarnation is obliterated. In effect, it is the delicate synthesis of bringing the new from the old—bearing witness to what has gone before, but not being limited or constrained by it.

The need to bring new meaning and fresh insights from the Bible whilst remaining connected to the traditions that have informed the collective whole that is Holy Scripture has always been the high challenge presented to black preachers. It is the challenge to bring a fresh word for the immediate context without doing violence to the text from which one's inspiration is drawn.[55] Essentially, I am arguing that black preachers within the ongoing dynamic that is black worship are improvisers and that improvisation provides a helpful framework for helping us to move beyond the limited binary of evangelical and liberal arguments around biblical authority.

Jesus Was a Jazz Musician

I believe that Jesus shows us how to improvise within the context of his ministry. The numerous encounters Jesus has with others as detailed in the Gospels (I have always found Luke's accounts of particular help in this regard) are reminders of the power of improvisation. It is the power of responding to circumstances in such a way that the "giveness" of the context is radically realtered and something startling and new emerges. Whether it is Jesus' encounter with the Canaanite women (Matthew 15: 21–28) or the rich young man (Mark 10:17–22), the engagement with others inspires Jesus to bring about new insights and learning. This engagement is one that straddles the tension between that which exists (the tradition of Judaism) and that which is becoming (the reinterpretation of that tradition, leading to the emergence of Christianity).

Just as the jazz musician must engage with the context in which he or she is located, so too must the preacher. Whilst John Coltrane might play one of his celebrated compositions *Chasin' the Trane* hundreds of time in any one year, every individual performance of that piece would be unique. The context in which it might be performed, even if within the same club for an audience that might have heard this composition before, perhaps only some few hours previously, still remains a unique one. No two performances are ever the same, because the audience and how they respond to the time and space in which they are housed at that precise moment is never the same. The motivation, the concerns, and themes that exist outside of that time and space, from which they have emerged, is never identical.

The context in which the performance is housed is a unique cocktail of numerous pressures, expectations, and needs. The good musician is not only aware of these subtle nuances within the context, he or she responds to them, utilizing this stimulus to create new art from within the midst of existing knowledge and truth.

In this respect, the preacher is no different. Whatever our thoughts on the efficacy of reusing old sermons (I come from the school of "If it was worth preaching once then it can stand repetition"), the nature of worship and the encounter of each new context should bring new meaning to old words. If we are preaching in the power of the Holy Spirit, the dynamic interchange between the various elements that coexist in that time and space should ensure that our words are never stale. Playing the music of the sermon with panache and style should engage the congregation in such a fashion that their response galvanizes the preacher to new examples of improvisation.

From Contextual Theorizing to Textual Improvisation

In this section I want to offer an approach to conceptualizing black theology, which utilizes an improvisatory aesthetic in order to enable black people to rethink and reimagine what it means to be human within particular cultural milieus. In order to do this, I have returned to the methodology adopted in previous pieces of work as a means of attempting to bring this jazz-inspired conception to life. In *Acting in Solidarity*[56] and *Dramatizing Theologies*[57] I have used drama as a means of undertaking theological reflection.

Now I want to revisit this method and add to it the important mechanism of improvisation in order to help black people reflect upon the meaning of black religion and faith in the twenty-first century. The impetus for using jazz and improvisation as a heuristic for black theology arose from an encounter with a group of black young people in the West Midlands conurbation of Britain.

In my meeting with this group of black young people, I was struck by the extent to which many of them had become detached from the historic religiocultural mores of their parents and grandparents. All six members in the group had been socialized within, what one might term, a traditional black church setting. Yet, despite these strong formational religious roots, none of them in the group felt the black church remained a home in which they could continue to reside and express their speculative journeys of faith. I was struck by the realization that black theology for them seemed a distant and unrecognizable construct to which they had no relationship.

Dealing with the Realities of an Emerging Generation

One of the characteristics of the early industrial age of the nineteenth century was the homogeneity between people of different generations. I have written about this phenomenon in a previous publication.[58] Cultural icons such as Freud[59] and pyschosocial thinkers in the likes of Erikson[60] have written about the importance of compact and homogeneous settings. In using this phrase, such commentators are speaking of sociocultural contexts in which there is an appearance of sameness and a sense of continuity between people of different generations. This continuity and sameness ensured for an ongoing dissemination of cultural values between succeeding generations. This process ensured that the story of the community (and the sense of identity and matrices of values) was passed on with each newly emerging generation inheriting the codified cultural barometers that confer meaning from their elders.

Charles Foster has commented on the importance of each generation inheriting the narrative of the community. This inheritance should be formed in such a way as to enable the cultural transmission of those values, social mores, and cultures that leads to the preservation of such things, which enable any group to gain a sense of assurance for their continued existence.[61] As a religious educator, Foster's chief frame of reference is the church and the importance of each religious community passing on the faith to succeeding generations. Within a British context, where there does not exist the same self-conscious, overarching sociocultural and economic Christian framework that exists in the United States, there are, nonetheless, important questions of cultural transmission, not necessarily located solely within a Christian purview.

Before I attempt to identify the hallmarks of the increasingly visible phenomenon of youth culture within what one might term a postmodern epoch, I think it prudent that I highlight another important feature of the era that is modernity, from which we have moved.[62]

An important characteristic of modernity, particularly in the early years of industrialization, was the static nature of communities. It was assumed that there was little social or geographical mobility between or from within particular communities. It was thought unlikely that many young people would move extensively beyond the boundaries of the communities and social mores and value systems into which they had been nurtured. Clearly, this made the task of translating Christian faith and the values of Christian communities a relatively easier, if not a benign, task between generations.[63] Writers such as Anne Wimberly[64] and Joseph Crockett[65] have commented on the social cohesion between African Americans of different generations. This has been exemplified, primarily within the social phenomenon of the black church,[66] in order to explain the strong retention of cultural values within these often oppressed and marginalized communities.

It should be noted, however, that more recent work by the likes of Dennis Jacobsen[67] and Harold Dean Trulear has begun to challenge the traditional assumptions around notions of social location, sameness, and cultural values.[68]

In Britain, the prevalence of youth culture, as a distinct and marked alternative pattern of association and lived experience, provides one of the most significant challenges that face the nation in general and the church in particular. The age-old certainties of previous eras have disappeared. The certainties (some might argue the necessities) of each generation undoubtedly learning from the one that preceded it have gone.[69]

Many will argue that this development is not purely a postmodern phenomenon. The seeds for this change can be traced as far back as the 1950s and the post–World War II social dislocation of the old order that had existed prior to 1945. The rise in consumer culture and the development of young people, as distinct entities beyond the confines of the adult world (prolonged by the extension of tertiary education),[70] meant that the homogeneous thread that ran through many Western societies was broken. This development is indeed not new. Many will have lived through the epoch that saw young people dressing differently from their elders and the development of subcultures and forms of youth association from which older people were excluded.[71]

What marks out this era as markedly different from any that has preceded it is the sense that the proliferation of youth culture is no longer an internalized self-defining process of identity formation and boundary demarcation but mass consumerism driven by corporate business under the aegis of globalization.

I wonder to what extent the established theories for youth culture as subversive bottom-up constructs that imply a democratization of knowledge and the development of the self are now collapsing. Writers such as Borgman,[72] Epstein,[73] and Ward[74] are beginning to chart the new developments in youth cultures and their implications for youth ministry and the mission of the church.

Without wishing in any sense to sound either apocalyptic or defeatist, I want to provide a telling example of how youth culture has become a brand commodity, one in which, to a large extent, it is no longer controlled by young people themselves, but by those who see them as a blank tableau on which they can create their popularist images in order to extend their profit margins.

It can be argued that from the moment the Bobby Sox generation was manipulated into creating the young Frank Sinatra as a cultural icon (his clothes were made conveniently of flimsy substances in order that they would tear away when pulled by young girls), consumer marketing has been in evidence.

More recent creations from Doc Martins to face paint, studs, and zips to body piercing, there has been an interesting struggle between self-definition, generated from the bottom-up by young people, and consumer and media domination from the top-down. In our present age, it would appear that as our capacities to know have increased, chiefly through the proliferation of media outlets, conversely, our ability to make independent decisions may have diminished. The governance of what is "in" and what is not appears to be controlled by an ever increasing oligarchy of vested interests.

Yesterday Does Not Exist . . .

By way of an example, let me share with you an incident I witnessed a few years ago. One of the three main commercial television channels in Britain, Channel Four, commissioned a national poll to find the musical artists of the twentieth century. The poll was divided into a number of categories, from best solo artist to the best group, and so on. The results of this poll were hugely illuminating and, in many respects, highlight the unique and peculiar nature of the present age in which we are living.

I watched this program as a researcher in youth ministry, conscious of being (at the time) in my mid-thirties. Whilst undoubtedly past it, I was at least comforted (so I imagined) by the fact that I was not irrevocably estranged from the hinterland of youth culture and the experiences of modern youth.

My sense of complacency was to be rudely interrupted. The results of the poll illustrated clearly the postmodern feature of self-definition and knowledge of the "now" at the expense of any significant understanding of recent history or the antecedents of what is currently in vogue. The respondents to the poll, mainly young people between the ages of 14 and 25, identified their present heroes and heroines from present age—the MTV generation as the greatest performers of the century. Robbie Williams was greater than Frank Sinatra. Madonna was greater than Aretha Franklin. Oasis was better than the Rolling Stones. My memory of the revelatory evening was the sight of Beverley Knight, a highly respected black R&B singer in Britain, locked in an almost catatonic state, repeatedly exclaiming "Madonna, a better singer than Aretha Franklin? Hell, no, that can't be right? It just can't be right!"

The age divide was clearly evident for all to see. The ageing worthies on the panel were visibly shocked at the poll results. Could this really be the case? Well, obviously, it was. No amount of platitudinous and sententious moralizing was going to change the reality of these young people. In a postmodern era, for many young people, yesterday does not exist. Existence and truth is dominated by the here and now.

In some respects, this has always been the case. I am sure that my preference for the "now" of late 1970s Britain superseded my parent's love for Jamaican popular culture circa the late 1950s. The difference, however, was in my knowledge of the late 1950s Jamaican culture. I knew what I did not like, or could make a conscious comparison between the two eras. Many of these young people, when subsequently interviewed, were simply unaware of the claims of the icons that had preceded them.

Yet, speak to any cultural commentator and youth specialist and they will tell you that the features I have outlined in brief narrative is not the whole story. There is another story to be told. It is a story that involves a search for transcendence. This is a struggle for wholeness—a desire and a search for a viable spirituality by which they can live. David Hay has conducted important research over a number of years into the prevalence of spirituality in our seemingly postreligious age.[75] His investigations into the work of Alaistair Hardy, and the links between spirituality and zoology, have led Hay to ponder whether human beings are preprogrammed to incorporate a notion of spirituality within our being,[76] that is, are we "hot-wired" as spiritual beings?

The search for a viable framework that can transform the inner self and give meaning to external encounters with the "other" offer, I believe, is an important entrée for the Church to engage with the plural, constantly mutating realities that are youth cultures. The Church of Christ is the custodian of a metanarrative that contains within it the resources for transcendence and redemption. Questions of redemption are never far from the surface of human existence. Despite the bravado of some young people, one still hears the plaintive query, "Is this all there is?" The challenge for the church is to find ways of attempting to harness the realities of youth culture and the perceived all-pervasive nature of the global media that drives and feeds this ongoing development.

The critical failures of faith communities in the past when faced with this powerful synergy of youthful participation and media promulgation of lifestyle and consumer goods was the attempt to stand in the marketplace and denounce all such developments in the name of the Lord. This missiological enterprise was ill founded and hopeless.

In my work, I have attempted to create a schema that challenges young people to enter into dialogue with the antecedents of their existence, namely, to provide a context that can enable people of different generations to be in dialogue with one another.[77]

What this approach attempts is to locate a pragmatic and strategic method for enabling young people to improvise upon the narrative of their lives alongside that of the Gospel. This method is one that moves beyond the limitations of the unhelpful dichotomy between a rigid ultra conservatism that simply wants to replicate the past and an extreme form of liberalism that is seemingly prepared to jettison the past at the altar of contemporary relevance.

The process of sharing conversations between people of different generations[78] is one that attempts to bring the richness of the past and the resources that have affirmed and given meaning into dialogue with the present in order to help reframe and influence the future.

The challenge is not an easy one. The subversive nature of much that is youth culture (summed up in the often quoted adage "If you don't know, then you weren't meant to know") often defies categorization and oversight. The global powers of capitalism and mass marketing will not be easily deterred. Stoical inaction is not an option. Neither, for that matter, is inappropriate mock triumphalism. The challenge presents itself, but the church remains mandated to offer Christ as a response to the ongoing questions of being human in this and every age.

The question, then, remains: how can black theology provide a means of enabling postmodern black youth to interrogating their inner being in a manner that is cognizant of the past, but not wedded to it in a rigid, reified form? I believe a jazz hermeneutic for black theology provides a helpful way forward.

In order to put my theory in practice, I invited this group of six black young people to improvise on a dramatic text I had written. I wanted to see how using an improvisatory, jazz hermeneutic, this group of black young people could be encouraged to ask critical questions of their lives and the wider social context in which they lived.

The group was introduced to the following script, after we had spent several hours (over the course of three meetings) reflecting on our familial patterns, using the methodology I had first developed in *Faith, Stories and the Experience of Black Elders*.[79] The methodology in this book invites younger black people and children to enter into dialogue with their elders in order to ascertain how notions of continuity and discontinuity are expressed in their extended families.[80]

What emerged from these sessions were a number of concerns related to the experiences of these young adults with their older relatives, particularly grandparents. Their grandparents were all born in the Caribbean and had traveled to Britain in the 1950s and 1960s. Alongside the question of intergenerational tensions were an alternative set of concerns connected with identity and language. Many of the young people were keen to adopt stylized forms of speech patterns that mimicked Jamaican idioms as a means of affecting a form of identity that could be immediately construed as oppositional or subversive. These forms of signifying are reflective of more recent studies undertaken by the likes of Tomlin and Willis.[81]

The following dramatic piece will pose some difficulties for the bulk of African Americans, as it is written in Jamaican patois, a syncretistic dialect/language, which is reflective of the sociocultural identities of the predominantly rural, agrarian proletariat of that island. I adopted this form of idiom in order to pay homage to the eclectic and subversive nature of black linguistic speech patterns and the mythical social location and space it afforded these black young people. I hope that my North American friends will feel able to battle with the language and glean from the script some of the intergenerational tensions that exist in this fictional account of black, African Caribbean life in Britain.

The script is a humorous look at a particular dimension of black life in Britain. The young people enjoyed reading and performing the script and, through their utilization of an improvisatory jazz framework, were enabled to interpret and reinterpret the piece, going beyond the scripted drama in order create their own hermeneutic of this black cultural scenario.

What is the Real Deal?

By Anthony Reddie

No. 1: Now I'm sure that for many of us who have grown up in families with grandparents who originally came from the Caribbean, there has been one question that has been on our minds for a very, very long time. That question is, when your grandparents are angry and they begin to chat the hard, back a yard talk . . . What do they mean and what are they trying to tell us?

No. 2: Well, at great cost and after much research we have now have the real deal. The truth behind the tough talk!

No. 1: So, as say they down at the local Conservative club when they want to hear a nice tune again.

No. 2: Wheel and come again my selector.

No. 1: (*Doubtful*) Yes! So let us begin. We give you a guide to understanding the real meaning behind those phrases they use. For instance, when your grandmother looks at you hard one Sunday morning and says

No. 2: Kiss mi neck back!

No. 1: What she really means is

No. 2: Yu blin' or jus' stupid? You mean fi put on dem dutty crease up blue jean an' wear dem to church dis marning? Yu 'ave noh shame? Yu nah walk nex' to mi wi dem hugly tear up sint-ting "pon yu behin." Gallang!

No. 1: On the other hand there is another situation to mention. Your grandfather has just told you off and you decide to pull a face because you don't like what he said. Unfortunately, your grandfather sees you pulling the face when you think he isn't looking. He is not pleased. In actual fact he is vex. He looks at you and says

No. 2: See yu? Yu face favour ginny fowl. If yu would a' come from the Guinea Coast dem would a shoot yu.

No. 1: What he means by this statement is

No. 2: First, if yu t'ink sey yu is too old fi some ol' fashion lashing, yu is wrong. An' second, stop pull dat hugly face. Face like dat go'n spoil de milk.

No. 1: He finishes by saying

No. 2: An' nuh bodder t'ink sey yu can use fi my shaver again. Now yu is man, or so yu t'ink, yu better buy yu own bart'room business an' leave fe me t'ings alone. Yu wort'less wretch yu!

No. 1: Dinner times are usually times for a great deal of bodderation and argument. You know the situation. At the dinner table your grandmother stares at you as you begin to eat down the whole house. She shouts.

No. 2:   But wha' mek unno pickney so craven hi?

No. 1:   When your grandmother says these words she means

No. 2:   How com' yu wan' eat off de las' piece a' chicken wen mi not even get one piece fi eat yet? Dis, after you niam five piece a' chicken, three plate a' rice, four boiled dumplins, a whole heap a' salad and two big glass of carrot juice. Yu t'ink me can liv' 'pon fresh air?

No. 1:   She looks at you hard and then says

No. 2:   Bwoy, yu craven fi real.

No. 1:   At this point, it's no good trying to hand back that last piece of chicken when you've already taken two big bites out of it. This does not please your grandmother. She shouts.

No. 2:   But wait! Yu a' han' mi fi yu bite up chicken? Is who yu t'ink mi is? Darg?

No. 1:   The next area of contention is the question of money. Or to be precise the lending of money. You can imagine the situation. You need some money desperately, so you approach your grandfather and ask him. Your grandfather looks at you and says

No. 2:   Bwoy pickney, if yu wan' good den yu nose mus' run.

No. 1:   When your grandfather says this what he means is

No. 2:   So wha' wrong wi yu han'? Yu sick or somet'ing? Yu 'fraid a' wok? Yu wan' mi fi gi yu money so yu can skylark an' mek fool, while ol' man like mi 'ha' fi wrestle ol' iron seven day a' week? Bwoy, yu mus' tek mi fe idiot.

No. 1:   But you reply, "I'll pay you back. I need that money." Your grandfather kisses his teeth and says

No. 2:   *(Kisses teeth)* Wanty wanty nuh getty getty. Getty getty nuh wanty wanty.

No. 1:   Yeah! Right! Thanks Pops.

No. 2:   And one las' t'ing. Nuh bodder pull dat hugly face again. Mi nuh wan' yu fi crack de mirror. Yu know how dis ya family bad lucky already.

No. 1:   Another situation I would like to bring to your attention is this one. You are going out to a beach party. Beach appearance is absolutely necessary. So you put on your most outrageous clothes you can find and are about to leave the house when both your grandmother and grandfather see you. They throw their hands into the air and exclaim.

No. 2:   Massi Puppa mi dead.

No. 1:   Now at this point I have to be honest. There isn't any translation for this. You simply grab your coat and run out of the house shouting, "I'll see you later. Don't wait up for me." As you leave you can see your grandparents shaking their heads. Your grandfather looks at your grandmother and says

No. 2:   De bwoy get 'im stuppidness from yu, yu know?

No. 1:   Your grandmother disagrees. She says

No. 2:   But wha' mek yu love tell lie so? Is your family who all fuh-fool. See dem? De whol' a' unno fool to ra . . .

No. 1:   I think we'd better stop that conversation right there. I don't think the church is the right place for such talk. But any one who has ever seen their grandparents arguing will know that when the child returns from the beach party next morning, the grandparents are still stood on the doorstep having exactly the same argument they were having before. Now your grandfather is saying to your grandmother

No. 2:   My family nuh fool. See your family? All a' dem a' stiff idiot. Yu nuh rememba yu Uncle Desmond? De man so fool 'til . . . De whole neighbourhood always call 'im "dutty face Desmond." 'im so fuh-fool, 'im not even know how fi wash imself. De man frownsey like tom-cat.

No. 1:   At this point you walk past them into the house and go to bed, leaving them arguing on the doorstep. They've been arguing for so long, neither of them knows what the argument is about. They certainly don't remember that it was over you that they began to argue in the first place. The next difficult situation you run into is when your grandmother finds that one of her prize glasses has been broken. You know that prize glass? The one inside the glass cabinet in the front room! That glass cabinet that has not been opened for twenty years. The glass cabinet that only big people over the age of fifty can open. That prize glass is in that cabinet which is in that room where no unruly pickney should ever set foot. But the glass is broken and your grandmother says to you

No. 2:   Tell me somet'ing! Is yu who break fi me expensive glass? Tell de trut' an' shame de devil.

No. 1:   What your grandmother really means is

No. 2:   No bodder tell mi no bare face lie. Mi know it yu who bruk de glass. No odder somemaddy live in a' dis ya house. An it nuh yu Puppa or yu Mumma who bruk de glass, so it mus' a' yu. Yu know how lang mi did 'ave dat glass? An' now yu com' wi yu disruptive self an' mash it up. Well, yu betta know dis. Yu go'n pay fi dat glass. Mi wan' every last red cent fi pay fi it. Yu 'ear mi?

No. 1:   Yes Granny. You see. There are somethings that will never change. Grandparents will buy things and children

No. 2:   Pickney!

No. 1:   Yes, pickney will mash them up. It's part of the contract. Grandparents buy and pickney destroy. That is how it goes. Now the final area of contention is when it comes to the question of chores. Duties in the house. Your Grandmother has just told you to get out of bed and vacuum the floor. But you were out 'til late the previous night partying. Fi yu body tired. You just cannot get out of bed. Your grandmother fires open the door and shouts.

No. 2:   But wha' mek big bwoy love sleep sleep so?

No. 1:   When your grandmother says this, what she really means is

No. 2:   But mi dyin' trial. Mi never see such a' lazy, wort'less, gravillicious, slabba-slabba yout' in all a' me days. Com' out a de bed now!

No. 1:   At this point a broom handle is introduced into the proceedings. The broom jucks yu right in your stomach and you have to come out of bed. Your grandmother tries to juck you with the broom handle again, but this time you catch hold of it and say, "But granny, there's no need to do that. I'm getting out of bed." But you have made a big mistake. You shouldn't have tried to catch hold of the broom handle. Your grandmother says.

No. 2:   Ah oh! So yu wan' fight me now? So yu tin'k sey mi an' yu is size? Well mi go'n show yu somet'ing.

No. 1:   At this point, your grandmother runs to get that big belt your grandfather wears to hold up his best trousers that are really too big for him, whilst you flash on your clothes and begin to run for the door. Your grandmother is following you shouting.

No. 2:   Is wey yu a' go? Mi nuh don' wi yu yet. Com' back an' tek lick.

No. 1:   You shout out, "Granny, I'll come back later. When you're in a better mood." Your grandmother shouts.

No. 2:   Nuh ax' mi ax yu. A' tell mi a' tell yu. Com' back.

No. 1:   But you're not coming back. You run off into the blue wide yonder, with the voice of your grandmother shouting after you.

No. 2:   Mi a' wait fi yu. Yu should a' stay an' burn, nuh turn an' run.

No. 1:   After some ten hours you think it is safe to return home. You slip back into the house with a big bunch of flowers in your hand. The house is empty. Perhaps your grandmother has gone out? All is quiet. She's probably asleep you think to yourself. She'll have forgotten. I'll put the flowers on the table with a nice little note saying I'm sorry for staying in bed when I should have been vacuuming the floor. I'll go to bed, and in the morning everything will be all right. All of sudden you see out of the corner of your eye the broom handle flying towards you, followed by the words . . .

No. 2:   So yu t'ink sey mi done? Mi not even start yet.

No. 1:   Grandparents, especially our grandmothers are like elephants. They don't stand for no foolishness.

No. 1 and 2:   And they never forget.

No. 1:   Thank you.

No. 2:   The end.

Reflections on the Sketch

This script, and the approach within it, draws upon my previous research in which drama was used for undertaking theological reflection. In it, I have attempted to juxtapose two realities—namely the past and the historic values of hard work, thrift, duty, and responsibility, as represented by the black elders—alongside the future and the seemingly rebellious response of the youth. This sketch is a humoros exploration of the tensions involved in intergenerational discourses, in which questions of continuity and discontinuity are never far from the surface. It is an essentialist/nonessentialist dialectic, in which the struggles between the established and the emerging are constantly at war with one another.

The sketch was used with these young people in order that they might explore how, through using an improvisatory framework from jazz music, it might be possible to navigate a middle way between the two competing cultural extremes.

The sketch was used on a subsequent occasion with a group of older black people all of whom were preachers (lay and ordained) in their different denominations, where I challenged them to see how an improvisatory framework applied to this text might enable them to create a jazz hermeneutic for their preaching. How might one address issues of conflict resolution and intracommunal tensions such as the ones found in early Christian communities, by reflecting on this sketch using a jazz hermeneutic?

Questions of Language

The sketch makes extensive use of Jamaican patois, which operates as a form of signifying, alerting us to the subversive and complex positionality of black language when used within a black subcultural setting.[82] In using this script with the group, I was interested in exploring the use of language amongst these African Caribbean young people, all of whom were in their late teens. To what extent does Jamaican patois function as a legitimizing code for black self-authentication? It was interesting to note that some members of the group seemed more at ease with the language than others. Constraints of time prevent any significant analysis of the outcomes of the particular form of interaction with these black youths.

By utilizing an improvisatory model of engagement within this Jamaican/Caribbean form of dialogical discourse through the medium of drama and dialogue, it is my hope that there may arise from this conceptual framework a dialectical form of knowledge that affirms the theory and the practice of black theology.

The sketch, highlighting as it does, complex issues of black relationships, models of authority, changing values between the generations, and use of language in black discourse, provides an interactive and accessible model for constructing black God-talk. If God is black within the context of black ontological and existential experience, then *she* speaks in Patois, Ebonics, or some other linguistic code or idiom that is indicative of black selfhood and identity.

A feature of this sketch is the seeming breach between the contemporary experiences of the younger person and the two older people. I do not want to suggest that the scenario in this sketch group is in any sense archetypal of the experiences and cultural mores of all postmodern black British youth. Clearly, not all young people are informed by an eclectic and pluralistic set of environmental and psychological factors that affect these yang adults. Also, their initial socialization within a Jamaican-influenced context is one that is not representative of all black people of African descent within the religiocultural landscape of this country or in other contexts across the length and breadth of the African Diaspora.

Reinterpreting *What is the Real Deal* in Light of a "Jazz Hermeneutic for Black Theology" and Ministry

In order to locate my rereading of this dramatic sketch in terms of black theology, I want to return, once again, to the practical theological discipline of preaching. The art, discipline, and practice of preaching in light of the black experience in black majority church settings have always carried with it a distinct ideological and theological stance. The subjugated selfhood of black people, distorted and abused by the ravages of racism and white hegemony, has responded to and taken their cue from the preacher for a positive vision of what it means to be a black human being.[83] Grant Shockley has outlined the educational role played by the pastor in many black churches, whether in an explicit dialogical form in the sermon, or more implicitly, in the realms of pastoral care.[84]

I now want to look at this sketch through a dialectical approach, one that interrogates the text, in addition to utilizing the creative engagement of the participants, whose presence brings the flat script to life. What the participant brings to the text by way of his/her performance is as valuable in terms of interpretation as are the perspectives of the author. The author does not have the last word.[85]

This dialectical relationship between the text and the performer finds echoes in the world of biblical interpretation.[86] The similarities, however, extend way beyond biblical studies. This dialectical exchange is also reflective of the relationship between the jazz musician and the inherited melody, and the preacher in their relationship with the biblical text and Christian tradition in the sermon.

In the sketch, the different characters are engaged in an ongoing process of negotiation about truth. Each of the three characters try to assess their relationship with another and their understanding of black cultural life, moral values, and familial practices. This ongoing negotiation is reflective of the relationship between jazz musicians and other members of the band. The band requires the active involvement and engagement of all members in order for it to function optimally.

In the sketch, the different characters are each trying to impose their perspective on the truth of that situation on their peers. This tendency, although perfectly natural[87] is, nonetheless, a misguided process, for it simply weakens the corporate whole. The effective working of the collective,[88] whether within the drama, the jazz band, or in worship, requires the cooperation of all individuals.[89]

Similarly, within the context of black worship at its best, the preacher is negotiating with the text and the congregation. The ongoing dynamic that is worship within many black majority churches is, to me, reminiscent of many of the features in evidence in the sketch. Speculating on the life of the characters beyond the written text, I am convinced that their sense of well being would be enhanced, if they were able to seriously engage with one another as I have outlined in a "Jazz Hermeneutic for black Theology."

Remaking the Moment Every Time

Just as the jazz musician has to respond to the unique context of every performance, bringing new knowledge to life, in the split second, so too must the preacher. The preacher has to respond to the promptings of the spirit and the expectations and needs of the congregation. The preacher cannot rely upon what was said the previous week or in a past service—the past in this respect is a foreign country to which there is no return. Even replaying the old sermon, repeating the existing words of the text, is never the same, even second time around.

The uniqueness of each occasion demands a freshness of approach and ingenuity of the occasion. The new performance remains connected to past versions of the melody. Whilst the two performances are similar, they are never the same. Similarly, with the preacher, past dramatic performances of the sermon in worship may influence the present, but each new enacted sermon is unique in its own right.

The performative integrity of the preacher in bringing new knowledge to life within the context of worship is reflected in the ongoing dynamic of action and reflection in the dramatic performance of the sketch. Working with the group who performed *What is the Real Deal?* on no less than six occasions was an interesting process. What emerged from the various performances were a number of reflections, which highlighted the differing perspectives and perceptions of the six participants. Each new performance gave rise to new insights and knowledge. Romney Moseley argues that a process of repeated performance and the ongoing analysis of reality and subjective selfhood aid critical reflection.[90]

Just as the participants in the drama constantly re-engage and re-negotiate with the text, this is equally the case with the preacher and the jazz musician. The improvisation of the jazz musician is built around the process of engaging with the inherited melody and then having the confidence to go beyond the fixed nature of the text. The improvisation is the link between the fixity of the text and the openness of the context.

In the many performances of *What is the Real Deal?* I have witnessed, it has been interesting to observe the ways in which the various participants are enabled by repeated performance to go beyond the limits of the text. Whilst the improvisatory process often lacks the sheer verve and loose-limbed creativity often found in jazz or in preaching, there is, nonetheless, a genuine development of new ideas and thinking, which takes the participant beyond the conventional limits of the drama.

What Does This Suggest for Working with a Postmodern Generation?

Working within the framework of a jazz hermeneutic for black theology is to appreciate that there exists a means by which one can be faithful to one's oral traditions and heritage of faith,[91] whilst being open to the future possibilities of a new epoch. Jazz music reminds us that we are not restricted to the binary of "either or," rather, it is "both and."

The realities of the postmodern epoch is that we can no longer assume that the old, old story of how we got over will captivate or energize a younger generation for whom there exists new contextual struggles and dangers. Of course, many of us of an older vintage will recognize that these new struggles are simply the old ones in new clothes; but each generation must discover this fact for itself.

A jazz-inspired approach to black theology will challenge the church to extricate itself once and for all from the bulwark of nineteenth-century white, European-inspired evangelicalism and its fixed, reified, none improvisatory approach to Christian faith. This approach is one, that has emerged from a tainted source, as black people know, at their cost.

A jazz-inspired approach to black theology will eschew the rigid biblical literalism that is causing many of our educated and critically thinking black young people to despair of the black church, seeing it as a haven for nonthinking, simplistic rhetoric, as opposed to the prophetic laboratory of conscientization it has been in its historic past.[92]

Guiding Principles for a Jazz Inspired Approach to Being the Black Church in the Twenty-First Century

The theological and anthropological point of departure; remains the conviction that we are all created in God's image and are valuable in God's sight. This needs to be reaffirmed constantly, because at various times in history, particular ideologies have attempted to create hierarchies of importance based on specific, elected groups of people.[93] In many respects, all human beings are more alike than they are different.[94] Not only are we all created in God's image, *in some respects, the transformed life of spirit transcends all our differences and makes them of limited or even no importance.*

The previous point is in italics because it encapsulates one of the enduring tensions within human communities. It is one of the tensions that confronts the black church as we step hesitantly into the twenty-first century. How important is our particular ethnicity and the cultures and traditions that arise from that? Ethnicity, and culture are all part and parcel of what it means to be human.[95]

There are dangers when we become too fixated on issues of race, ethnicity, cultures, and notions of being different.[96] Those who focus on blackness as essential in the construction of one's identity will usually use ideas around black cultures as a central point in their argument. In seeking to reflect upon the ongoing influence of blackness, we must be careful not to invest this area of black experience with notions of mythical and romanticized power. Cultures should not be seen as distinct material entities in and of themselves. Cultures are constructed by human action and imagination.[97]

To focus upon black culture as a material entity in and of itself, as if it has a static existence beyond the experiences of the people who are constantly recreating it, is to run the risk of romanticizing black culture. Such romantic myths surrounding black culture are often used to create forms of counterresistance to white power and authority. Examples can be seen in various forms of black nationalism, in which people who are not black (particularly white people) are often demonized.[98]

Yet, there are dangers in ignoring the realities of our differences, particularly those around what it means to be black. The notion of affirming ones' blackness has been a reaction to the reality and the sin of white supremacy.[99] How can we deal with imbalances in power and influence if we do not deal with the reality of who we are and what constitutes our identities? Many will argue that acknowledging and celebrating blackness is a way of affirming the basic sense of one's identity.[100]

Things We Can Learn from Pentecost—A Model of Handling Difference

In a previous chapter on Christian education, I used a case study based on Acts chapter 2 and Pentecost as a means of offering us a pneumatological paradigm for reimaging the Godly inspired notions of being community. This notion of community is one that eradicates the restricted, discriminatory, and bounded realities in which we presently live. Given the central importance of the spirit in black religiosity,[101] I want to return, albeit briefly, to Pentecost once again, as a means of helping black Christianity to deal with postmodern difference within its own ranks.

Cain Hope Felder, the respected biblical scholar, in his commentary on the Pentecost narrative, identifies the references to Mesopotamia, Pamphylia, Egypt, and parts of Libya near Crete[102] as being places connected with Africa. Felder and others[103] are asserting both a black presence in the Bible and a black, African-centered form of interpretation for reading the Bible. There is 'difference' at the heart of this story. The people are transformed but their differences—the uniqueness of their identities—does not disappear. Many of these people at the heart of the story are black, so being black is important and should not be relegated or downplayed as being of no consequence or value. Just as the Incarnation—Jesus' historical presence in the world shows that being flesh, being human, and living in a particular time and space is important,[104] so too does Pentecost. Pentecost shows that the Holy Spirit does not eradicate our differences, rather the Spirit celebrates them.

Life in the Spirit is about being one in Christ, in fellowship with each other. Being in community with each other and with Christ can transcend what it means to be linked to a particular identity—in this case, being black, male, female, gay, or straight. The status that is often linked to particular identities (being male, or being a Jew, for example.) is exploded. The Spirit transcends all this.[105]

So there is a tension between these two differing ways of seeing identity, that in Christ, the differences around ethnicity or gender are overcome and made irrelevant; but also the counter view, that in Christ, we come to celebrate those very things as essential parts of who we are. How can both be true?

Back to this Jazz Thing Again!

For an answer, let us look again at the practice of jazz music. Jazz musicians are constantly reworking an established melody in order to create something new and spontaneous for that split moment in time in mid performance. It is a negotiation between the individual musician, their fellow musicians (or the vocalist in the band if there is one), and the inherited melody written by the composer.

For all the great jazz musicians, their art is a delicate balance between that which is given and the newness of each performance or individual encounter with the tradition, which in turn yields new insights and knowledge.[106] In effect, Jazz is never "a" or "b," but is always "a + b," that is, improvisation means that you are never stuck in one place doing simply one thing without it changing. Human beings are never locked into being just one thing. Just as a jazz musician can improvise upon a melody, thereby, being able to build on what has gone before without ever completely forgetting about it, so too can human beings. Our identities and subjectivities are never fixed.

Black people are able to celebrate what it means to be black and can acknowledge that their blackness is essential to their identity and their sense of self; but they are not locked into it. It does not define them completely. They can improvise on it.

Using a jazz hermeneutic for black theology, for example, we can see how one can celebrate particular characteristics of being who we are (in terms of race, ethnicity, cultures, gender, sexuality), but that celebration brings us into communion with others rather than separates us.

Due to the prevalence of racism, however, and other imbalances in power, disadvantaged groups will always need to create their own (exclusive) networks in order that they can become more complete and full members of the body of Christ. This has been and remains the enduring genius of the black church.

Remaining Lessons to Be Learnt by the Black Church

As I outlined in chapter 4, one of my scholarly heroes was the late Grant Shockley. Grant Shockley was, for over 30 years, one of the most urgent and insistent voice for a perspective on the teaching and learning of the Christian faith that engaged with the realities of the black experience.

In one of his most withering polemics, he asked the urgent question (I am paraphrasing in the interests of brevity) *when will the Protestant church begin to practice what it preaches?*[107] Shockley, reflecting upon the African American experience of racism, marginalization, and prejudice, often at the hands of good white Christians, wondered what had been the prevailing understanding of Christianity amongst the white Christian majority in the United States.

I hold a very similar view. Britain, although less pronouncedly religious than the United States, nevertheless, has a rich and distinctive history that is reflective of Christian values and the language of the Christian faith. And yet, despite this impressive heritage, it has not stopped racist ideas and bogus assumptions about black people inflicting the practice of being church.[108]

Once again, white majority churches failed to bridge the gap between "talking the talk and walking the walk."[109] While the rhetoric has been eloquent and persuasive, the practice has been a great let down. In fact, I would argue that the practice has not only left a great deal to be desired in its blatant contradiction of the fundamental tenets of the gospel, it has disgraced the name of Christ, and been a perversion of God's redemptive act of grace displayed in the life, death, and resurrection of Jesus.[110]

We Must Move beyond Neoconservatism

In order to address the challenge of postmodernism, the black church, inspired by an improvisatory approach to black theology, will gain the confidence to move beyond the strictures of a stultifying form of conformity into which so many of us have been herded. In a previous work I have questioned the conformist strains of many black churches, which, in many instances are governed by twin concerns of "shame" and "racism."[111] Scholars such as Kelly Brown Douglas,[112] Robert Beckford,[113] Jacquelyn Grant,[114] and myself[115] have all explored in our many differing ways, the challenge faced by the black church to move beyond the seemingly endemic forms of conservative thinking and practice that has limited the scope of its prophetic agency.

As the black church seeks to engage with the challenge of attempting to assist a postmodern and disaffected younger generation to see the merits of Christian faith within its own auspices, one is forced to ask a crucial set of questions: Into what entity are we hoping to socialize these young people? What are they and we to learn? To what end are we all being nurtured as disciples?

In the last section of this text I want to flesh out some important characteristics of a postmodern black church that is open to real and dynamic learning and nurturing. This is a form of transformative learning, which draws on the aesthetics of jazz music and improvisation, in order that we can learn to be different, a form of difference that is more open and capable of being inspired by the Spirit of God to become a new dynamic sign of God's reign or rule.[116] I have highlighted these important markers for a new way of being church under three headings.

1. *Open to embracing difference*—The maxim "unity in diversity" is one I have lived with since the heady days of the antiapartheid movement of the 1970s and 1980s.[117] As a black male born in Britain, I have witnessed the attempts of many black churches in my own country to be truly countercultural by speaking out against the seemingly all-pervasive racism and reactionary tendencies of the so-called white Middle England; yet, despite these laudable attempts, they still manage to be wonderfully exclusive and reactionary in their own ecclesiological practices.

To be open to embracing difference is to be open to the spirit of God that unites us (not as the same) into one dimension—The body of Christ. Our way of being church must move beyond the tyranny and blandness of homogeneity into a new way of being the people of God, where we are constantly asking ourselves, "Is this way of being church reflective of *all the* experiences of *all the* people represented within Christ's body?" Are our liturgies, prayers, stories of faith, Bible study groups, and fellowship meetings enabling all people to be themselves? who 'wins' and 'loses' in our present way of being church?

2. *Open to enabling all people to be their authentic selves*—One of the most unhelpful legacies of church history and the development of Christian thought has been the dichotomy between matters spiritual and temporal. The early Church Fathers, many of whom had drunk rather too liberally from the well of Hellenistic thought, were notorious for creating an unhelpful dichotomy between spirit and matter.[118] The spirit and the abstract became more important and preferable to that which might be seen as the material and concrete. This form of dichotomy found its way into the thinking of the early church and became enshrined in Christian thought, particularly in the area of sexual matters.[119]

In our present age, as we bask in the early dawn of the third millennium, we are still struggling with a host of dichotomies: the divide between secular and religious, between Sunday and the remainder of the week—the latter being the place that houses the self, which lives in such a dichotomous unholy existence. Our communities of faith must be places where people can be their authentic selves—that is, the multiple "I's" and the 'warts and all I' which spends the majority of its life in an imperfect world, rather than the often self-conscious mannered universe that is the black church.[120]

In many respects, the creation of this open and inclusive church where people can be themselves is not a wholly novel idea. Speaking as a Methodist, I look back with a modicum of pride, at the ingenuity and farsightedness of John Wesley, who knew that the quest for scriptural holiness could not be affected within the wider arena of secular self-interest or in a setting of self-conscious church piety.[121] He advocated that the saints meet in small "class meetings" in order to work through and develop the necessary qualities for their growth in grace.[122]

I realize that the realities of the twenty-first century are a world away from the high water benchmark of eighteenth-century Methodism and the evangelical revival, but we must find new ways of doing old and trusted things. People need to find a place where the good, the bad, and the down right ugly can hang out and get a hearing. Finally, we need to embrace the courage to look at the Bible anew.

3. *Open to a critical rereading of Scripture*—By this I mean that we need to embrace the insights of Postcolonial readings of Scripture, and to hear the muted voices of the poor and marginalized in God's purposes for God's own creation. Writers such as Sugirtharajah and his seminal text *Voices from the Margin*,[123] plus Musa Dube,[124] and Justin Ukpong, and others[125] have much to teach us about a critical rereading of the Bible in which the perspectives of the silent majority of the earth are heard, with their viewpoints becoming the focal point for a shared learning and empowerment of all people.

This is a process of looking at the Bible through the eyes of the poor and the marginalized in a manner that extends beyond the parameters of simply race and racism. This will enable us to learn radically new insights about what it means to be church and to be the people of God, instituted by the spirit, in order to bear witness to the Gospel of Jesus Christ. A radical rereading will enable us to see Paul's injunction in Galatians 3:28 no longer as a proof text to justify a constructed notion of sameness—in effect, a color blind theology that has captured many black evangelicals; but rather, it becomes a radical ideal in which distinctions between "in groups" and "out groups" are obliterated. A new reading moves us into a model that affirms difference, but outlaws preferential treatment based on ideas of election and preordained acceptance for some and the exclusion of others on grounds of race, gender, or sexuality.[126]

Similarly, this new form of rereading for a radically new way of engaging with Scripture will enable us to see the cautionary tale of Babel (Genesis, chapter 11), not as a spiritualized rebuke to human kind and its vanity, but as a challenge to accept that corporate aggrandizement and globalized power, masquerading as allegiance to God will not be tolerated. Black people know first hand what it means to be on the receiving end of powers and principalities that seek to disguise their evil intent by wrapping themselves in the alleged word of God. Postcolonial theologies are reminding us that there is another tale to be told, and that God's word should never be equated solely with the voice of the winners in history.[127]

In conclusion, then, to be open to being new black churches in the twenty-first century is to fashion new understandings, relearning old tricks, and finding new ways of interpreting the word of God. Until and unless this form of learning and nurturing is embraced, we will fail to be all that we can and should be.

And in the end . . .

This study has been my attempt to chart my own personal journey as a black theologian and educator. I have sought to retrace my steps, looking from inside my own context, at the wider expanse of the black Atlantic, in order to learn from the established older sibling that is African American black theology. In order to accomplish the second half of this theological conceit, I have had to adopt the position of an outsider, looking into a foreign context, namely the United States.

This text has sought to both acknowledge the huge debt black religious scholars from the various locations in which the black experience is housed owe to our African American brothers and sisters, and attempt to critique that ongoing dominance. I have written as a black British theologian and educator, whose work has been heavily influenced by North American black and womanist theologies.

This study has attempted to bring these two seminal influences—British and the American—into a dialectical conversation surrounding the efficacy, influence, and future trajectory of black theology. I am aware that many of my colleagues in Britain, particularly those who have Caribbean roots like myself, will be dismayed at the extent to which I have favored the United States at the expense of the Caribbean. My engagement with the United States as opposed to the Caribbean has been in part a product of my self-conscious identity as a black male. African American thought with its unambiguous identification with blackness has often inspired me in ways which the sometimes Jamaican/Caribbean obfuscation has not. In terms of the latter, I have often found the Jamaican motto "out of many, one people," a politically expedient aphorism to justify white minority rule in a black majority country. I will acknowledge this failing, but can only report the truth as I have experienced it in my own formative development as a black religious scholar. The truth is my own development as a black theologian and educator owes much to the United States. I know that the British context has been infused by my Caribbean roots and that these formative influences will always remain within and around me. At no point have I sought to construct this narrative as a normative one. I am not suggesting that America should be so predominant in my own mind or that of the collective entity, which is black theology in Britain. The efficacies of such hegemony should be challenged, and I am pleased to report that black theology in Britain is coming of age and is increasingly less reliant on North America for its raison d'etre. But it would be a strange and unfortunate form of historical revisionism that sought to expunge the influence of the United States from the annals of black British theological historicity.

In the final analysis, this is my subjective story. It is the first of its kind, but hopefully, it won't be the last.

Notes

Introduction

1. The Handsworth and Lozells areas of Birmingham have been home to migrant black communities since the 1950s. The first generation of black migrants came from the Caribbean to this area as part of the post—World War II mass movement of people from the "New Commonwealth" of Britain. Since that initial wave of migrants, succeeding generations of people were born in and have grown up in the urban context of inner city Birmingham in these areas.
2. See Gayraud S. Wilmore and James H. Cone (eds.) *Black Theology: A Documentary History, 1966–1979* (Maryknoll, NY: Orbis Books, 1992).
3. James H. Cone *Black Theology and Black Power* (Maryknoll, NY: Orbis Books, 1997).
4. James H. Cone *A Black Theology of Liberation* (Maryknoll, NY: Orbis Books, 1990).
5. Gayraud S. Wilmore *Black Religion and Black Radicalism* (Maryknoll, NY: Orbis Books, 1983).
6. For the development of the concept of the black Atlantic as the thematic frame and a trope for articulating Diasporan African intellectual and cultural thought, see Paul Gilroy *The Black Atlantic: Modernity and Double Consciousness* (London: Verso, 1993).
7. This now seemingly clichéd phrase was uttered by Tony Blair when he was campaigning for the 1997 General Elections in Britain as leader of the official opposition, the Labour Party.
8. See Paul Gilroy *Between Camps: Nations, Cultures and the Allure of Race* (London: Allen Lane, Penguin Press, 2000).
9. See forthcoming Michael N. Jagessar and Anthony G. Reddie (eds.) *Black Theology in Britain: A Reader* (London: Equinox Publishing, 2007).
10. See A. Elaine Crawford "Womanist Christology and the Wesleyan Tradition." *Black Theology: An International Journal* (Vol. 2, No. 2, July 2004), pp. 213–220.
11. The British Methodist Church is the "Mother" church of the Wesleyan Methodist Movement and is a white majority denomination. In ecclesial terms, it is the equivalent of the United Methodist Church (UMC) in the United States. For a history of the British Methodist Church, see Barrie Tabraham *The Making of Methodism* (Peterborough: Epworth Press, 1995).

12. Anthony Reddie "Book Review of Charles R. Foster and Fred Smith." *Black Religious Experience: Conversations on Double Consciousness and the Works of Grant Shockley* (Nashville, TN: Abingdon Press, 2004). In *Black Theology: An International Journal* (Vol. 3, No. 1, January 2005), pp. 119–121.

I Historical Developments

1. See Anthony G. Reddie *Nobodies to Somebodies* (Peterborough: Epworth Press, 2003), pp. 1–36 and Robert Beckford *Jesus is Dread* (London: Darton, Longman and Todd, 1998), pp. 42–58.

2. See Dwight N. Hopkins *Heart and Head: Black Theology, Past, Present and Future* (New York and Basingstoke, Hampshire: Palgrave Macmillan, 2002), pp. 127–154.

3. See Anthony G. Reddie *Growing into Hope, 2 vols.* (Peterborough: Methodist Publishing House, 1998, 1), p. 1. Also, see Anthony G. Reddie "An Unbroken Thread of Experience." Joan King (ed.) *Family and All That Stuff* (Birmingham: National Christian Education Council [NCEC], 1998), pp. 153–160.

4. Janice E. Hale *Unbank The Fire: Visions of the Education of African American Children* (Baltimore: Johns Hopkins University Press, 1991), pp. 25–131.

5. Robert Beckford *Dread and Pentecostal* (London: SPCK, 2000), pp. 106–112.

6. See Barry Chevannes *Rastafari: Roots, and Ideology* (Syracuse: Syracuse University Press, 1994).

7. See Kortright Davis *Emancipation Still Comin': Explorations in Caribbean Emancipatory Theology* (New York: Orbis books, 1990), pp. 12–49.

8. See Devon Dick *Rebellion to Riot: The Jamaican Church in Nation Building* (Kingston, Jamaica: Ian Randle, 2003). See also Noel L. Erskine *Decolonizing Theology: A Caribbean Perspective* (Maryknoll, NY: Orbis Books, 1981).

9. See Anne H. Pinn and Anthony B. Pinn *Black Church History* (Minneapolis: Fortress Press, 2002).

10. See Dwight N. Hopkins *Down, Up, and Over: Slave Religion and Black Theology* (Minneapolis: Augsburg Press, 2000).

11. See Dilip Hiro *Black British, White British: A History of Race Relations in Britain* (London: Paladin) and Ron Ramdin *The Making of the Black Working-Class in Britain* (London: Gower, 1987).

12. See Anthony G. Reddie *Faith, Stories and the Experience of Black Elders* (London: Jessica Kingsley, 2001), for a more detailed exploration of the religious convictions and spirituality of black elders.

13. See John Munsey Turner *Methodism, revolution and social change* (Wesley Historical Society: West Midlands Branch, 1973), Ted Jennings *Good News to the Poor: John Wesley's Evangelical Economics* (Nashville, TN: Abingdon Press, 1990). See also David Hempton *The Religion of the People: Methodism and Popular Religion* (London: Routledge, 1996).

14. Rupert E. Davies *Methodism* (Peterborough: Epworth Press, 1985), pp. 56–104.

15. See Philip Cliff *The Rise and Development of the Sunday School Movement in England 1780–1980* (Birmingham: National Christian Education Council—NCEC, 1986).

16. Peter Sedgwick "The Sectarian Future of the Church and Ecumenical Schools." Jeff Astley and David Day (eds.) *The Contours of Christian Education* (Great Wakering, Essex: McCrimmons, 1992), pp. 245–265.

17. Douglas S. Hubery *Teaching the Christian Faith Today* (Surrey: Denholm House Press, 1965), *Christian Education and the Bible* (Birmingham: REP, 1967) and *The Teaching Methods of Jesus* (London: Chester House Publications, 1970). The influence of the British Methodist Churches Division of Education and Youth (MDEY) can be seen in the creation of *Partners in Learning*, a comprehensive program for Christian worship and learning based upon principles of experiential education since the late 1960s. More recently, the division was actively involved in the development of *Kaleidoscope and Spectrum* (training programs for lay volunteers working with children and young people) and *Unfinished Business* (a report published by the Churches Consultative Group on Ministry among Children [CGMC] concerned with issues of Christian nurture and the place of children in the church). The successor to MDEY is the "Worship and Learning" office of the Connexional British Methodist Church. The Worship and Learning Office has been instrumental in the development of *Roots: Worship and Learning for the Whole Church*. *Roots* is an ecumenical, monthly Christian education and liturgical resource for the whole church in Britain. It is based on two resource books, which are supplemented by additional material on the web.

18. See the Report to the British Methodist Conference of 2001 in Ipswich *Learning and Developing as the Whole People of God*—Agenda, *Vol 1* (Peterborough: Methodist Publishing House, 2001).

19. I deal with this issue in *Growing into Hope: Christian Education in Multi-Ethnic Churches, Vol. 2—Liberation and Change*, pp. 9–10. Here, I describe the pressures of being a black person in a white dominated society, trying to live in two different worlds.

20. Reddie "An Unbroken Thread of Experience," pp. 153–160.

21. See Doreen McCalla (ed.) *Black Success: Essays in Racial and Ethnic Studies* (Cambridge: DMee: Vision Learning Ltd and Cambridge University Press, 2003).

22. See Volume 1 of *Growing Into Hope: Believing and Expecting*, p. 8. This training exercise was constructed (using data from the 1991 census) to assist predominantly white leaders who work with black children to understand both the context in which black people live in Britain, and the psychological and emotional effects of being a minority in a white dominated country. Black people who predominantly live in inner city areas have divided their existence in this country into areas of familiarity. Black children move interchangeably, from areas of great familiarity (where black people although a minority are suddenly in the majority) to other situations where they become seemingly insignificant. This pattern has not changed appreciably since the postwar wave of mass African Caribbean migration to this country. This interchangeability of African Caribbean life, which is centered on differing contexts has given rise to issues of cultural dissonance.

23. Selective literature includes R.B. Davidson *Black British* (Oxford: Oxford University Press, 1966), R.A. Easterlin *Immigration* (Cambridge MA: Oxford University Press, 1982), Paul Hartman and Charles Hubbard Charles, *Immigration and the Mass Media* (London: Davis-Poynter, 1974), Edward Scobie *Black Britannia: A History of Blacks in Britain* (Chicago: Johnson Publishing & Co., 1972), Ken Pryce *Endless Pressure* (Bristol: Classical Press, 1979), Winston James and Clive Harris *Migration, Racism and Identity* (London: Verso, 1993).

24. Ian Duffield "Blacks in Britain: History and the Historians." *History Today* (Vol. 31, September 1981), p. 34.

25. Peter Fryer *Staying Power: The History of Black People in Britain* (London: Pluto Press, 1984), p. 10.

26. Ceri Peach *West Indian Immigration to Britain* (London: Oxford University Press, 1968), p. 82. Documentary evidence attesting to the significant black presence in Britain in the post-Renaissance period can be found in James Walvin *Black and White: The Negro and English Society 1555–1945*. (London: Allen Lane, 1973). *The Black Presence: A Documentary History of the Negro in England, 1550–1860* (London: Orbach and Chambers, 1971). F.O. Shyllon *Black People in Britain: 1555–1833* (London: Institute of Race Relations and Oxford University Press, 1977) Douglas A. Lorimer *Colour, Class and the Victorians* (Leicester: Leicester University Press, 1978). An important biography to note is Mary Seacole's *Wonderful Adventures*, Ziggy Alexander and Audrey Dewjee (eds.) (London: Falling Wall Press, 1984).

27. The first significant positive sense of my own self-worth within the Methodist church came with the publication of Heather Walton *A Tree God Planted: Black People in British Methodism* (London: Methodist Church, 1985).

28. Mary Prince was a black slave in the nineteenth century who published her autobiography in 1831 detailing her experiences of hardship, struggle, and emancipation. Her book was entitled *The History of Mary Prince, a West Indian Slave. Related by Herself. With a Supplement by the Editor. To Which Is Added, the Narrative of Asa-Asa, a Captured African* (London: Published by F. Westley and A. H. Davis, 1831). Her book was a key text in the abolitionary movement of the nineteenth century.

29. See Vincent Caretta (ed.) *Olaudah Equiano: The Interesting Narrative and Other Writings* (New York and London: Penguin Books, 1995).

30. See Vincent Caretta (ed.) *Letters of the Late Ignatius Sancho, an African* (New York and London: Penguin Books, 1998).

31. Fryer *Staying Power*, p. 10.

32. See Caretta (ed.) *Letters of the Late Ignatius Sancho, an African*.

33. See Mary Prince *The History of Mary Prince, a West Indian Slave*.

34. For useful analysis of this struggle see A.A. Sivanandan *A Different Hunger: Writings on Black Resistance* (London: Pluto Press, 1982). See also Roger Fieldhouse *Anti Apartheid: A History of the Movement in Britain* (London: Merlin Press, 2005).

35. For the latest development on this work see the forthcoming Michael N. Jagessar and Anthony G. Reddie (eds.) *Black Religion and Black Theology in Britain: A Reader* (London: Equinox Publishing, 2007).

36. See Heather Walton *A Tree God Planted: Black People in British Methodism* (London: Ethnic Minorities in Methodism Working Group, Methodist Church, 1984) and *Inheritors Together: Black people in the Church of England* (London: Race, Pluralism, and Community Group Board for Social Responsibility, Church of England, 1985). See also John Wilkinson *Church in Black and White: The Black Tradition in "Mainstream" Churches in England: A White Response and Testimony* (Edinburgh: St. Andrews Press, 1993).

37. For more information, see Claire R. Taylor *British Churches and Jamaican Migration: A Study of Religion and Identities, 1948–1965* (Unpublished Ph.D. thesis, Anglia Polytechnic University, 2002).

38. By historic mainline, I mean those established denominations of the Protestant tradition that account for the greater majority of the population that can be described and identified as church attendees and practicing Christians. The churches in question are Anglican, Methodist, Baptist, and United Reformed.

39. Emmanuel Y. Lartey "Editorial." *Black Theology in Britain: A Journal of Contextual Praxis* (No. 1, October 1998), pp. 7–9.

40. Ibid., p. 8.

41. Black churches in Britain are not confined to any one denomination. Just like their counterparts in the United States, black churches can be divided into three board categories. The first category and by far the most visible is the black majority Pentecostal churches. These churches owe their origin to black migrants who traveled from the Caribbean in the post—World War II mass movement of the last century. The first churches were offshoots of predominantly white Pentecostal denominations in the United States. These churches were first established in the early 1950s. The largest and most established of these churches are the New Testament church of God and the church of God of prophecy'. For further details, see Joe D. Aldred *Respect: A Caribbean British Contextual Theology* (Peterborough: Epworth Press, 2006). The second strand is black majority churches in white historic denominations. These churches are demographically determined, as their black majority membership has grown out of black migrants moving into inner city, urban contexts, coupled with the white flight of the middle-class. For further information, see Wilkinson *Church in Black and White*. The final strand is that of independent black majority NeoPentecostal churches. This group is, in many respects, a dynamic offshoot of those in the first category. These churches tend to be stand-alone entities that operate as independent communities of faith outside of any established national denominational structure. One of the most significant differences between the first and third categories is that whilst the first is almost exclusively black Caribbean in complexion, those in category three are a mixture of black Caribbean churches and black African ones.

42. See Lartey "Editorial," pp. 7–9.

43. For complete details of this phenomenon, see Eugene Genovese *Roll Jordan Roll* (New York: Vintage Books, 1980), Albert Rabateau *Slave Religion* (New York: Oxford University Press, 1978), Dwight N. Hopkins and George L. Cummings (eds.) *Cut Loose Your Stammering Tongue: Black Theology and the Slave Narratives* (New York: Orbis Books, 1991) and Hopkins *Down, Up and Over*.

44. Gus John *The New Black Presence* (London: British Council of Churches, 1976).
45. Robinson A. Milwood *Let's Journey Together* (London: The Division of Social Responsibility of the Methodist Church, 1980).
46. Ibid., pp. 1–4.
47. Ibid., p. 1.
48. Ibid., p. 11.
49. Ibid., pp. 17–20.
50. See the exercise entitled "The Meal Test." Reddie *Growing into Hope, Vol.1 Believing and Expecting* (Peterborough: Methodist Publishing House, 1998), pp. 6–7.
51. See Howard Thurman *Jesus and the Disinherited* (Boston, MA: Beacon Press, 1996).
52. I have sought to address questions of how contemporary black theologians attempt to engage with the religious discourse of their forbears, in a previous text. How can we do justice to what our forbears have written and articulated, in a manner that enables us to claim them as our own, without imposing upon them, nomenclatures, which they themselves would not have owned or of which they were barely conscious? See Reddie *Faith, Stories and the Experience of Black Elders*, Reddie *Dramatizing Theologies: A Participative Approach to Black God-Talk* (London: Equinox Publishing, 2006).
53. See Anita Jackson *Catching Both Sides of the Wind: Conversations with Five Black Pastors* (London: The British Council of Churches, 1985), pp. 31–64.
54. Ibid., p. 55.
55. See Robinson A. Milwood "Salvation as Liberation." Donald English (ed.) *Windows on Salvation* (London: DLT, 1994), pp. 109–121.
56. See Robinson A. Milwood *Liberation and Mission: A Black Experience* (London: African Caribbean Education Resource Centre (ACER), 1997).
57. Ibid., pp. 65–75.
58. See Roswith I.H. Gerloff *A Plea for British Black Theologies: the Black Church Movement in Britain, 2 vols.* (Unpublished Ph.D. thesis, University of Birmingham, 1991).
59. "Claiming the Inheritance" was founded in 1986 and based in Birmingham, in the West Midlands of Britain. It brought together predominantly black Christians to celebrate their history and heritage in order to create programs and resources that would challenge and overcome the various ills that afflicted black people in Britain. The movement came to an end in the late 1990s, having been instrumental in mobilizing and informing black (and white) people for many years. A number of black people who were active in their organization in its formative years have since moved into ordained (pastoral) ministry having "cut their teeth" in practical theological work by way of their involvement in CTI. See *Claiming The Inheritance: Ten Years On* (West Bromwich: Claiming The Inheritance, 1997).
60. See chapter 2 for a more in-depth assessment of the legacy of Robert Beckford.
61. See John L. Wilkinson "Church in Black and White": The Black Christian Tradition in 'Mainstream' Churches (Unpublished M.Litt theses, University of Birmingham, 1990).
62. See previous references in this chapter to *Church in Black and White*, 1993.

63. Kenneth Leech *Struggle in Babylon* (London: Sheldon Press, 1988).
64. Kenneth Leech *The Sky Is Red: Discerning the Sign of the Times* (London: DLT, 1997).
65. John Wilkinson, James H. Evans Jr., and Renate Wilkinson *Inheritors Together* (London: Race, Pluralism and Community Group of the Board for Social responsibility of the Church of England, 1985).
66. Ibid., pp. 54–71.
67. Ibid., p. 10.
68. John Wilkinson, James H. Evans Jr., and Renate Wilkinson *Inheritors Together*, p. 10.
69. See Renate Wilkinson "A Chance to Change." *Inheritors Together*, pp. 20–53.
70. James H. Evans Jr. *We Have Been Believers: An African American Systematic Theology* (Minneapolis: Fortress Press, 1992).
71. James H. Evans Jr. "The Struggle for Identity: Black People in the Church of England." *Inheritors Together*, pp. 54–71.
72. Ibid., p. 69.
73. Personal conversation with Robert Beckford, 14th April 2004.
74. See *Account of Hope: Report of a Conference on the Economic Empowerment of the Black Community* (London: Community and Race Relations Unit of the British Council of Churches, 1990).
75. Ibid., p. 39.
76. Ibid., pp. 39–40.
77. Ibid., pp. 14–17.
78. See Peter J. Paris *The Social Teaching of the Black Churches* (Minneapolis: Fortress Press, 1985), C. Eric Lincoln and Lawrence Mamiya *The Black Church in the African American Experience* (Durham and London: Duke University Press, 1990).
79. Raj Patel, Maurice Hobbs, and Greg Smith *Equal Partners: Theological Education and Racial Justice* (London: British Council of Churches, 1992).
80. Ibid., p. v. It is interesting to note that at the time of writing, my own institution (The Queen's Foundation for Ecumenical Theological Education) is the only one that has Black Theology as a mandatory part of the curriculum for ministerial training and formation. Most of the recommendations of the report are still not operational or discernible within the British Theological educational system.
81. Patel, Hobbs, and Smith *Equal Partners* "Wesley Daniel—Reflections." pp. 63–66.
82. Ibid., p. 65.
83. See "Black Power: Statement by the National Committee of Negro Churchmen, July 31, 1966." Gayraud S. Wilmore and James H. Cone (eds.) *Black Theology: A Documentary History, 1966–1979* (Maryknoll, NY: Orbis Books, 1979), pp. 23–30.
84. Paul Grant and Raj Patel (eds.) *A Time To Speak: Perspectives of Black Christians in Britain* (Birmingham: A Joint Publication of Racial Justice and the Black and Third World Theology Working Group, 1990).
85. Paul Grant and Raj Patel (eds.) *A Time To Act: Kairos 1992* (Birmingham: A Joint Publication of Racial Justice and the Black and Third World Theology Working Group, 1992).

86. See Frederick L. Ware *Methodologies of Black Theology* (Cleveland, OH: Pilgrim Press, 2002), pp. 39–65. See also Dwight N. Hopkins *Black Theology of Liberation [Introducing]* (Maryknoll, NY: Orbis Books, 1999), pp. 41–48 and "Black Theology of Liberation." *Black Theology: An International Journal* (Vol. 3, No. 1, January 2005), pp. 11–31.

87. See Harry Goulbourne "Collective Action and Black Politics." Doreen McCalla (ed.) *Black Success: Essays in Racial and Ethnic Studies* (Cambridge: DMee: Vision Learning Ltd and Cambridge University Press, 2003), pp. 9–38.

88. See Sivanandan *A Different Hunger.*

89. A useful text that discusses some of the differences, similarities, and socio-cultural positionalities of black, Hispanic, and Latino/a communities can be found in Anthony B. Pinn and Benjamin Valentin (eds.) *The Ties That Bind: African American and Hispanic American/Latino/a Theologies in Dialogue* (New York: Continuum, 2001).

90. T. Modood and P. Werbner (eds.) *The Politics of Multiculturalism in the New Europe* (London: Zed Books, 1997).

91. W.E.B. Dubois *The Souls of Black Folk* (New York: Bantam Books, 1989), p. 3.

92. See Cornel West *Democracy Matters: Winning the Fight Against Imperialism* (New York: Penguin Books, 2004).

93. Garnet Paris "Black Theology: The U.S. Experience." *A Time To Speak*, pp. 23–28.

94. Revd. Eve Pitts "Black Womanist Ethic." *A Time To Speak*, pp. 29–36.

95. See Revd. David Moore "Through a Black Lens: Telling Our History and Understanding Its Significance," *A Time To Speak*, pp. 11–16.

96. Grant and Patel (eds.) "Editorial." *A Time To Act*, p. 1.

97. Clarice Nelson and Sybil Phoenix "If the Church Was What It Professed To Be . . ." *A Time To Speak*, pp. 19–24.

98. Eric Pemberton "1492: An Evaluation." *A Time To Act*, pp. 37–40.

99. The Womanist Theology Group "A Womanist Bibliodrama." *A Time To Act*, pp. 25–32.

100. Julia Shervington "Immigration Controls—The Human Cost." *A Time To Act*, pp. 71–78.

101. See Beckford *Dread and Pentecostal* and *God and the Gangs* (London: DLT, 2004), pp. 168–182.

102. See Reddie *Nobodies to Somebodies*, pp. 67–73.

103. See Cone *A Black Theology of Liberation* (Maryknoll, NY: Orbis Books, 1990), pp. 110–128. See also Jacquelyn Grant *White Women's Christ and Black Women's Jesus* (Atlanta: Scholars Press, 1989), pp. 195–230 and Kelly Brown Douglas *The Black Christ* (Maryknoll, NY: Orbis Books,1994), pp. 97–117.

104. Reddie *Nobodies to Somebodies*, pp. 67–73.

105. See Beckford *Dread and Pentecostal*, pp. 168–182.

106. Wilmore and James H. Cone (eds.) *Black Theology: A Documentary History, 1966–1979* and *Black Theology: A Documentary History, Vol. 2 1980–1992.*

107. See Frederick L. Ware *Methodologies of Black Theology* (Cleveland, OH: Pilgrim Press, 2002).

108. See Clifford Geertz *The Interpretation of Cultures: Selected Essays* (London: Fontana Press, 1993) and *Local Knowledge* (New York: Basic Books, 1983). See also Lubna Nazir Chaudry "Researching 'My People,' Researching Myself: Fragments of a Reflexive Tale." *Qualitative Studies in Education* (Vol. 10, No. 4, 1997), pp. 441–451.

109. See Gretchen Gerzina *Black England: Life Before Emancipation* (London: John Murray, 1995).

110. Ron Ramdin *Reimaging Britain: 500 Years of Black and Asian History* (London: Pluto Press, 1999), pp. 193–306.

111. See Reddie *Nobodies to Somebodies*, pp. 14–15.

112. Fryer *Staying Power*, pp. 372–373.

113. Bob Carter, Clive Harris, and Shirley Joshi "The 1951–1955 Conservative Government and the Racialization of Black Immigration." Kwesi Owusu (ed.) *Black British Culture and Society: A Text Reader* (London: Routledge, 2000), pp. 21–36.

114. "Black Power: Statement by the National Committee of Negro Churchmen, July 31, 1966." Gayraud S. Wilmore and James H. Cone (eds.) *Black Theology: A Documentary History, 1966–1979*, p. 24.

115. James H. Cone "Theology's Great Sin: Silence in The Face of White Supremacy." *Black Theology: An International Journal* (Vol. 2, No. 2, July 2004), pp. 139–152.

116. James H. Cone *A Black Theology of Liberation* (Maryknoll, NY: Orbis Books, 1990), p. 6.

117. See Douglas *The Black Christ*, pp. 110–112.

118. Comment made by Professor John M. Hull in an address to the annual conference of the British Methodist Church, Southport, 1999.

119. JoAnne Marie Terrell *Power in the Blood?: The Cross in the African American Experience* (Marknoll, NY: Orbis Books, 1998), pp. 17–34.

120. See "Christian Jargon." Anthony G. Reddie *Acting in Solidarity: Reflections in Critical Christianity* (London: DLT, 2005), pp. 59–67.

121. See Mokgethi Mothlabi "The Problem of Ethical Method in Black Theology." *Black Theology: An International Journal* (Vol. 2, No. 1, January 2004), pp. 57–72. Mothlabi compares Cone's ethical method with those of some of his critics within the black theology movement.

122. A more detailed assessment of Robert Beckford's work will be undertaken in the following chapter.

123. It should be noted that Joe Aldred's trilogy of books does offer some insights into the differing theological and cultural expressions of black Christian faith in Britain from normative white Christianity. See Joe Aldred *Preaching With Power* (London: Cassells, 1998) and *Sisters with Power* (London: Continuum, 2000), and Joe Aldred *Praying With Power* (London: Continuum, 2000).

124. See Mark Lewis Taylor *The Executed God: The Way of the Cross in Lockdown America* (Minneapolis: Fortress Press, 2001).

125. See Robert E. Hood *Begrimed and Black and Black: Christian Traditions on Blacks and Blackness* (Minneapolis: Fortress Press, 1994), pp. 73–90.

126. See Vincent L. Wimbush *The Bible and African Americans: A Brief History* (Minneapolis: Fortress Press, 2003), pp. 63–75.

127. The African Caribbean Evangelical Alliance (ACEA) is an overarching organizational that seeks to act for and provide a structure, forum, and support mechanism for black-led and black majority churches in Britain. It was founded by the Revd. Philip Mobahir in 1984. ACEA exists within the larger and more generic "Evangelical Alliance."

128. See Alton B. Pollard, III and Love Henry Whelchek, Jr. (eds.) *How Long This Road: Race, Religion and the Legacy of C. Eric Lincoln* (New York: Palgrave Macmillan, 2003).

129. Cheryl Townsend Gilkes *If It Wasn't for the Women* (Maryknoll, NY: Orbis Books, 2001).

130. See Henry Goldschmidt and Elizabeth McAlister (eds.) *Race, Nation, and Religion in the Americas* (Oxford and New York: Oxford University Press, 2004) for an excellent treatment of the role of race in conjunction with religion within the popular imagination of North (and South) America.

131. See N. Lynne Westfield "Teaching for Globalized Consciousness: Black Professor, White Student and Shame." *Black Theology: An International Journal* (Vol. 2, No. 1, January 2004), pp. 73–83 for an excellent account of an apologetic black theological approach to working with white people in an attempt to address issues of identity and power within a pedagogical context.

132. See my analysis around a phenomenon I have termed "A Theology of Good Intentions." See Reddie *Nobodies to Somebodies*, pp. 155–171. See also the section entitled "Racial Justice/Black Theology." Reddie *Acting in Solidarity*, pp. 83–119.

133. Harold Dean Trulear "African American Religious Education." Barbara Wilkerson (ed.) *Multi-Cultural Religious Education* (Birmingham, AL: Religious Education Press, 1997), pp. 161–189.

134. Emmanuel Y. Lartey "Editorial." pp. 7–9.

135. See Timothy E. Fulop and Albert J. Rabateau (eds.) *African American Religion: Interpretive Essays in History and Culture* (New York and London: Routledge, 1997). See also Henry H. Mitchell *Black Church Beginnings: The Long-Hidden Realities of the First Years* (Grand Rapids, MI: Wm.B. Eerdmans, 2004).

136. Anthony B. Pinn *Terror and Triumph: The Nature of Black Religion* (Minneapolis: Fortress Press, 2003), pp. 133–157.

137. See Eric E. Pemberton *A Study of Caribbean Religions* (Unpublished M.Phil thesis, University of Birmingham, 1988). See also Aldred *Respect*.

138. In Britain, there is no settled agreement on the appropriate nomenclatures for the naming of black women's experiences. Some are happy to use the term Feminist, whilst others prefer the more African American term of womanist. See Marjorie Lewis "Diaspora Dialogue: Womanist Theology in Engagement with Aspects of the Black British and Jamaican Experience." *Black Theology: An International Journal* (Vol. 2, No. 1, January 2004), pp. 85–109.

139. Ibid., pp. 85–109.

140. Diane Watt "Traditional Religious Practices Amongst African Caribbean Mothers and Community OtherMothers." *Black Theology: An International Journal* (Vol. 2, No. 2, July 2004), pp. 195–212.

141. I will deal with this issue in detail in chapter 3 where I will look at the respective movements in womanist theology in both the contexts.

142. See Ware *Methodologies of Black Theology.*

143. See Peter J. Paris *The Spiritualities of African Peoples: The Search for a Common Moral Discourse* (Minneapolis: Fortress Press, 1995).

144. Anthony B. Pinn *Varieties of African American Religious Experience* (Minneapolis: Fortress Press, 1998).

145. Robert Beckford "Response to Dwight N. Hopkins' 'A New Heterosexual Male.' " *Black Theology in Britain: A Journal of Contextual Praxis* (Vol. 4, No. 2, May 2002), pp. 228–231.

146. See Cornel West *Democracy Matters: Winning The Fight Against Imperialism* (New York: Penguin Books, 2004).

147. Reddie *Growing into Hope.*

148. A more detailed appreciation of the work and legacy of Grant S. Shockley can be found in Charles R. Foster and Fred Smith (eds.) *Black Religious Experience: Conversations On Double Consciousness and the Work of Grant Shockley* (Nashville, TN: Abingdon Press, 2003). See also chapter 4 of this book and my *Nobodies to Somebodies*, pp. 47–48.

149. See Lartey *In Living Colour.*

150. This term seeks to denote an area in England that is north of the South East (principally London) and is south of those areas defined as the beginning of the north, such as Derbyshire and Yorkshire.

151. See Cain Hope Felder (ed.) *Troubling Biblical Waters: Race, Class, and Family* (Maryknoll, NY: Orbis Books, 1989) (The Bishop Henry McNeal Turner studies in North America) and *Stony the Road We Trod: African American Biblical Interpretation* (Minneapolis: Fortress Press, 1991).

152. See Randall C. Bailey and Jacquelyn Grant (eds.) *The Recovery of Black Presence: An Interdisciplinary Exploration* (Nashville, TN: Abingdon Press, 1995) and Randall C. Bailey (ed.) *Yet with a Steady Beat: Contemporary U.S. Afrocentric Biblical Interpretation* (Atlanta: Society for the Study of Biblical Literature, 2003).

153. Among the major works of James H. Cone are *Black Theology and Black Power* (1969, repr. Maryknoll, NY: Orbis Books, 1989), *A Black Theology of Liberation* (1970, repr. Maryknoll, NY: Orbis Books, 1990). Among his more recent books are *Martin, Malcolm and America* (Maryknoll, NY: Orbis Books, 1992) and *Risks of Faith* (Boston: Beacon Press, 1999).

154. See Major J. Jones *Christian Ethics for Black Theology* (Nashville, TN: Abingdon Press, 1974).

155. See J. Deotis Roberts *Liberation and Reconciliation: A Black Theology* (Maryknoll, NY: Orbis Books, rev. edn, 1994).

156. Preston N. Williams "James Cone and the Problem of a Black Ethic." *Harvard Theological Review* (No. 65, 1972), pp. 483–484.

157. See Karen Baker-Fletcher and Garth Kasimu Baker-Fletcher *My Sister, My Brother: Womanist and Xodus God-Talk* (Maryknoll, NY: Orbis Books, 1997).

158. See Douglas *The Black Christ*.
159. See Linda E. Thomas (ed.) *Living Stones in the Household of God: The Legacy and Future of Black Theology* (Minneapolis: Fortress Press, 2004).
160. Dwight N. Hopkins "Black Theology of Liberation." *Black Theology: An International Journal* (Vol. 3, No. 1, January 2005), pp. 11–31.
161. At the time of writing, there are a few (post) graduate students who are undertaking biblical studies at the University of Birmingham.
162. See Michael N. Jagessar *Full Life For All: The Work and Theology of Philip A. Potter: A Historical Survey and Systematic Analysis of Major Themes* (Zoetermeer, The Netherlands: Boekencentrum, 1997) and "Cultures in Dialogue: The Contribution of a Caribbean Theologian." *Black Theology: An International Journal* (Vol. 1, No. 2, May 2003), pp. 139–160.
163. See Aldred *Preaching With Power*.
164. See Michael J. Brown *Blackening of the Bible* (Harrisburg, PA: Trinity Press International, 2004).
165. See Vincent L. Wimbush *African Americans and the Bible: Sacred Texts and Social Textures* (New York: Continuum, 2000) and Vincent L. Wimbush *The Bible and African Americans: A Brief History* (Minneapolis: Fortress Press, 2003). See also Joseph V. Crockett "Engaging Scripture in Everyday Situations: An Interactive Perspective that Examines Psychological and Social Processes of Individuals as They Engage Scripture Texts." *Black Theology: An International Journal* (Vol. 3, No. 1, January 2005), pp. 97–117. These texts look at the various ways in which black people read and engage with biblical texts from a variety of perspectives.
166. See Beckford *Dread and Pentecostal*, pp. 152–156.
167. See Cone *A Black Theology of Liberation*, pp. 31–33 and *Introducing Black Theology of Liberation* (Maryknoll, NY: Orbis Books, 1999), pp. 41–42.
168. Wimbush *The Bible and African Americans*, pp. 83–85.

2 Friend or Foe?: Black Theologians and the Black Church

1. See C. Eric Lincoln and Lawrence H. Mamiya *The Black Church in the African American Experience* (Durham & London: Duke University Press, 1990) and Peter J. Paris *The Social Teaching of the Black Churches* (Minneapolis: Fortress Press, 1985). See also Anne H. Pinn and Anthony B. Pinn *Black Church History* (Minneapolis: Fortress Press, 2002) for a brief selection of an extensive literature in this area of black theological work.
2. Charles R. Foster and Fred Smith *Black Religious Experience: Conversations on Double Consciousness and the Work of Grant Shockley* (Nashville, TN: Abingdon Press, 2003), pp. 64–65.
3. See Dwight N. Hopkins *Introducing Black Theology of Liberation* (Maryknoll, NY: Orbis Books, 1999), pp. 43–44.
4. See James H. Harris *Pastoral Theology: A Black-Church Perspective* (Minneapolis: Fortress Press, 1991). See also Dale P. Andrews *Practical*

Theology for Black Churches: Bridging Black Theology and African American Folk Religion (Louisville: John Knox Press, 2002).

5. See A.H. Pinn and A.B. Pinn *Black Church History*.

6. See John L. Wilkinson *Church in Black and White: The Black Christian Tradition in "Mainstream" Churches in England: A White Response and Testimony* (Edinburgh: St. Andrews Press, 1993).

7. See Joe D. Aldred *Respect: A Caribbean British Theology* (Unpublished Ph.D. thesis, Department of Biblical Studies, University of Sheffield, 2004).

8. See Doreen McCalla "Black Churches and Voluntary Action: Their Social Engagement with the Wider Society." *Black Theology: An International Journal* (Vol. 3, No. 2, July 2004).

9. Mark Sturge *Look What the Lord Has Done!* (London: Scripture Union, 2005).

10. Arlington Trotman "Black, Black-Led or What?" Joel Edwards (ed.) *"Let's Praise Him Again": An African Caribbean Perspective on Worship* (Eastbourne: Kingsway Publications, 1992), pp. 12–35.

11. Robert Beckford *Dread and Pentecostal: A Political Theology for the Black Church in Britain* (London: SPCK, 2000), pp. 176–182.

12. See Robert Beckford *Jesus is Dread* (London: Darton, Longman and Todd, 1998), pp. 42–58, where Beckford outlines the various positions occupied by black people within white majority churches. I will deal with this issue in greater detail at a later point in this chapter.

13. See M. Byron *Post War Caribbean Migration to Britain: The Unfinished Cycle* (Aldershot: Averbury, 1994). See also R.B. Davidson *West Indian Migrants* (London: Oxford University Press, 1962) and R. Glass *Newcomers: The West Indians in London* (Assisted by Harold Pollins) (London: George Allen and Unwin, 1960) for a historical analysis of the presence of disproportionate numbers of black people living in inner urban conurbations in Britain.

14. Peter Brierley *The Tide is Running Out: What the English Church Attendance Survey Reveals* (London: Christian Research, 2000), p. 136.

15. Two notable exceptions of which I am aware are Romney M. Moseley *No Longer Strangers: Ministry in a Multicultural Society* (Toronto: Anglican Book store, 1987) and Grant S. Shockley (ed.) *Heritage and Hope: The African American Presence in United Methodism* (Nashville, TN: Abingdon Press, 1991).

16. David Isiorho "Black Theology in Urban Shadow: Combating Racism in the Church of England." *Black Theology: An International Journal* (Vol. 1, No. 1, November 2002), pp. 29–48.

17. Ibid., p. 47.

18. At the time of writing, Bishop John Sentamu, has just been appointed to the see of York, and will be the first black Archbishop in the Church of England. Sentamu was born and brought up in Uganda. Despite his elevation, I remain unconvinced about the extent to which his presence will change the structural and de facto whiteness of the established church in England.

19. Isiorho "Black Theology in Urban Shadow," p. 47.

20. Robert Beckford *God and the Gangs* (London: Darton, Longman and Todd, 2004), pp. 85–90.

21. See Doreen McCalla's work on the social teachings and engagement of the Church of God of Prophecy. Also, see Doreen McCalla "Black Churches and Voluntary Action: Their Social Engagement with the Wider Society."

22. See David Sheppard *Bias to the Poor* (London: Hodder and Staughton, 1983). *Faith in the City: Archbishop's Commission on Urban Priority Areas* (London: Church House Publications, 1985), *Anglicans and Racism* (London: Board of Social Responsibility, 1986) *Seeds of Hope: Report of a Survey on Combating Racism in the Diocese of the Church of England* (London: Church House Publications, 1991), *The Passing Winter: A Sequel to Seeds of Hope* (London: Church House Publications, 1996).

23. See Isiorho "Black Theology in Urban Shadow: Combating Racism in the Church of England," pp. 29–48. See also David Isiorho "Black Anglicans in Focus: Qualitative Data on Black Marginality." *Black Theology: An International Journal* (Vol. 2, No. 2, July 2004), pp. 221–238.

24. See Glynn Gordon Carter *An Amazing Journey: The Church of England's Response to Institutional Racism* (London: Church House Publications, 2003).

25. Beckford *Jesus is Dread* and *God of the Rahtid* (London: Darton, Longman and Todd, 2001).

26. Ibid.

27. Beckford *Dread and Pentecostal*.

28. The college has been renamed The Queen's Foundation for Ecumenical Theological Education. It comprises (1) the college, where men and women are trained for authorized, ordained public ministry in the Anglican, Methodist, and United Reformed Traditions. This training takes place on a full time, residential basis, (2) The West Midlands course that trains people for ordained ministry by means of a nonresidential course, and (3) The Research Centre for Applied Theology. The center is the newest component of the Queen's Foundation.

29. It is interesting to note the work of Valentina Alexander's Ph.D. thesis *To Break Every Fetter?: To What Extent Has the Black-Led Church in Britain Developed a Theology of Liberation?* (Unpublished Ph.D thesis, University of Warwick, 1996). See also Paul Grant and Raj Patel (eds.) *A Time To Speak* (Birmingham: Racial Justice and the Black Theology Working Group, 1990), Paul Grant and Raj Patel (eds.) *A Time To Act* (Birmingham: Racial Justice and the Black Theology Working Group, 1992) for other comparatively early examples of black British theological work prior to Beckford's Ph.D. thesis.

30. Beckford *Jesus is Dread*.

31. Ibid.

32. Beckford *Dread and Pentecostal*.

33. Beckford *God of the Rahtid*.

34. Beckford *God and the Gangs*.

35. Robert Beckford *Jesus Dub: Theology, Music and Social Change* (London: Routledge, 2005).

36. See James H. Cone A *Black Theology of Liberation* (Maryknoll, NY: Orbis Books, reprint, 1986) and *God of the Oppressed* (San Francisco: Harper Collins, 1975).

37. Trying to name different ecclesial bodies remains notoriously difficult. This particular term is an amalgam of several earlier manifestations and serves as a

useful point of departure. It is by no means an agreed upon or settled term, and is in its own way deeply problematic. But given that we have to name particular phenomena or institutions for purposes of definition and identification, I have chosen this particular term. See Beckford *Dread and Pentecostal*, pp. 35–66.

38. See Beckford *Jesus is Dread*, pp. 42–60.
39. See Beckford *Dread and Pentecostal* for an analysis of black majority church practices.
40. Beckford *Jesus is Dread*.
41. See James H. Cone *Black Theology and Black Power* (New York: Orbis Books, 1986), *God of the Oppressed* (San Francisco: Harper, 1975), and *A Black Theology of Liberation*.
42. Gustavo Gutteriez *A Theology of Liberation* (New York: Orbis, Books, 1973).
43. Leonardo and Clodovis Boff *Introducing Liberation Theology* (Tunbridge Wells: Burns and Oates, 1987).
44. Emmanuel Y. Lartey *In Living Colour* (London: Cassells, 1997).
45. See Cone *Black Theology and Black Power*.
46. See Dwight N. Hopkins (ed.) *Black Faith and Black Talk: Critical Essays on James H. Cone's Black Theology and Black Power* (Maryknoll, NY: Orbis Books, 1999).
47. Beckford *Jesus is Dread*, pp. 25–44.
48. See Horace Campbell *Rasta and Resistance: From Marcus Garvey to Walter Rodney* (London: Hansib, 1985).
49. See William David Spencer *Dread Jesus* (London: SPCK, 1999).
50. Beckford *Jesus is Dread*, pp. 61–129.
51. Ibid., pp. 117–119.
52. See Gayraud S. Wilmore *Black Religion and Black Radicalism* (Maryknoll, NY: Orbis Books, 1983).
53. See Henry H. Mitchell and Nicola Copper-Lewter *Soul Theology: The Heart of American Black Culture* (San Francisco: Harper and Row, 1986).
54. Theophus Smith *Conjuring Culture: Biblical Formations of Black America* (New York: Oxford University Press, 1994).
55. See Frederick L. Ware *Methodologies of Black Theology* (Cleveland, OH: Pilgrim Press, 2002), p. xvi.
56. By historic mainline, I mean those established denominations of the Protestant tradition that account for the greater majority of the population that can be described and identified as church attendees and practicing Christians. The churches in question are Anglican, Methodist, Baptist, and United Reformed.
57. Beckford *Jesus is Dread*, pp. 42–58.
58. Beckford *Jesus is Dread*, pp. 47–58.
59. Beckford *Jesus is Dread*, pp. 42–58.
60. Anne and Anthony Pinn's book *Black Church History* clearly highlights the important role Methodism (particularly the AME, AMEZ, and the CME) has played in the ongoing struggle for black liberation within the United States. My comments are clearly directed at the white majority British Methodist Church.

61. The research project on which this study is based was given the title "Birmingham Initiative." Revd. Christopher Hughes Smith, the then general secretary of the Division of Education and Youth, having formerly been a minister and district chairman in Birmingham, was aware of the deficiencies in the existing Christian education work sponsored by the Methodist church amongst black children and young people. The project ran from May 1995 to August 1999.

62. Anthony G. Reddie *Growing into Hope: Believing and Expecting (Vol.1)* (Peterborough: Methodist Publishing House, 1998) and *Growing into Hope: Liberation and Change (Vol.2)* (Peterborough: Methodist Publishing House, 1998).

63. *Faithful and Equal.*

64. Anthony G. Reddie *Faith, Stories and the Experience of Black Elders: Singing the Lord's Song in a Strange Land* (London: Jessica Kingsley, 2001).

65. This term refers to the mass migratory movement of African and African Caribbean people from the New Commonwealth to Britain. This movement began on June 22, 1948 with the arrival of 492 Jamaicans on the *S.S. Empire Windrush* at Tilbury docks. Over the next 20 years, approximately 500,000 people made this journey to Britain. This movement was effectively ended in the early late 1960s by a succession of punitive immigration bills that were passed by Conservative and Labour administrations, with the specific intention of halting black immigration, which was seen as a threat to the body politic of the country. See Peter Fryer *Staying Power: The History of Black People in Britain* (London: Pluto Press, 1992), pp. 372–386.

66. Reddie *Faith, Stories and the Experience of Black Elders*, pp. 13–46.

67. Beckford *God of the Rahtid.*

68. Ibid., pp. 1–29.

69. Ibid., pp. 27–30.

70. Ibid., pp. 8–10.

71. Ibid., pp. 38–65.

72. Revd. Dr. Emmanuel Lartey was the founding editor of *Black Theology in Britain: A Journal of Contextual Praxis* (Sheffield Academic Press, 1998), which is the first and to date the only black theological journal in Britain. The journal came into existence in October 1998. Emmanuel is credited with being one of the founders of the black theology in Britain Forum that first met in 1992. Along with Revd. Dr. George Mulrain, Robert Beckford, and others, the forum met in order to establish a conducive space in which the development of black theology in Britain could be undertaken. The forum has met monthly since that time.

73. Emmanuel Y. Lartey *In Living Colour: An Inter-Cultural Approach to Pastoral Care and Counselling* (London: Cassell, 1997).

74. Ibid., pp. 9–14.

75. Ibid., pp. 85–111.

76. Ibid., p. 87.

77. Leonardo and Boff *Introducing Liberation Theology.*

78. Matthew 25:31–46. The attributed words of Jesus "Truly, I say to you, as you did it to the least of these my brethren, you did it to me" in verse 40 has been

seen by many Liberation theologians as an essential proof text and a key theological motif for their commitment and solidarity with the poor.

79. Lartey *In Living Colour*, pp. 87–88.

80. Mary R. Sawyer "The 'American Dilemma' in the Life and Scholarship of C. Eric Lincoln." Alton B. Pollard, III and Love Henry Whelchel, JR. (eds.) *How Long This Road: Race, Religion and the Legacy of C. Eric Lincoln* (New York: Palgrave-Macmillan, 2003), pp. 43–62.

81. See Joe Aldred *Respect: Understanding Caribbean British Christianity.* (Peterborough: Epworth, 2005).

82. See Joe Aldred *Preaching With Power* (London: Cassells, 1998), *Sisters with Power* (London: Continuum, 2000), and *Praying With Power* (London: Continuum, 2000).

83. See J. Deotis Roberts *Liberation and Reconciliation: A Black Theology* (Maryknoll, NY: Orbis Books, rev. edn., 1994).

84. See Victor Anderson *Beyond Ontological Blackness* (New York: Continuum, 1995).

85. See Aldred *Respect: A Caribbean British Theology.*

86. Anderson *Beyond Ontological Blackness*, pp. 86–93.

87. See Robert E. Hood *Must God Remain Greek?: Afro-Cultures and God-Talk* (Minneapolis: Fortress Press, 1990). See also Gay L. Byron *Symbolic Blackness and Ethnic Difference in Early Christian Literature* (New York: Routledge, 2002).

88. See Dwight N. Hopkins *Down, Up and Over: Slave Religion and Black Theology* (Minneapolis: Fortress Press, 2000), pp. 13–50. See also Delores S. Williams *Sisters in the Wilderness: The Challenge of Womanist God-Talk* (Maryknoll, NY: Orbis Books, 1993), pp. 84–107.

89. See Clarence E. Hardy III *James Baldwin's God: Sex, Hope, and Crisis in Black Holiness Culture* (Knoxville, TN: University of Tennessee Press, 2003).

90. Ibid., p. 34.

91. James H. Cone *God of the Oppressed* (San Francisco: Harper, 1975), pp. 196–206.

92. Miguel A. De La Torre "Scripture." Miguel A. De La Torree (ed.) *Handbook of U.S. Theologies of Liberation* (St. Louis: Chalice Press, 2004), pp. 85–86.

93. Ibid., p. 85.

94. Ibid., p. 86.

95. See the dramatic sketch "Grasping the Chaos" Anthony G. Reddie (ed.) *Acting in Solidarity: Reflections in Critical Christianity* (London: DLT, 2005), pp. 127–135.

96. Wilmore *Black Religion and Black Radicalism*, pp. 103–135.

97. Vincent L. Wimbush *The Bible and African Americans: A Brief History* (Minneapolis: Fortress Press, 2003), pp. 63–67.

98. Ibid., p. 66.

99. At the time of writing, the *Black Boys Can* project of the Church of God of Prophecy in Britain is a direct case in point of a black church seeking to empower and affirm black young people.

100. Edward Coard *How the West Indian Child is Made Educationally Subnormal in the British School System: The Scandal of the Black Child in Britain* (London: New Beacon Books, 1971).
101. David Gillborn *Race, Ethnicity and Education: Teaching and Learning in Multi-Ethnic Schools* (London: Allen and Unwin, 1990).
102. Tony Sewell *Black Masculinities and Schooling* (Stoke-On-Trent: Trentham Books, 1997).
103. Trentham Books, a radical antiracist publisher based in Stoke-On-Trent and headed by Gillian Klein and Barbara Wiggins, has done more than most other publishers to articulate a plausible and committed apologetic for the presence of minority ethnic people in Britain. One of their most important publications is the journal *Race Equality Teaching* published three times a year by Trentham.
104. An address given at the annual greenbelt festival, Castle Ashby, Northamptonshire, 1988.
105. Cornel West "Black Theology and Human Identity." Dwight N. Hopkins (ed.) *Black Faith and Public Talk: Critical Essays on James Cone's Black Theology and Black Power* (Maryknoll, NY: Orbis Books, 1999), pp. 11–19.
106. See Anthony G. Reddie "Pentecost—Dreams and Visions (A Black Theological Reading)." Maureen Edwards (ed.) *Discovering Christ: Ascension and Pentecost* (Birmingham: IBRA, 2001), pp. 27–42.
107. See Erik H. Erikson *Identity: Youth and Crisis* (New York: W.W. Norton, 1984). This book remains the classic text that details the development of human identity throughout the course of the human lifespan. In particular, Erikson analyzes how childhood exerts a disproportionate influence upon the development of the self.
108. Cain Hope Felder "The Bible—Re-Contextualisation and the Black Religious Experience." Gayraud Wilmore (ed.) *African American Religious Studies: An Interdisciplinary Anthology* (Durham and London: Duke University Press, 1989), pp. 158–162.
109. Ibid., pp. 158–162.
110. Grant S. Shockley "Black Theology and Religious Education." Randolph Crump Miller (ed.) *Theologies of Religious Education* (Birmingham, AL: Religious Education Press, 1995), pp. 321–333.
111. Cain Hope Felder (ed.) *Stony the Road We Trod: African American Biblical Interpretation* (Minneapolis: Fortress Press, 1991).
112. Thomas Hoyt Jr. "Interpreting Biblical Scholarship for the Black Church Tradition." Cain Hope Felder (ed.) *Stony the Road We Trod: African American Biblical Interpretation* (Minneapolis: Fortress Press, 1991), pp. 17–39.
113. "The Hermeneutical Dilemma of the African American Biblical Student." *Stony the Road We Trod*, pp. 40–56.
114. "Reading Her Way Through the Struggle: African American Women and the Bible." Cain Hope Felder (ed.), pp. 57–80.
115. "Beyond Identification: The Use of Africans in Old Testament Poetry and Narratives." Cain Hope Felder (ed.), pp. 165–186.
116. "Race, Racism, and the Biblical Narratives." Cain Hope Felder (ed.), pp. 127–145.

117. In the third year of the study, it was agreed by the management committee of the project that the material in the curriculum (which hitherto had been in draft form in five separate sections) should be published and made available for wider use across the country. The material was published by the Methodist Publishing House on June 17, 1998 in two volumes. Both the volumes were given the general title of *Growing Into Hope*, Vol. 1 was subtitled *Believing and Expecting*, Vol. 2 *Liberation and Change*.

118. Reddie *Growing into Hope*, pp. 76–78.

119. See Anderson *Beyond Ontological Blackness: An Essay on African American Religious and Cultural Criticism* (New York: Continuum, 1995), pp. 130–158.

120. See Anderson *Beyond Ontological Blackness*. Anderson is critical of the heroism that pervades black religious and cultural thought, which constantly highlights seemingly extraordinary characters at the expense of the countless nameless and faceless individuals who are the more accurate representation of any community or ethnic grouping, pp. 130–158.

121. Reddie *Faith, Stories and the Experience of Black Elders*.

122. Ibid., pp. 13–15.

123. See Roswith I.H. Gerloff *A Plea for British Black Theologies: The Black Church Movement in Britain—Vol.1. and Vol.2* (Unpublished Ph.D. thesis, University of Birmingham, 1991).

124. Iain MacRobert *Black Pentecostalism: Its Origins, Functions and Theology* (Unpublished Ph.D. thesis, University of Birmingham, 1989).

125. See Reddie "Black Voices."*Acting in Solidarity*, pp. 109–119.

126. Brierley *The Tide is Running Out*, p. 136.

127. See Cornel West and Eddie S. Glaude Jr. (eds.) *African American Religious Thought: An Anthology* (Louisville: Westminster John Knox Press, 2003).

128. See Beckford *Jesus is Dread, Dread and Pentecostal* and *God of the Rahtid*.

129. However, it should be noted that the increasing numbers of black Methodists in Britain, particularly in London, are now of West African descent, not Caribbean.

130. Heather Walton *A Tree God Planted: Black People in British Methodism* (London: Methodist Church, 1984).

131. See David Sheppard *Bias to the Poor, Faith in the City: Archbishop's Commission on Urban Priority Areas, Anglicans and Racism* (Church House Publications, 1986), *Faithful and Equal:* The Report Adopted at the Portsmouth Methodist Conference (The Methodist Church, 1987), *Rainbow Gospel* (London: British Council of Churches, 1988), *Seeds of Hope: Report of a Survey on Combating Racism in the Diocese of the Church of England* (London: Church House Publications, 1991), *The Passing Winter.*

132. Robinson Milwood *Liberation and Mission* (London: ACER, 1997).

133. Naboth Muchopa (with Sandra Ackroyd and Marjorie Lewis Cooper) *Strangers No More: Transformation Through Racial Justice* (London: Methodist Church, 2001).

134. See Reddie *Faith, Stories and the Experience of Black Elders*.

135. Reddie *Growing into Hope*.

136. Anthony G. Reddie (ed.) *Legacy: Anthology in Memory of Jillian Brown* (Peterborough: Methodist Publishing House, 2000).
137. See A. Elaine Crawford *Hope in the Holler: A Womanist Theology* (Louisville: John Knox Press, 2002), pp. 15–40.
138. See Lewin L. Willaims *Caribbean Theology* (New York: Peter Lang, 1994) and George Mulrain "The Caribbean." John Parratt (ed.) *An Introduction to Third World Theologies* (Cambridge: Cambridge University Press, 2004), pp. 163–181.
139. See Devon Dick *Rebellion to Riot: The Jamaican Church in Nation Building* (Kingston: Ian Randle Publishers, 2002).
140. See John Munsey Turner *Methodism, Revolution and Social Change* (West Midlands: Wesley Historical Society, 1973), Ted Jennings *Good News to the Poor: John Wesley's Evangelical Economics* (Nashville, TN: Abingdon Press, 1990). See also David Hempton *The Religion of thePpeople: Methodism and Popular Religion* (London: Routledge, 1996).
141. Reddie, *Growing into Hope.*
142. For a U.S. perspective on black Methodism, see Foster and Smith (eds.) *Black Religious Experience.*
143. See Inderjit S. Bhogal "Citizenship." Reddie *Legacy*, pp. 137–141.
144. See Theodore Runyan *The New Creation: John Wesley's Theology Today* (Nashville, TN: Abingdon Press, 1998), pp. 146–206.
145. It is interesting to note that two of the most renowned black theologies and womanist theologies in the United States—James Cone and Jacquelyn Grant—are members of the African Methodist Episcopal Church (AME). It is a moot point, however, as to the extent to which their Christological formulations have been overtly influenced by their Methodist roots. See Cone *A Black Theology of Liberation*, pp. 110–128 and Jacquelyn Grant *White Women's Christ and Black Women's Jesus* (Atlanta: Scholar's Press, 1989), pp. 195–230.
146. See William R. Herzog III *Jesus, Justice and the Reign of God: A Ministry of Liberation* (Louisville: Westminster John Knox Press, 2000), pp. 191–216.
147. Jacquelyn Grant *White Women's Christ and Black Women's Jesus* (Atlanta: Scholar's Press, 1989), pp. 195–230.
148. See also Reddie "Pentecost—Dreams and Visions (a Black theological reading)." Maureen Edwards (ed.) *Discovering Christ: Ascension and Pentecost* (Birmingham: International Bible Reading Association, 2001), pp. 27–42.
149. The overarching authority for overseeing policing in the capital city, London.
150. The BMLU is the national campaigning and representative organization within British Methodism that seeks to challenge the structures in order to make the national church more inclusive and less racist. The group also undertakes a strategy of empowerment programs for individual and groups of black Methodists. There are, quite naturally, equivalent groups in the United Methodist Church in the United States.
151. See Beckford *Dread and Pentecost* for an examination of the ecclesiology and underlying theology of the black-led, black majority Pentecostal church in the United Kingdom. See also Aldred *Respect.*
152. James H. Cone *My Soul Looks Back* (Maryknoll, NY: Orbis Books, 2000), pp. 70–82.

153. See Sybil Phoenix *Willing Hands* (London: Pilgrim Books, 1984).
154. Doreen McCalla "Syble's Successful Children." Doreen McCalla (ed.) *Black Success in The U.K.: Essays in Racial and Ethnic Studies* (Birmingham: Cambridge University Press and DMee: Vision Learning Ltd., 2003), pp. 125–150.

3   Bring on the Sistas

1. At a later point in this chapter I pose the question as to whether womanist theology is a related branch of black theology or a wholly separate discipline in its own right.
2. Issues of the appropriate nomenclature for womanist theology is addressed at a later point in this chapter.
3. Alice Walker *In Search of Our Mothers' Gardens: Womanist Prose* (London: Women's Press, 1984).
4. Ibid., p. xi.
5. James H. Cone *A Black Theology of Liberation [Twentieth Anniversary Edition]* (Maryknoll, NY: Orbis Books, 1990).
6. Delores S. Willaims "James Cone's Liberation: Twenty Years Later." Cone *A Black Theology of Liberation*, pp. 189–195.
7. "Black Theology: Statement by the National Committee of Black Churchmen, June 13, 1969." Gayraud S. Wilmore and James H. Cone (eds.) *Black Theology: A Documentary History, 1966–1979* (Maryknoll, NY: Orbis Books, 1979), pp. 100–102.
8. Ibid., p. 102.
9. See my analysis of the dramatic sketch "My God," where I imagine God as a black woman. This can be found in chapter 3 of *Dramatizing Theologies: A Participative Approach to Black God-Talk* (London: Equinox, 2006).
10. Demetrius K. Williams "The Bible and Models of Liberation in the African American Experience." Randall C. Bailey (ed.) *Yet with a Steady Beat: Contemporary U.S. Afrocentric Biblical Interpretation* (Atlanta: Society of Biblical Literature, 2003), pp. 33–59.
11. Ibid., pp. 48–59.
12. Demetrius K. Williams *An End to this Strife: The Politics of Gender in African American Churches* (Minneapolis: Fortress Press, 2004).
13. Ibid., pp. 9–10.
14. See Dwight N. Hopkins *Head and Heart: Black Theology, Past, Present and Future* (New York: Palgrave Macmillan, 2002), pp. 89–105.
15. See Karen Baker-Fletcher and Garth Kasimu Baker Fletcher *My Sister, My Brother: Womanist and Xodus God Talk* (Eugene, OR: Wipf and Stock Publishers, 2002).
16. See Anthony G. Reddie (ed.) *Legacy: Anthology in Memory of Jillian Brown* (Peterborough: Methodist Publishing House, 2000).
17. See Elaine Foster "Women and the Inverted Pyramid of the Black Churches in Britain." G. Saghal and N. Yuval-Davis (eds.) *Refusing Holy Orders: Women and Fundamentalism in Britain* (London: Virago, 1992).

18. Walker *In Search of Our Mothers' Gardens*, pp. xi–xii.
19. Ibid., pp. xi–xii.
20. If "black" is seen as a term denoting ugliness, immorality, and is a state to be pitied, which in turn is linked to the depressed and subjugated humanity of a set of people, then God, in Christ, who sides with and identifies with the struggles of these people, is black. It is interesting to note that the only positive term that has the prefix or suffix of black in common parlance in Britain is namely when you have money in the bank; then, you are said to be "In the Black." For those within the British context, who are followers of cricket, when the West Indies cricket team toured England in 1984 and won the five test match series 5–0, the usual term of "white-wash" was inverted, and instead, it was stated that the largely all black West Indies team had "black-washed" the largely all white English team. For the ways in which the term black is inverted and given new meaning in theological terms, see Cone *A Black Theology of Liberation*, pp. 21–39.
21. In ways not dissimilar to the term "black," Beckford has sought to reconceptualize our understanding of the term "dread." Dread, often taken to mean catastrophe, fear, and anxiety in Caribbean and British idioms, is inverted and seen as a term denoting empowerment and freedom. Beckford juxtaposes this term with Jesus, in order to create a "Dread Christology." In effect, Jesus becomes Dread. See Robert Beckford *Jesus is Dread* (London: Darton, Longman and Todd, 1998), pp. 144–152.
22. The term Rahtid is often used in Jamaican/Caribbean idiom as a mild expletive and slightly less offensive word to express outrage and anger as opposed to other more extreme forms of expletives. As such, it is viewed with ambivalence in black Caribbean religiocultural contexts as a barely acceptable term. Beckford again inverts this term in order to identify Jesus' praxis and the work for the reign of God as part of process of what he terms "redemptive vengeance," in which the word "Rahtid" becomes an exemplifier for a radical and prophetic anger that is committed to challenging and overthrowing injustice. See Robert Beckford *God of the Rahtid*, pp. 38–65.
23. Stephanie Y. Mitchem *Introducing Womanist Theology* (Maryknoll, NY: Orbis Books, 2002), pp. 46–64.
24. Kate Coleman "Black Theology and Black Liberation: A Womanist Perspective." *Black Theology in Britain: A Journal of Contextual Praxis* (No. 1, October 1998), pp. 59–69.
25. See the dramatic sketch and subsequent reflections related to "Black Voices." Anthony G. Reddie *Acting in Solidarity: Reflections in Critical Christianity* (London: DLT, 2005), pp. 109–119.
26. Maxine Howell-Baker "Towards a Womanist Pneumatological Pedagogy: An Investigation into the development and Implementation of a Theological Pedagogy by and for the Marginalized." *Black Theology: An International Journal* (Vol. 3, No. 1, January 2004), pp. 32–54.
27. Ibid., p. 34.
28. See Katie G. Canon *Black Womanist Ethics* (Atlanta: Scholar's Press, 1988) and Katie G. Canon *Katie's Canon* (New York: Continuum, 2002) for excellent

examples of how black women's experience provides the raw material and is also a method for undertaking theological discourse.

29. Kelly Brown Douglas *The Black Christ* (Maryknoll, NY: Orbis Books, 1994), pp. 97–117.
30. Howell-Baker "Towards a Womanist Pneumatological Pedagogy," p. 35.
31. Victor Anderson *Beyond Ontological Blackness* (New York: Continuum, 1995), pp. 104–111.
32. Ibid., pp. 112–114.
33. Dwight N. Hopkins *Introducing Black Theology of Liberation* (Maryknoll, NY: Orbis Books, 1999), pp. 44–45.
34. Ibid., pp. 42–43.
35. See Lorraine Dixon "Are Vashti and Esther Our Sistas?" Reddie *Legacy*, pp. 97–107.
36. See Reddie *Faith, Stories and the Experience of Black Elders* (London: Jessica Kingsley, 2001).
37. Anderson *Beyond Ontological Blackness*, pp. 108–109.
38. Walker *In search of our Mothers' Garden: Womanist Prose*, pp. xi–xii.
39. See Cheryl J. Sanders "Christian Ethics and Theology in Womanist Perspective." James H. Cone and Gayraud S. Wilmore (eds.) *Black Theology: A Documentary History—Vol. 2: 1980–1992* (Maryknoll, NY: Orbis Books, 1993), pp. 336–344.
40. Ibid., p. 338.
41. See Coleman "Black Theology and Black Liberation: A Womanist Perspective," pp. 59–69. See also Kate Coleman "Black Women and Theology." *Black Theology in Britain: A Journal of Contextual Praxis* (No. 3, 1999), pp. 51–65 and Kate Coleman "Woman, Single and Christian." Joe Aldred (ed.) *Sisters With Power* (London: Continuum, 2000), pp. 10–23.
42. Coleman "Black Women and Theology," p. 52.
43. See John M. Hull *Mishmash: A Study in Metaphor—Religious Education in Multicultural Britain* (Birmingham: Christian Education Movement and University of Birmingham, 1991).
44. See Penny Thompson *Whatever Happened to Religious Education?* (Cambridge: Lutterworth Press, 2004).
45. Aldred (ed.) *Sisters With Power*.
46. Reddie (ed.) *Legacy*.
47. Kate Coleman "Woman, Single and Christian," pp. 10–23.
48. Lorraine Dixon "A Black Woman and Deacon: A Womanist Reflection on Pastoral Ministry." Aldred (ed.) *Sisters With Power*, pp. 50–64.
49. Mukti Barton "Hermeneutical Insubordination Toppling Wordly Kingdoms." Aldred (ed.) *Sisters With Power*, pp. 24–35.
50. Christine Russell Lumby "Women Leadership." Aldred (ed.) *Sisters With Power*, pp. 75–88.
51. Andrea Encinas-Meade "The Strong Black Woman." Aldred (ed.) *Sisters With Power*, pp. 148–160.
52. Joe Aldred (ed.) "Introduction." *Sisters With Power*, pp. v–vi.
53. Ibid., p. vi.

54. Lorraine Dixon "A Black Woman and Deacon: A Womanist reflection on pastoral ministry."

55. Dionne Lamont "Deconstructing Patriarchy," pp. 36–49.

56. Lorraine Dixon "Are Vashti and Esther our Sistas?" Reddie (ed.) *Legacy*, pp. 97–108 and Lorraine Dixon "bell hooks: Teller of Truth and Dreamer of Dreams," pp. 129–135.

57. Valentina Alexander "A Black Woman in Britain Moves towards an Understanding of Her Spiritual Rites." Reddie (ed.) *Legacy*, pp. 119–125.

58. Jillian Brown "Part One—The Work of Jillian M. Brown." Reddie (ed.) *Legacy*, pp. 1–78.

59. See Marjorie Lewis "Diaspora Dialogue: Womanist Theology in Engagement with Aspects of the Black British and Jamaican experience." *Black Theology: An International Journal* (Vol. 2, No. 1, January 2004), pp. 85–109.

60. See Diane Watt "Traditional Religious Practices Amongst African Caribbean Mothers and Community OtherMothers." *Black Theology: An International Journal* (Vol. 2, No. 2, July 2004), pp. 195–212.

61. Maxine E. Howell-Baker "Towards a Womanist Pneumatological Pedagogy: An Investigation into the Development and Implementation of a Theological Pedagogy by and for the marginalized." *Black Theology: An International Journal* (Vol. 3, No. 1, January 2005), pp. 32–54.

62. Lewis "Diaspora Dialogue," pp. 100–109.

63. Ibid., p. 100.

64. Diane Watt "Traditional Religious Practices Amongst African Caribbean Mothers and Community OtherMothers," pp. 195–212.

65. Maxine E. Howell-Baker "Towards a Womanist Pneumatological Pedagogy." *Black Theology: An International Journal* (Vol. 3, No. 1, January 2004), pp. 32–54.

66. See Paul Gilroy *The Black Atlantic: Modernity and Double Consciousness* (London: Verso, 1993).

67. See Lee *Back Between Home and Belonging: Critical Ethnographies of Race, Place and Identity* (London: Centre for New Ethnicities Research, 1999). See also Les Back *New Ethnicities and Urban Culture: Racisms and Multiculture in Young Lives* (London: University College of London Press, 1996).

68. Jacquelyn Grant *White Women's Christ and Black Women's Jesus* (Atlanta: Scholars Press, 1989).

69. Cone *Black Theology and Black Power.*

70. Cone *A Black Theology of Liberation.*

71. James H. Cone *God of the Oppressed* (San Francisco: Harper, 1975).

72. See "Postsketch Reflections for 'A problem Shared,' " Reddie (ed.) *Acting in Solidarity*, pp. 72–74.

73. Anthony G. Reddie *Nobodies to Somebodies: A Practical Theology for Education and Liberation* (Peterborough: Epworth Press, 2003), pp. 11–12.

74. Josiah Young "Envisioning the Son of Man." *Black Theology: An International Journal* (Vol. 2, No. 1, January 2004), pp. 11–17.

75. Cham Kaur-Mann "Who Do You Say I am?: Images of Jesus." *Black Theology: An International Journal* (Vol. 2, No. 1, January 2004), pp. 19–44.

76. Grant *White Women's Christ and Black Women's Jesus*, pp. 9–62.

77. This term emanates from a Jamaican woman by name of Hilary Robertson-Hickling who has been resident in Britain. See Hilary Robertson-Hickling "For Absent Friends." Reddie (ed.) *Legacy*, pp. 112–114.
78. Katie Geneva Canon *Katie's Canon: Womanism and the Soul of the Black Community* (New York: Continuum, 1995).
79. Ibid., pp. 47–56.
80. Ibid., pp. 55–56.
81. Ibid., p. 56.
82. Walker *In Search of Our Mother's Gardens*, pp. xi–xii.
83. Canon *Katie's Canon*, p. xii.
84. See Stacey Floyd-Thomas and Laura Gillman " 'The Whole Story is What I'm After': Womanist Revolutions and Liberation Feminist Revelations through Biomythography and Emancipatory Historiography." *Black Theology: An International Journal* (Vol. 3, No. 2, July 2005) pp. 176–199.
85. Heidi Safia Mirza (ed.) *Black British Feminism: A Reader* (London: Routledge, 1997).
86. Amina Mama *Beyond the Masks: Race, Gender and Subjectivity* (London and New York: Routledge, 1995).
87. See Audre Lorde *Sister Outsider: The Essays and Speeches* (Freedom, CA: Crossing Press, 1984). See also Audre Lorde *Zami: A New Spelling of My Name* (London: Sheba, 1984).
88. Patricia Hill Collins *Black Feminist Thought: Knowledge, Consciousness and the Politics of Empowerment* (New York & London: Routledge, 2000).
89. Grant *White Women's Christ and Black Women's Jesus*.
90. See Valentina Alexander *To Break Every Fetter?: To What Extent Has the Black-Led Church in Britain Developed a Theology of Liberation?* (Unpublished Ph.D. thesis, University of Warwick, 1996).
91. See Carol J. Tomlin *Black Preaching Style* (Unpublished M.Phil. thesis, University of Birmingham, 1988).
92. See Elaine F. Foster *Black Women in Black-Led Churches: A Study of Black Women's Contribution to the Growth and Development of Black-Led Churches in Britain* (Unpublished M.Phil. thesis, University of Birmingham, 1990).
93. Extracts of Alexander's doctoral thesis will be published in Michael N. Jagessar and Anthony G. Reddie (eds.) *Black Theology and Black Religion in Britain: A Reader* (London: Equinox Publishing, c. 2007).
94. Mukti Barton *Scripture as Empowerment for Liberation and Justice: The Experience of Christian and Muslim Women in Bangladesh* (Bristol: Centre For Comparative Studies in Religion and Gender, University of Bristol, 1999).
95. Mukti Barton *Rejection, Resistance and Resurrection: Speaking Out on Racism in the Church* (London: DLT, 2005).
96. Dwight N. Hopkins "A New Black Heterosexual Male." *Black Theology in Britain* (Vol. 4, No. 2, May 2002), pp. 214–227.
97. Kate Coleman "Black Women and Theology." *Black Theology in Britain: A Journal of Contextual Praxis* (No. 3, 1999), pp. 51–65.
98. See the postsketch reflection to "In The Psychiatrist's Chair." Reddie (ed.) *Acting in Solidarity: Reflections in Critical Christianity* (London: DLT, 2005),

pp. 19–21 for a brief discussion on the ethnocentric concentration on white Euro-American values and assumptions in much that is considered generic in scholarly British theological work.

99. See Foster *Black Women in Black-Led Churches*.
100. Yvette Hutchinson "When Being a Woman Is Not Enough." Joe Aldred (ed.) *Sisters With Power* (London and New York: Continuum, 2000), pp. 1–9.
101. See Robert Beckford *Dread and Pentecostal* (London: SPCK, 2000), pp. 35–66.
102. See postsketch reflections to "It Could Have Happened Like This." Reddie *Acting in Solidarity*, pp. 50–52.
103. Doreen Morrison "Resisting Racism—By Celebrating 'Our' Blackness." *Black Theology: An International Journal* (Vol. 1, N0. 2, May 2003), pp. 209–223.
104. See Anderson *Beyond Ontological Blackness*, pp. 142–158.
105. See Reddie *Dramatizing Theologies*.
106. See E. Hammond Oglesby *O Lord, Move This Mountain* (St. Louis, MO: Chalice Press, 1998).
107. See Cannon *Black Womanist Ethics*, pp. 1–23.
108. See Evelyn L. Parker *Twenty Seeds of Hope: Religious Moral Values in African American Adolescents in Chicago and Implications for Christian Education in the Black Church* (Unpublished Ph.D. thesis, Garret/Northwestern University Program in Religious and Theological Studies, 1996), pp. 46–147. See also Evelyn L. Parker *Trouble Don't Always Last: Emancipatory Hope Among African American Adolescents* (Cleveland, OH: Pilgrim Press, 2003).
109. See Emilie Townes *In a Blaze of Glory* (Nashville, TN: Abingdon Press, 1995).
110. See N. Lynne Westfield *Dear Sisters: A Womanist Practice of Hospitality* (Cleveland, OO: Pilgrim Press, 2001). See also N. Lynne Westfield "Towards A Womanist Approach to Pedagogy." *Religious Education* (Vol. 98, No. 4, Fall 2003), pp. 521–532 (520).
111. See Chapter 5: "Theology from the Bottom Up: Developing an Inclusive Methodology for Engaging with the Voiceless." Reddie (ed.) *Dramatizing Theologies*.
112. Townes *In a Blaze of Glory*, p. 11.
113. N. Lynne Westfield "Kitchen Table Banter." *Religious Education* (Vol. 96, No. 3, Summer 2001), pp. 423–429.
114. Karen Baker-Fletcher and Garth Kasimu Baker-Fletcher *My Sister, My Brother*, pp. 16–18.
115. James H. Cone *A Black Theology of Liberation*, p. xvi.
116. Karen Baker-Fletcher and Kasimu Baker-Fletcher *My Sister, My Brother*.
117. Ibid., pp. 15–16.
118. See Reddie *Acting in Solidarity* and *Dramatizing Theologies*.
119. Among the major works of James H. Cone are *Black Theology and Black Power* and *A Black Theology of Liberation*. Among his recent books are *Martin, Malcolm and America* (Maryknoll, NY: Orbis Books, 1992) and *Risks of Faith* (Boston: Beacon Press, 1999).

120. See Major J. Jones *Christian Ethics for Black Theology* (Nashville, TN: Abingdon Press, 1974).
121. See J. Deotis Roberts *Liberation and Reconciliation: A Black Theology* (Maryknoll, NY: Orbis Books, rev. edn, 1994).
122. Preston N. Williams "James Cone and the Problem of a Black Ethic." *Harvard Theological Review* (No. 65, 1972), pp. 483–484.
123. Anthony B. Pinn *Noise and Spirit: The Religious and Spiritual Sensibilities of Rap Music* (New York: New York University Press, 2003).
124. Dwight N. Hopkins *Being Human: Race, Culture and Religion* (Minneapolis: Fortress Press, 2005).
125. See Beckford *God of the Rahtid*.
126. See Cannon *Black Womanist Ethics*.
127. See Townes *In a Blaze of Glory*.
128. Williams *An End to this Strife*, pp. 9–10.
129. Beckford describes this phenomenon as passive radicalism. See Beckford *Dread and Pentecostal*, pp. 46–48.
130. See Vincent L. Wimbush *The Bible and African Americans: A Brief History* (Minneapolis: Fortress Press, 2003), pp. 63–70.
131. See Cone *God of the Oppressed*, pp. 62–83 and Vincent L. Wimbush (ed.) *African Americans and The Bible: Sacred Texts and Social Textures* (New York: Continuum, 2000) for a comprehensive appraisal of the myriad ways in which African Americans have engaged with the Bible.

4   Education, Education, Education

This now seemingly clichéd phrase was uttered by Tony Blair, when he was campaigning for the 1997 general elections in Britain as leader of the official opposition party, the Labour Party.

1. See Frederick L. Ware *Methodologies of Black Theology* (Cleveland, OH: Pilgrim Press, 2002) for an excellent overview of the various methodological approaches employed by black theologians over the past 40 years.
2. See Dale P. Andrews *Practical Theology for Black Churches: Bridging Black Theology and African American Folk Religion* (Louisville: John Knox Press, 2002), and James H. Harris *Pastoral Theology: A Black-Church Perspective* (Minneapolis: Fortress Press, 1991).
3. See Dwight N. Hopkins (ed.) *Black Faith and Public Talk: Critical Essays on James H. Cone's Black Theology and Black Power* (Maryknoll, NY: Orbis Books, 1999) and Linda E. Thomas (ed.) *Living Stones in the Household of God* (Minneapolis: Fortress Press, 2004) that are excellent examples of texts written in honor of and in response to the legacy of James Cone.
4. Examples of this terminology can be found in the work of such scholars as George L. Champion, Sr. *Christian Education for the African American Church* (Riviera Beach, FL: Port Printing Company, 1990) and Lora-Ellen McKinney *Christian Education in The African American Church* (Valley Forge, PA: Judson Press, 2003).

5. See Peter J. Paris *The Social Teaching of the Black Churches* (Minneapolis: Fortress Press, 1985) and C. Eric Lincoln and Lawrence Mamiya *The Black Church in the African American Experience* (Durham and London: Duke University Press, 1990).

6. James H. Cone *For My People* (Maryknoll, NY: Orbis Books, 1984), pp. 99–121.

7. See Dwight N. Hopkins *Head and Heart* (New York: Palgrave MacMillan, 2003), pp. 109–154.

8. Jeremiah A. Wright Jr. "Unashamedly Black and Unapologetically Christian." Michael I.N. Dash, L. Rita Dixon, Darius L. Swann, and Ndugu T'Ofori-Atta (eds.) *African Roots: Towards an Afrocentric Christian Witness* (Lithonia, GA: SCP/Third World Literature, 1994), pp. 178–195.

9. See my account of and reflections on the phenomenon of Prosperity Gospel in "The Plain Old Honest Truth?" Anthony G. Reddie (ed.) *Acting in Solidarity: Reflections in Critical Christianity* (London: DLT, 2005), pp. 44–153.

10. Olivia Pearl Stokes "Black Theology: A Challenge to Religious Education." Norma H. Thompson (ed.) *Religious Education and Theology* (Birmingham AL: Religious Education Press, 1982), p. 71.

11. James H. Cone *Black Theology and Black Power* (New York: Seabury Press, 1969), pp. 62–90.

12. James H. Cone *God of the Oppressed* (San Francisco: Harper, 1975), p. 18.

13. James H. Cone *A Black Theology of Liberation* (Maryknoll, NY: Orbis Books, 1990), p. 1.

14. Ibid., p. 5.

15. Albert J. Raboteau *Slave Religion* (Oxford: Oxford University Press, 1978), pp. 44–150.

16. Eric Williams *Capitalism and Slavery* (London: Andre Deutsch, 1964), pp. 30–168.

17. See Dwight N. Hopkins *Being Human: Race, Culture and Religion* (Minneapolis: Fortress Press, 2005), pp. 118–160.

18. W.E.B. Dubois "The African Roots of War (1915)." Meyer and Wenberg (eds.) *W.E.B. Dubois: A Reader* (New York: Harper and Row, 1970), pp. 360–371.

19. Walter Rodney *How Europe Underdeveloped Africa* (London: Bogle-L'Ouverture, 1972), p. 69.

20. David Northrup (ed.) *The Atlantic Slave Trade* (Lexington, MA: D.C. Heath & Co., 1994), pp. 12–35. See also Carter G. Woodson *The Miseducation of the Negro* (1933, repr. Trenton, NJ: Africa World Press, 1990), pp. xii–xiii.

21. Bob Marley "Redemption Song." from the album *Uprising* (Bob Marley Music: Island Records, 1980).

22. Matthew 5:1–12.

23. The best example of this work can be seen in my previous text—Anthony G. Reddie *Nobodies to Somebodies: A Practical Theology for Education and Liberation* (Peterborough: Epworth Press, 2003).

24. See Joseph V. Crockett *Teaching Scripture from an African American Perspective* (Nashville, TN: Discipleship Resources, 1991).

25. See Anne Streaty Wimberly *Soul Stories: African American Christian Education* (Nashville, TN: Abingdon Press, 1994).
26. See Michael I.N. Dash, Jonathan Jackson, and Stephen C. Rasor (eds.) *Hidden Wholeness: An African American Spirituality for Individuals and Communities* (Cleveland, OH: United Church Press, 1997).
27. Yolanda Y. Smith *Reclaiming the Spirits: New Possibilities for African American Christian Education* (Cleveland, OH: Pilgrim Press, 2004).
28. Ibid., p. 2.
29. Ibid., p. 3.
30. Ibid., pp. 9–54.
31. Ibid., pp. 55–82.
32. Ibid., pp. 83–101.
33. Ibid., pp. 102–115.
34. Ibid., pp. 102–115.
35. See Anthony B. Pinn *Terror and Triumph: The Nature of Black Religion* (Minneapolis: Fortress Press, 2003), pp. 133–156.
36. See Charles R. Foster and Grant S. Shockley (eds.) *Working With Black Youth: Opportunities for Christian Ministry* (Nashville, TN: Abingdon Press, 1989).
37. Grant S. Shockley "Historical Perspectives," pp. 9–29.
38. Ibid., pp. 22–26.
39. Ibid., p. 23.
40. Charles R. Foster and Fred Smith (eds.) *Black Religious Experience: Conversations on Double Consciousness and the Work of Grant Shockley* (Nashville, TN: Abingdon Press, 2003).
41. This issue is addressed in part by Elaine Crawford. See A. Elaine Crawford "Womanist Christology and the Wesleyan Tradition." *Black Theology: An International Journal* (Vol. 2, No. 2, July 2004), pp. 213–220.
42. Foster and Smith (eds.) *Black Religious Experience*, pp. 25–44.
43. Ibid., pp. 45–74.
44. Ibid., pp. 125–152.
45. See Grant S. Shockley "Black Liberation, Christian Education and Black Social Indicators." *Duke Divinity School Review* (Vol. 40, Spring 1975), pp. 109–125.
46. Foster and Smith (eds.) *Black Religious Experience*, p. 73.
47. See Cone *For My People*.
48. N. Lynne Westfield *Dear Sisters: A Womanist Practice of Hospitality* (Cleveland, OH: Pilgrim Press, 2001).
49. Ibid.
50. Ibid., p. 5.
51. Ibid., pp. 40–77.
52. Ibid., pp. 40–103.
53. Ibid., pp. 40–77.
54. See bell hooks *Teaching to Transgress* (New York: Routledge, 1994).
55. Westfield *Dear Sisters*, pp. 40–77.
56. See Emilie Townes *In a Blaze of Glory* (Nashville, TN: Abingdon Press, 1995).

57. N. Lynne Westfield "Kitchen Table Banter." *Religious Education* (Vol. 96, No. 3, Summer 2001), pp. 423–429.
58. Wimberly *Soul Stories* and Anne Streaty Wimberly (ed.) *Honoring African American Elders: A Ministry in the Soul Community* (San Francisco: Jossey-Bass Publishers, 1997).
59. Maxine Howell-Baker "Towards a Womanist Pneumatological Pedagogy: An Investigation into the Development and Implementation of a Theological Pedagogy by and for the Marginalized." *Black Theology: An International Journal* (Vol. 3, No. 1, January 2004), pp. 32–54.
60. See Anthony G. Reddie "Pentecost: Dreams and Visions—A Black Theological Reading." Maureen Edwards (ed.) *Discovering Christ: Ascension and Pentecost* (Birmingham: IRBA, 2001), pp. 27–42.
61. Birmingham is situated in the West Midlands of Britain, and is the second largest city, with a population of approximately 1.2 million people.
62. Bob Marley and the Wailers "Survivors" on the album *Survival* (Island records, 1979).
63. See Michael Joseph Brown *The Blackening of the Bible* (Harrisburg: Trinity Press International, 2004) for an excellent overview on the differing ways in which African American biblical scholars have constructed varying forms of hermeneutics for reading the Bible.
64. See Dwight N. Hopkins *Down, Up and Over: Slave Religion and Black Theology* (Minneapolis: Fortress Press, 2000), pp. 13–41.
65. Grant Shockley "From Emancipation to Transformation to Consummation. A Black perspective." Marlene Mayr (ed.) *Does the Church Really want Religious Education?* (Birmingham, AL: Religious Education Press, 1988), p. 228.
66. See Cain Hope Felder "Race, Racism and Biblical Narratives." *The Original African Heritage Study Bible* (Nashville, TN: The James C. Winston Publishing Company, 1993), p. 1572.
67. Verses 5–12.
68. Cain Hope Felder (ed.) *The Original African Heritage Study Bible* (Nashville, TN: The James C. Winston Publishing Company, 1993), p. 1572.
69. Cain Hope Felder (ed.) *Stony the Road We Trod: African American Biblical Interpretation* (Minneapolis: Augsburg Press, 1991). See also Randall C. Bailey and Jacquelyn Grant (eds.) *The Recovery of Black Presence: An Interdisciplinary Exploration* (Nashville, TN: Abingdon Press, 1995).
70. Black British theologian Robert Beckford uses the term *Dread that* denotes, mighty, powerful, and dynamic. See Robert Beckford *Jesus is Dread* (London: Darton, Longman and Todd, 1998).
71. Hopkins *Head and Heart*, pp. 127–154.
72. See Robert Beckford *God of the Rahtid* (London: DLT, 2001), pp. 1–30.
73. The notable reggae performer and poet Linton Kwesi Johnson details the litany of black deaths in police custody in his track "T'ings and Times" on the album *Tings and Times* (London: LKJ Records, 1991).
74. Beckford *God of the Rahtid*, pp. 31–38.
75. Janice Hale "The Transmission of Faith to Young African American Children." Bailey and Grant (eds.) *The Recovery of Black Presence* (Nashville, TN: Abingdon Press, 1995), p. 207.

76. Cone *God of the Oppressed*, pp. 17–29.
77. Dwight N. Hopkins *Black Theology of Liberation*, pp. 23–28.
78. Harold Dean Trulear "African American Religious Education." Barbara Wilkerson (ed.) *Multicultural Religious Education* (Birmingham, AL: Religious Education Press, 1997), p. 162.
79. Anthony G. Reddie *Faith, Stories and the Experience of Black Elders* (London: Jessica Kingsley, 2001).
80. This term refers to the mass migratory movement of black people from the Caribbean and Africa to Britain. This movement began on June 22, 1948, when the *SS. Windrush* deposited 492 Jamaicans at Tilbury docks. Over the course of the next 20 years, approximately half a million people came to Britain. The black young people in "Survivors" are their immediate descendants.
81. The overarching authority for overseeing policing in the capital city, London.
82. See Report of An Inquiry by Sir William MacPherson of Cluny, Advised by The Right Revd. Dr. John Sentamu and Dr. Richard Stone: Presented to Parliament by the Secretary of State for the Home Department by Command of Her Majesty (London: Her Majesty's Stationary Office (HMSO), 1999).
83. I have challenged notions of this "Commonsense" refusal by white authority to engage with racial injustice in a previous piece of work. See my exercise entitled "The Quest for Racial Justice." Reddie *Acting in Solidarity*, pp. 109–119.
84. See Doreen McCalla (ed.) *Black Success in the UK: Essays in Racial and Ethnic Studies* (Birmingham, UK: DMEE, Vision Learning Ltd. and Cambridge University Press, 2004).
85. See Beckford *God of the Rahtid*.
86. Cheryl Bridges Johns *Pentecostal Formation: A Pedagogy among the Oppressed* (Sheffield: Sheffield Academic Press, 1993), pp. 91–110.
87. See Mukti Barton "I am Black and Beautiful." *Black Theology: An International Journal* (Vol. 2, No. 2, July 2004), pp. 167–187.
88. Cheryl Bridges Johns *Pentecostal Formation*, pp. 30–35.
89. James H. Cone *Risks of Faith* (Boston: Beacon Press, 1999), pp. 130–145.
90. Bhikpu Parekh *Rethinking Multiculturism: Cultural Diversity an Political Theory* (Basingstoke, Hampshire: Macmillan, 2000).
91. Nancy Lynne Westfield "Teaching for Globalized Consciousness: Black Professor, White Student and Shame." *Black Theology: An International Journal* (Vol. 2, No. 1, January 2004), pp. 73–83.
92. See my analysis of the psychosocial dimensions of liberation in the dramatic sketch "Love Is the Answer."Anthony G. Reddie *Dramatizing Theologies: A Participative Approach to Black God-talk* (London: Equinox Publishing, 2006).
93. See Robert Beckford *Dread and Pentecostal* (London: SPCK, 2000). Beckford identities Pentecost as the key theological motif for black British theology, for it encapsulates the vision of a pneumataologically inspired ideal for community and belonging—one in which difference and racialized categories are exploded.
94. Mary A. Love "Musings on Sunday School in the Black Community." D. Campbell Wyckoff (ed.) *Renewing the Sunday School and the CDD* (Birmingham, AL: Religious Education Press, 1986), pp. 155–161.

95. Enoch H. Oglesby "Ethical and Educational Implications of Black Theology in America." *Religious Education* (Vol. 69, No. 4, January–February 1974), pp. 406–411.

96. See Cornell West *Democracy Matters* (New York: Penguin, 2004).

97. Evelyn L. Parker *Trouble Don't Always Last* (Cleveland, OH: Pilgrim Press, 2003), pp. 1–10.

98. Janice Hale "The Transmission of Cultural Values to Young African American children." *The Journal of Young Children* (Vol. 46, No. 6, 1990), pp. 9–13.

99. Reddie *Nobodies to Somebodies*, pp. 152–171.

5   Published and Be Damned—Reassessing the Role and Development of the Black Theology Journal

1. *Black Theology in Britain: A Journal of Contextual Praxis–BTIB* [1st published in October 1998] (Issue No.1) (Sheffield Academic Press). Last issue was published as Vol. 4, No. 2, in May 2002. In total, eight issues were published under this original title.

2. *Black Theology: An International Journal* was the successor to BTIB, although with a similar editorial team. The change in name was partly commercially driven, but also to reflect the growing confidence of the journal, in that it was now seeking to work on an international canvass, rather than a purely British one. The first issue under this new title was published in November 2002. The publisher was Continuum. At the time of writing, the journal remains under the present title and is now published by Equinox.

3. *Contact: The Interdisciplinary Journal of Pastoral Studies* ISSN 1352. 0806. <www. contactpracticaltheology.org>

4. *Contact: Practical Theology and Pastoral Care* ISSN 1352. 0806. <www. contactpracticaltheology.org>

5. Robert Beckford "Black Sexual Representation and Pastoral Care." *Contact*, 118, 1995, pp. 15–24.

6. George Mulrain "Bereavement Counselling among African Caribbean people." *Contact*, 118, 1995, pp. 9–16.

7. Jeffrey Brown "Young, Gifted and Black." *Contact*, 122, 1997, pp. 11–16.

8. Emmanuel Y. Lartey "African Perspectives on Pastoral Liturgy." *Contact*, 112, 1993, pp. 3–12.

9. Lorraine Dixon "Reflections on Pastoral Care from a Womanist perspective." *Contact*, 132, 2000, pp. 3–10.

10. See postsketch reflections to "In The Psychiatrist's Chair" Anthony G. Reddie *Acting in Solidarity: Reflections in Critical Christianity* (London: DLT, 2005), pp. 15–21.

11. See E. Hammond Oglesby *O Lord, Move This Mountain* (St. Louis, MO: Chalice Press, 1998).

12. Anthony G. Reddie "Towards a Black Christian Education of Liberation: The Christian Education of Black Children in Britain." *Black Theology in Britain: A Journal of Contextual Praxis* (Vol. 1, October 1998), pp. 46–58.

13. The source for this research is minutes of committee meetings dating from February 1997 through June 2001. All meetings were held at the Centre for Black and White Christian Partnership, Selly Oak, Birmingham.

14. Minutes of editorial committee held at the Centre for Black and White Christian Partnership, Birmingham, England, July 3, 1997.

15. See Inderjit S. Bhogal *A Table for All: A Challenge to Church and Nation* (Sheffield: Penistone Publications, 2000). See also Inderjit S. Bhogal "Citizenship." Anthony G. Reddie (ed.) *Legacy: Anthology in Memory of Jillian Brown* (Peterborough: Methodist Publishing House, 2000), pp. 137–141 and Inderjit S. Bhogal *On the Hoof: Theology in Transit* (Sheffield: Penistone Publications, 2001).

16. Inderjit Bhogal was elected to the annual post of "President of the Methodist Conference in 2000. This post is the highest representative office in the life of the British methodist church.

17. Bhogal *A Table for All*, p. 14.

18. Paul Grant and Raj Patel (eds.) *A Time To Speak: Perspectives of Black Christians in Britain* (Birmingham: Racial Justice and the Black Theology Working Group, 1990).

19. Paul Grant and Raj Patel (eds.) *A Time To Act: Kairos 1992* (Birmingham: Racial Justice and the Black and Third World Theology Working Group, 1992).

20. Minutes of the editorial committee held at the Centre For Black and White Christian Partnership, Birmingham, England, October 27, 1997.

21. Joe D. Aldred (ed.) *Sisters with Power* (London: Continuum, 2000), p. v.

22. Minutes of the editorial committee held at the Centre for Black and White Christian Partnership, Birmingham, England, October 27, 1997.

23. Ibid., November 10, 1997.

24. Ibid., November 7, 1997.

25. Ibid., February 10, 1998.

26. See James H. Harris *Pastoral Theology: A Black-Church Perspective* (Minneapolis: Fortress Press, 1991).

27. Dale P. Andrews *Practical Theology for Black Churches: Bridging Black Theology and African American Folk Religion* (Louisville: John Knox Press, 2002).

28. See my dramatic sketch entitled "We Know Best" in chapter 1 of Anthony G. Reddie *Dramatizing Theologies: A Participative Approach to Black God-Talk* (London: Equinox Publishing, 2006).

29. See the reflections prior and after "It Could Have Happened Like This?" Reddie *Acting in Solidarity*, pp. 45–53.

30. Minutes of the editorial committee held at the Centre for Black and White Christian Partnership, Birmingham, England, February 10, 1998.

31. Ibid., October 7, 1997.

32. Valentina Alexander "Afrocentric and Black Christian Consciousness: Towards an Honest Intersection." *Black Theology in Britain: A Journal of Contextual Praxis* (Issue No. 1, October 1998), pp. 11–19.

33. See Cheryl Sanders *Living the Intersection* (Minneapolis: Fortress Press, 1995).

34. Ron A. Nathan "Caribbean Youth Identity in the United Kingdom: A Call for a Pan-African Theology." *Black Theology in Britain* (Issue No.1, 1998), pp. 19–34.

35. See Josiah U. Young *A Pan-African Theology* (Trenton, NJ: Africa World Press, 1992).
36. George Mulrain "The Music of African Caribbean Theology." *Black Theology in Britain*, pp. 35–45.
37. Anthony G. Reddie "Towards a Black Christian Education of Liberation: The Christian Education of Black Children in Britain." *Black Theology in Britain* (Issue No. 1, 1998), pp. 46–58.
38. Kate Coleman "Black Theology and Black Liberation: A Womanist Perspective." *Black Theology in Britain* (Issue No. 1, 1998), pp. 59–69.
39. Paul Grant "Back to the Future: On Globalization and Political Mobilization." *Black Theology in Britain: A Journal of Contextual Praxis* (Issue No. 2, April 1999), pp. 47–56.
40. Eric Pemberton "African Slave Religions in the Caribbean." *Black Theology in Britain*, pp. 90–116.
41. Lorraine Dixon " 'Teach it, Sister!': Mahalia Jackson as Theologian in Song." *Black Theology in Britain* (Issue No. 2, 1999), pp. 72–89.
42. Lena Robinson "Black and Mixed Parentage Adolescents in Britain: An Overview of Racial Identity Issues." *Black Theology in Britain: A Journal of Contextual Praxis* (Issue No. 4, May 2000), pp. 113–125.
43. Roswith Gerloff "An African Continuum in Variation: The African Christian Diaspora in Britain." *Black Theology in Britain: A Journal of Contextual Praxis* (Issue No. 4, May 2000), pp. 84–112.
44. Diana L. Hayes "Women's Rights are Human Rights: A Womanist Perspective." *Black Theology in Britain: A Journal of Contextual Praxis* (Issue No. 5, November 2000), pp. 51–67.
45. Dwight N. Hopkins "A New Black Heterosexual male." *Black Theology in Britain: A Journal of Contextual Praxis* (Vol. 4, No. 2, May 2002), pp. 214–227.
46. Anthony B. Pinn "Rope, Neckties and Lynchings: A Discussion of Terror as an impetus for Black Religion." *Black Theology: An International Journal* (Vol. 1, No. 1, November 2002), pp. 11–28.
47. Josiah U. Young "Envisioning the Son of Man." *Black Theology: An International Journal* (Vol. 2, No. 1, January 2004), pp. 11–17.
48. A. Elaine Crawford "Womanist Christology and Wesleyan Tradition." *Black Theology: An International Journal* (Vol. 2, No. 2, July 2004), pp. 213–220.
49. James H. Cone "Theology's Great Sin: Silence in the Face of White Supremacy." *Black Theology: An International Journal* (Vol. 2, No. 2, July 2004), pp. 139–152.
50. See Beckford *Jesus is Dread, God of The Rahtid*, and *God and The Gangs*.
51. Minutes of the editorial committee held at the Centre for Black and White Christian Partnership, Birmingham, England, July 3, 1997.
52. See Gayraud S. Wilmore and James H. Cone (eds.) *Black Theology: A Documentary History, 1966–1979* (Maryknoll, NY: Orbis Books, 1979), pp. 112–219.
53. See postsketch reflections to "In The Psychiatrist's Chair" Reddie *Acting in Solidarity*, pp. 15–21.

54. See Anthony G. Reddie *Nobodies to Somebodies: A Practical Theology for Education and Liberation* (Peterborough: Epworth Press, 2003), pp. 141–146.

55. Ibid., p. 144.

56. Nancy Lynne Westfield "Teaching for Globalized Consciousness: Black Professor, White Student and Shame." *Black Theology: An International Journal* (Vol. 2, No. 1, January 2004), pp. 73–83.

57. Mark Lewis Taylor "A Dictionary for Resisting Empire: Celebrating the *Dictionary of Third World Theologies.*" *Black Theology in Britain: A Journal of Contextual Praxis* (Issue No. 6, 2001), pp. 87–105.

58. Roswith Gerloff "An African Continuum in Variation: The African Christian Diaspora in Britain." *Black Theology in Britain: A Journal of Contextual Praxis* (Issue No. 4, 2000), pp. 84–112.

59. Roswith I.H. Gerloff *A Plea for British Black Theologies: The Black Church Movement in Britain in Its Transatlantic Cultural and Theological Interaction,* 2 Vols. (Frankfurt and New York: Peter Lang, 1992).

60. See Valentina Alexander *To Break Every Fetter?: To What Extent Has the Black-Led Church in Britain Developed a Theology of Liberation?* (Unpublished Ph.D. thesis, University of Warwick, 1996). See also Robert Beckford *Dread and Pentecostal* (London: SPCK, 2000), Joe Aldred *Respect: A Caribbean British Contextual Theology* (Peterborough: Epworth Press, 2006), Mark Sturge *Look What the Lord Has Done!: An Exploration of Black Christian Faith in Britain* (London: Scripture Union, 2005).

61. See Anthony G. Reddie *Faith, Stories and the Experience of Black Elders: Singing the Lord's Song in a Strange Land* (London: Jessica Kingsley, 2001), pp. 107–110.

62. See Virginia Fabella and R.S. Sugirtharajah (eds.) *Dictionary of Third World Theologies* (Maryknoll, NY: Orbis Books, 2000).

63. Taylor "A Dictionary for Resisting Empire," p. 89.

64. See Virginia Fabella and R.S. Sugirtharajah (eds.) *Dictionary of Third World Theologies* (Maryknoll, NY: Orbis Books, 2000).

65. Taylor "A Dictionary for Resisting Empire," p. 91.

66. See Rebecca Chopp and Mark Taylor (eds.) *Reconstructing Christian Theologies* (Minneapolis: Fortress Press, 1994).

67. Taylor *The Executed God.*

68. See Reddie *Dramatizing Theologies.*

69. Clive Marsh "Black Christs in White Christian Perspective: Some Critical Reflections." *Black Theology: An International Journal* (Vol. 2, No. 1, January 2004), pp. 45–56.

70. See chapter 1 of this book.

71. See postsketch reflections to "Issues For The City" Reddie *Acting in Solidarity,* pp. 136–143 where I argue that one of the underexplored areas within British Urban theology (which remains largely the preserve of white scholars) is the nature of white flight by the white middle class. In the exercise from which these reflections have been drawn, many black people have commented ruefully on the continuing tendency of white people to make a run for

it when too many black folk move into the area and are perceived to have taken over the wider community and the church.

72. Maitland M. Evans *Counselling for Community Change: A Study Which Engages African-Caribbean Beliefs and Core Values to Construct a Missio-Cultural Counselling Model and to Further Examine Its Effectiveness in Engendering Mature Personhood and Community Change* (Unpublished Ph.D. thesis, University of Birmingham, 1999).

73. V. Clarice C. Barnes *The Montserrat volcanic disaster: A study of meaning, psycho-social effects, coping and intervention* (Unpublished Ph.D. thesis, The University of Birmingham, 2000).

6   Where We Headed Now?

1. See Anthony G. Reddie *Acting in Solidarity: Reflections in Critical Christianity* (London: DLT, 2005) and *Dramatizing Theologies: A Participative Approach to Black God-Talk* (London: Equinox Publishing, 2006).
2. See James H. Cone *A Black Theology of Liberation* (Maryknoll, NY: Orbis Books, 1990).
3. See J. Deotis Roberts *Liberation and Reconciliation: A Black Theology* (Maryknoll, NY: Orbis Books, rev. edn, 1994).
4. Gayraud S. Wilmore *Black Religion and Black Radicalism* (Maryknoll, NY: Orbis Books, 1983).
5. See also Jacquelyn Grant *White Women's Christ and Black Women's Jesus* (Atlanta: Scholar's Press, 1989).
6. Katie Geneva Canon *Katie's Canon: Womanism and the Soul of the Black Community* (New York: Continuum, 1995).
7. Emile M. Townes M. *Womanist Justice, Womanist Hope* (Atlanta, GA, Scholars Press, 1993).
8. For further information on the Skatalites, see <http://www.skatalites.com/>, which is the official website of the group.
9. See Reddie *Acting in Solidarity* and *Dramatizing Theologies*.
10. Ibid.
11. Ibid.
12. Reddie *Dramatizing Theologies*.
13. Ward and Burns describe jazz as the music of America. See Geoffrey C. Ward and Ken Burns *Jazz: A History of America's Music* (London: Pimlico, 2001).
14. For the development of the notion of the black Atlantic as the thematic frame and a trope for articulating diasporan African intellectual and cultural thought see Paul Gilroy *The Black Atlantic: Modernity and Double Consciousness* (London: Verso, 1993).
15. See Robert Beckford *God of the Rahtid* (London: DLT, 2001), pp. 113–118, *Jesus DubTheology, Music and Social Change* (London: Routlege, 2006).
16. See Reddie *Acting in Solidarity*.
17. See Anthony G. Reddie "An Interactive Odyssey: Black Experiential Preaching." Geoffrey Stevenson (ed.) *Pulpit Journeys* (London: DLT, 2006).

18. John Coltrane *A Love Supreme* [Deluxe edition] (Impulse Records, Ref No. 314–589–945–2, 2002).

19. Miles Davis *A Kind of Blue* (Columbia/Legacy Records. Ref no. CK 64935, 1997).

20. There is a church in San Francisco named after John Coltrane, which plays his music as a part of its liturgy and has styled him a latter day Saint —"The Church of John Coltrane." See <www.saintjohncoltrane.org.>

21. See Ward and Burns *Jazz*.

22. Anthony B. Pinn *Terror and Triumph: The Nature of Black Religion* (Minneapolis: Fortress Press, 2003), pp. 1–80.

23. See Ashley Kahn *A Love Supreme: The Creation of John Coltrane's Classic Album* (London: Granta Books, 2002).

24. Ward and Burns, pp. 290–291.

25. See George Cole *The Last Miles: The Music of Miles Davis 1980–1991* (London: Equinox Publishing, 2005).

26. See Coleridge Goode and Roger Cotterell *Bass Line: A Life Jazz* (London: Northway Publications, 2002), pp. 114–134.

27. Ibid. for an important account of Coleridge Goode, a black pioneer of the British jazz scene in the 1950s and 1960s.

28. Bruce J. Malina *The Social Gospel of Jesus: The Kingdom of God in Mediterranean Perspective* (Minneapolis: Fortress Press, 2001), pp. 113–140.

29. Personal conversations with jazz musicians in Birmingham, West Midlands, Britain.

30. Matthew 22: 38–39.

31. Dwight N. Hopkins *Being Human: Race, Culture, and Religion* (Minneapolis: Fortress Press, 2005), pp. 81–117.

32. See Gay L. Byron *Symbolic Blackness and Ethnic Difference in Early Christian Literature* (New York: Routledge, 2002) whose excellent book looks at the struggles within early Christian communities to define the boundaries and limits regarding what it meant to be part of the Body of Christ.

33. See Ward and Burns *Jazz*.

34. See, for example, Zygmunt Bauman *Intimations of Postmodernity* (London: Routledge, 1992).

35. See James H. Harris *The Word Made Plain* (Minneapolis: Fortress Press, 2004), pp. 1–50.

36. See Henry H. Mitchell *Black Belief* (New York: Harper and Row, 1975).

37. William A, Jones Jr, "Confronting the System." Gayraud Wilmore (ed.) *African American Religious Studies: An Interdisciplinary Anthology* (London: Duke University Press, 1989), pp. 429–457.

38. Grant S. Shockley "From Emancipation, to Transformation to Consummation." Marlene Mayr (ed.) *Does the Church Really Want Religious Education?* (Birmingham, AA: Religious Education Press, 1988), pp. 234–236.

39. Theophus H. Smith *Conjuring Culture: Biblical Formations of Black America* (New York: Oxford University Press, 1994), pp. 4–6.

40. See Dale P. Andrews *Practical Theology For Black Churches* (Louisville: John Knox Press, 2002).

41. James H. Cone *The Spirituals and the Blues* (Maryknoll, NY: Orbis Books, 1972).
42. Carlyle Fielding Stewart, III *Black Spirituality and Black Consciousness* (Trenton, NY: Africa World Press, 1999), pp. 105–120.
43. Andrews *Practical Theology for Black Churches*, pp. 6–23.
44. Carol Tomlin *Black Language Style in Sacred and Secular Contexts* (New York: Caribbean Diaspora Press, 1999), pp. 125–166.
45. Harris *The Word Made Plain*.
46. Tomin *Black Language Style in Sacred and Secular Contexts*, p. 126.
47. See Joe D. Aldred (ed.) *Preaching with Power* (London: Cassell, 1998).
48. Ermal Kirby "Black Preaching." *The Journal of The College of Preachers* (July 2001), pp. 47–49.
49. See Kirk Byron Jones *The Jazz of Preaching: How to Preach with great freedom and joy* (Nashville, TN: Abingdon Press, 2004), pp. 79–98.
50. Vincent L. Wimbush *The Bible and African Americans: A Brief History* (Minneapolis: Fortress Press, 2003), pp. 63–70.
51. Ibid., pp. 19–46.
52. Ibid., p. 24.
53. James H. Cone *God of the Oppressed* (San Francisco: Harper-San-Francisco, 1975), pp. 62–83.
54. Robert Beckford *God and the Gangs* (London: Darton, Longman and Todd, 2004), pp. 102–103.
55. Ermal Kirby "Black Preaching," p. 48.
56. Reddie *Acting in Solidarity*.
57. Reddie *Dramatizing Theologies*.
58. See Reddie *Faith, Stories and the Experiences of Black Elders*.
59. Sigmund Freud *Address to the Society of B'Nai of B'rith, rev. edn.*, 20: 273 (London: Hogarth Press, 1959).
60. Erik H. Erikson *Identity: Youth Crisis* (London: Faber and Faber, 1968), pp. 16–58.
61. Charles R. Foster 'The Pastor: Agent of Vision in the Education of a Community of Faith" Robert L. Browning (ed.) *The Pastor as Religious Educator* (Birmingham, AL: Religious Education Press, 1987), pp. 22–25. See also Charles R. Foster *Educating Congregations* (Nashville, TN: Abingdon Press, 1994).
62. In the interests of brevity I am guilty of conflating a number of important considerations regarding the existence and identification of the phenomenon that has become known as "postmodernity." There are seemingly as many views as there are people who have commented on the existence, nature, and timescale of postmodernism. See, for example, Zygmunt Bauman *Intimations of Postmodernity* (London: Routledge, 1992).
63. See Andrew Walker *Telling the Story: Gospel, mission and culture* (London: SPCK, 1996), who addresses the issue of the translation of the faith between generations and cultures in his work.
64. Anne Wimberly *Soul Stories* (Nashville, TN: Abingdon Press, 1996).
65. Joseph Crockett *Teaching Scripture from an African American Perspective* (Nashville, TN: Discipleship Resources, 1989).

66. See Anne H. Pinn and Anthony B. Pinn *The Black Church* (Minneapolis: Fortress Press, 2002).
67. Dennis A. Jacobsen *Doing Justice: Congregations and Community Organizing* (Minneapolis: Fortress Press, 2001).
68. Harold Dean Trulear "African American Religious Education." Barbara Wilkerson (ed.) *Multi-Cultural Religious Education* (Birmingham, AL: Religious Education Press, 1997), pp. 1–189.
69. See Gordon Lynch *After Religion: Generation X' and the search for Meaning* (London: DLT, 2002).
70. See Erik H. Erikson *The Life Cycle Completed* (London: Norton, 1993).
71. See Dick Hedbidge *Cut 'N' Mix: Culture, Identity and Caribbean Music* (London: Routledge, 1987).
72. Dean Borgman *When Kumbaya is not enough: A Practical Theology for Youth ministry* (Peabody, MA: Hendrickson, 1997).
73. Jonathan S. Epstein (ed.) *Youth Culture: Identity in a Postmodern World* (Massachusetts: Blackwell, 1999).
74. Pete Ward *Growing up Evangelical: Youthwork and the Making of a Subculture* (London: SPCK, 1996).
75. See David Hay (with Rebecca Nye) *The Spirit of the Child* (London: HarperCollins, 1998).
76. Ibid.
77. See Reddie *Faith, Stories and the Experiences of Black Elders*.
78. Ibid., pp. 54–61.
79. Ibid.
80. Ibid., pp. 54–61.
81. See Tomlin *Black Language Style in Sacred and Secular Contexts* and Lerleen Willis "All Things to All Men? Or What Has Language to Do with Gender and Resistance in the Black Majority Church in Britain." *Black Theology in Britain* (Vol. 4, No. 2, May 2002), pp. 195–213.
82. Ibid., pp. 195–213.
83. Andrew White "The Role of the Black Church in the Liberation Struggle." *Spectrum* (No. 47, July–September 1971), pp. 10–12.
84. Grant S. Shockley "Black Pastoral Leadership in Religious Education." Robert L. Browning (ed.) *The Pastor as Religious Educator* (Birmingham, AA: Religious Education Press, 1987), pp. 179–206.
85. See Will Coleman *Tribal Talk: Black Theology, Hermeneutics and African/American Ways of "Telling the Story"* (Pennsylvania: University of Pennsylvania Press, 2000), pp. 153–170.
86. See *Reading the Bible in the Global Village: Global Perspectives on Biblical Scholarship* (Atlanta: Society for Biblical Literature, 2002). See also Gerald O. West "Contextual Bible Study in South Africa: A Resource for Reclaiming and Regaining Land, Dignity and Identity." McGlory T. Speckman and Larry T. Kaufmann *Towards an Agenda for Contextual Theology: Essays in Honour of Albert Nolan* (Pietermaritzburg, South Africa: Cluster Publications, 2001), pp. 169–184.
87. Black, womanist, and liberation theologians have long asserted that all talk about God is filtered through the lens of our experience, thereby making all

theologies deeply contextual. There is no basis for asserting that any theology is universal or generic irrespective of context or experience. See Speckman and Kaufmann *Towards an Agenda for Contextual Theology*.

88. This may be a church, a base community, or some other form of ecclesial configuration.
89. See Ward and Burns *Jazz*, pp. 397–400.
90. Romney Moseley *Becoming a Self Before God: Critical Transformations* (Nashville, TN: Abingdon Press, 1991), pp. 88–100.
91. Ella P. Mitchell "Oral Tradition: The Legacy of Faith for the Black Church." *Religious Education* (Vol. 81, No. 1, 1986), pp. 93–112.
92. See Iva Carruthers, Frederick D. Haynes III and Jeremiah A. Wright Jr (eds.) *Blow the Trumpet in Zion: Global Vision and Action for the 21st Century Black Church* (Minneapolis: Fortress Press, 2005).
93. See Emmanuel C. Eze *Race and the Enlightenment* (Massachusetts: Blackwell, 1997).
94. Emmanuel Y. Lartey *In Living Colour: An Intercultural Approach to Pastoral care and Counselling* (London: Cassell, 1997), pp. 9–14.
95. See Hopkins *Being Human*, pp. 118–160.
96. See Victor Anderson *Beyond Ontological Blackness* (New York: Continuum, 1995), pp. 86–93.
97. Anne Hope and Sally Timmel *Training for Transformation*, Vol.4 (Southampton: Intermediate Publications, 1999), pp. 186–209.
98. See Martha Lee *The Nation of Islam: An American Millenarian Movement* (New York: Syracuse University Press, 1988), pp. 1–115 and Mattia Gardell *Countdown to Armageddon: Louis Farrakhan and the Nation of Islam* (London: C. Hurst, 1996), pp. 1–30.
99. James H. Cone "Theology's Great Sin: Silence in the Face of White Supremacy." *Black Theology: An International Journal* (Vol. 2, No. 2, July 2004), pp. 139–152.
100. Doreen Morrison "Resisting Racism—By Celebrating 'Our' Blackness." *Black Theology: An International Journal* (Vol. 1, No. 2, May 2003), pp. 209–223.
101. See Smith *Conjuring Culture* and Robert Beckford *Dread and Pentecostal* (London: SPCK, 2000).
102. Verses 5–12, Cain Hope Felder "Commentary on the Apostles." Cain Hope Felder (ed.) *The Original African Heritage Study Bible* (Nashville, TN: James C. Winston Publishing Company, 1993), p. 1572.
103. Cain Hope Felder (ed.) *Stony the Road We Trod: African American Biblical Interpretation* (Minneapolis: Augsburg, 1991), Randall C. Bailey and Jacquelyn Grant (eds.) *The Recovery of Black Presence: An Interdisciplinary Exploration* (Nashville, TN: Abingdon Press, 1995).
104. Robert Beckford "Theology in the Age of Crack: Crack age, Prosperity Doctrine and 'Being There.' " *Black Theology in Britain: A Journal of Contextual Praxis* (Vol. 4, No. 1, November 2001), pp. 9–24.
105. See Galatians 3:22.
106. Ward and Burns *Jazz*, pp. 290–291.
107. See Marlene Mayr (ed.) *Does the Church Really Want Religious Education?* pp. 221–248.

108. For an analysis of this point, see my *Faith, Stories and the Experience of Black Elders*.

109. David Ishiorho "Black Theology in Urban Shadow: Combating Racism in the Church of England." *Black Theology: An International Journal* (Vol. 1, No. 1, November 2002), pp. 29–48.

110. See Cone *Black Theology and Black Power*, pp. 71–81.

111. See my postsketch reflections to "It Could Have Happened Like This?" Reddie *Acting in Solidarity*, pp. 45–53.

112. See Kelly Brown Douglas *Sexuality and the Black Church: A Womanist Perspective* (Maryknoll, NY: Orbis Books, 1999).

113. Robert Beckford *Jesus is Dread* (London: DLT, 1998), pp. 61–78.

114. Jacquelyn Grant "Freeing the Captives: The Imperative of Womanist Theology." Iva Carruthers, Frederick D. Haynes III, and Jeremiah A. Wright Jr (eds.) *Blow the Trumpet in Zion: Global Vision and Action for the 21st Century Black Church* (Minneapolis: Fortress Press, 2005).

115. See my dramatic sketch entitled "Black Voices" Reddie *Acting in Solidarity*, pp. 109–119.

116. Beckford *Dread and Pentecostal*, pp. 160–204.

117. See Jean Knighton-Fitt *Beyond Fear* (Cape Town: Pretext Publishers, 2003) for a moving insider account of the anti apartheid struggle in South Africa. This insider's narrative sits alongside the many outsiders who marched and protested in solidarity with those who were experiencing the brutalities of the apartheid regime first hand so to speak.

118. See David Willows *Divine Knowledge: A Kierkegaardian Perspective on Christian Education* (Aldershot: Ashgate, 2001), pp. 8–26.

119. See Beckford *Jesus is Dread*, pp. 61–78 and Douglas *Sexuality and the Black Church*.

120. See Lee Butler "The Spirit Is Willing and the Flesh Is Too: Living Whole and Holy Lives through Integrating Spirituality and Sexuality." Anthony B. Pinn and Dwight N. Hopkins (eds.) *Loving the Body: Black Religious Studies and the Erotic* (New York: Palgrave Macmillan, 2005), pp. 111–120.

121. Margaret Jones "Growing in Grace and Holiness." Clive Marsh, Brian Neck, Angela Shier-Jones, and Helen Wareing (eds.) *Unmasking Methodist Theology* (London and New York: Continuum, 2004), pp. 155–165.

122. David Carter *Love Bade Me Welcome: A British Methodist Perspective on the Church* (Peterborough: Epworth Press, 2002), pp. 58–67.

123. R.S. Sugirtharajah (ed.) *Voices from the Margin* (Sheffield: Sheffield Academic Press, 1991).

124. See Musa W. Dube *Postcolonial Feminist Interpretation of the Bible* (St. Louis: Chalice Press, 2000).

125. *Reading the Bible in The Global Village*.

126. See Demetrius K. Williams *An End to This Strife: The Politics of Gender in African American Churches* (Minneapolis: Fortress Press, 2004).

127. See Catherine Keller, Michael Nausner, and Mayra Rivera (eds.) *Postcolonial Theologies: Divinity and Empire* (St. Louis: Chalice Press, 2004).

Index